Worksheets for

Drafting & Design

Engineering Drawing Using Manual and CAD Techniques

by

Clois E. Kicklighter, CSIT

Dean Emeritus, School of Technology
Professor Emeritus of Construction Technology
Indiana State University
Terre Haute, IN

and

Walter C. Brown

Publisher
The Goodheart-Willcox Company, Inc.
Tinley Park, Illinois
www.g-w.com

The Goodheart-Willcox Company, Inc. Brand Disclaimer: Brand names, company names, and illustrations for products and services included in this text are provided for educational purposes only and do not represent or imply endorsement or recommendation by the author or the publisher.

The Goodheart-Willcox Company, Inc. Safety Notice: The reader is expressly advised to carefully read, understand, and apply all safety precautions and warnings described in this book or that might also be indicated in undertaking the activities and exercises described herein to minimize risk of personal injury or injury to others. Common sense and good judgment should also be exercised and applied to help avoid all potential hazards. The reader should always refer to the appropriate manufacturer's technical information, directions, and recommendations; then proceed with care to follow specific equipment operating instructions. The reader should understand these notices and cautions are not exhaustive.

The publisher makes no warranty or representation whatsoever, either expressed or implied, including but not limited to equipment, procedures, and applications described or referred to herein, their quality, performance, merchantability, or fitness for a particular purpose. The publisher assumes no responsibility for any changes, errors, or omissions in this book. The publisher specifically disclaims any liability whatsoever, including any direct, indirect, incidental, consequential, special, or exemplary damages resulting, in whole or in part, from the reader's use or reliance upon the information, instructions, procedures, warnings, cautions, applications, or other matter contained in this book. The publisher assumes no responsibility for the activities of the reader.

Introduction

The *Worksheets* are designed for use with the textbook *Drafting & Design: Engineering Drawing Using Manual and CAD Techniques*. The drawing problems and activities are intended to:

- Help develop basic drafting skills.
- Make the study of drafting more interesting and productive for you by increasing the number of learning activities and eliminating much of the tedious, repetitive work.
- Provide opportunities to apply problem-solving skills.

Many of the *Worksheets* problems have been carefully selected from the drafting rooms and engineering facilities of industry to provide realistic experiences. The problems can be solved using traditional drafting techniques or computer-aided drafting (CAD) methods.

The *Worksheets* problems are closely correlated to the textbook. The problems are organized to follow the sequence of chapters in the textbook. Note that all chapters are not listed in the Contents; only those containing problems are listed.

The majority of the *Worksheets* problems are provided in electronic format on the Instructor's CD as a part of the teaching package for *Drafting & Design: Engineering Drawing Using Manual and CAD Techniques*. The problems are provided as drawing files (DWG files) and can be completed using a CAD system.

Used with the textbook, the *Worksheets* problems are designed to give you a better understanding of the drafting field and the many career opportunities in drafting. Striving to complete the problems to the best of your ability will help you increase your drafting expertise and expand your problem-solving abilities.

Clois E. Kicklighter
Walter C. Brown

Contents

	Textbook Page	Worksheets Page

Section 1—Introduction to Drafting

Chapter 2
Traditional Drafting Equipment and Drawing Techniques..................41................7

Chapter 5
Sketching, Lettering, and Text..................131................23

Section 2—Drafting Techniques and Skills

Chapter 6
Basic Geometric Constructions..................163................35

Chapter 7
Advanced Geometric Constructions..................213................43

Chapter 8
Multiview Drawings..................241................45

Chapter 9
Dimensioning Fundamentals..................281................60

Chapter 10
Section Views..................315................68

Chapter 11
Pictorial Drawings..................347................83

Section 3—Descriptive Geometry

Chapter 12
Auxiliary Views..................407................97

Chapter 13
Revolutions..................441................107

Chapter 14
Intersections..................463................114

Chapter 15
Developments..................509................123

	Textbook Page	Worksheets Page

Section 4—Advanced Applications

Chapter 16
Geometric Dimensioning and Tolerancing ....549.................135

Chapter 17
Working Drawings...587.................141

Chapter 18
Threads and Fastening Devices ....615.................158

Chapter 19
Cams, Gears, and Splines ....651.................163

Section 5—Drafting and Design Specializations

Chapter 22
Architectural Drafting...715.................168

Chapter 24
Electrical and Electronics Drafting.......................................749.................169

Chapter 25
Map and Survey Drafting..761.................172

Chapter 26
Welding Drafting ....779.................174

Chapter 27
Technical Illustration ....795.................176

Chapter 28
Graphs and Charts...805.................178

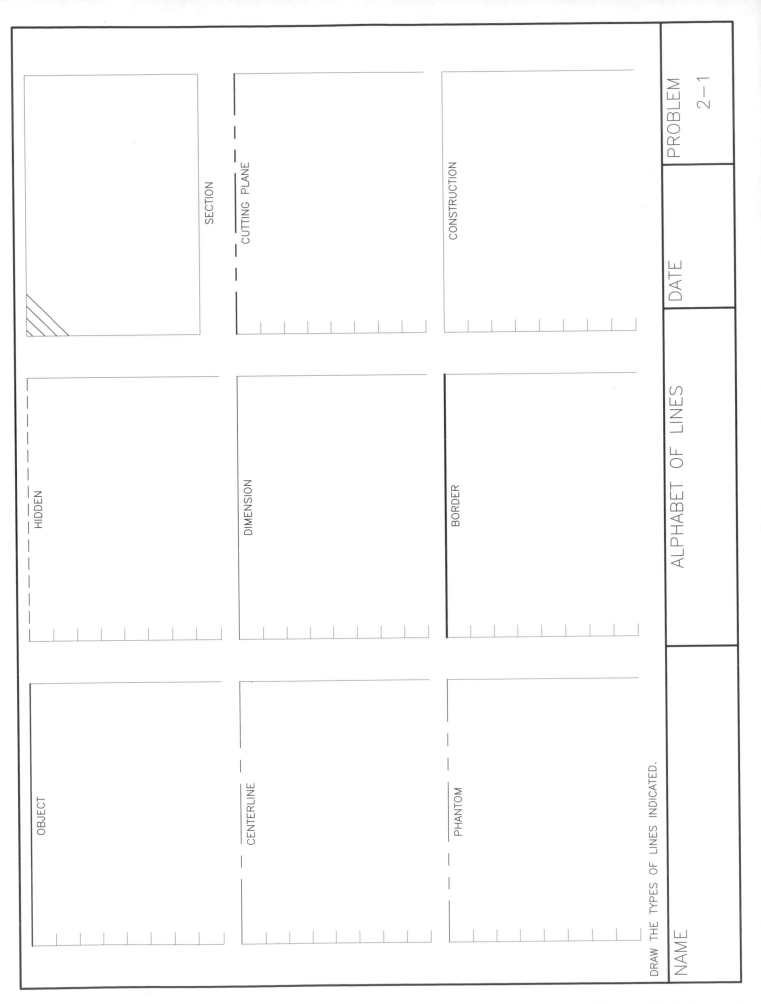

SECTION

CUTTING PLANE

CONSTRUCTION

HIDDEN

DIMENSION

BORDER

OBJECT

CENTERLINE

PHANTOM

DRAW THE TYPES OF LINES INDICATED.

NAME

ALPHABET OF LINES

DATE

PROBLEM

2-1

Lay off each line to the given length at the scale indicated. Make a short vertical mark to clearly indicate the length.

SCALE	LENGTH OF LINE
1" = 1"	6¾"
FULL SIZE	5⅛"
1" = 1'– 0"	7'– 3½"
¼" = 1'– 0"	30'– 9"
¼" = 1'– 0"	22'– 5"
1½" = 1'– 0"	3'– 7½"
QUARTER SIZE	2'– 2¼"
½" = 1'– 0"	14'–11"
⅛" = 1'– 0"	62'–10"
1" = 1'– 0"	6'– 4¾"
3/16" = 1'– 0"	40'– 6"
3/32" = 1'– 0"	81'– 0"

NAME

DATE

PROBLEM
2–2

ARCHITECT'S SCALE

Lay off each line to the given length at the scale indicated. Make a short vertical mark to clearly indicate the length.

SCALE	LENGTH OF LINE
1" = 10" (USE 10 SCALE)	9.80"
1" = 10' – 0"	4.40'
1" = 30" (USE 30 SCALE)	226.00"
FULL SIZE (USE 50 SCALE)	6.375"
FULL SIZE	3.187"
FULL SIZE	7.250"
FULL SIZE	6.125"
FULL SIZE	4.020"
FULL SIZE	5.825"
1" = 500 MILES (USE 50 SCALE)	2475 MILES
1" = 500'	4250.5'
1" = 2" (USE 20 SCALE)	14.75"

DECIMAL INCH SCALES

NAME			DATE	PROBLEM
				2-3

Chapter 2   Traditional Drafting Equipment and Drawing Techniques   9

Lay off each line to the given length at the scale indicated. Make a short vertical mark to clearly indicate the length.

SCALE	LENGTH OF LINE
1:1 (USE 1:100 SCALE)	127 mm
1:1	98.5 mm
1:1	152.25 mm
1:1	106 mm
1 cm = 1 m (USE 1:100 SCALE)	17.54 m
1 cm = 1 m	13.08 m
1 cm = 1 km (USE 1:100 SCALE)	16.55 km
1 cm = 1 km	20.6 km
FULL SIZE (USE 1:100 SCALE)	105.2 mm
FULL SIZE	86.5 mm
HALF SIZE (USE 1:20 SCALE)	382 mm
HALF SIZE	264 mm

NAME

METRIC SCALE

DATE

PROBLEM 2–4

Draw horizontal lines.

Draw vertical lines.

Draw lines 45° to the right.

Draw lines 30° to the left.

Draw lines 60° to the right.

Draw lines 75° to the left.

Draw lines 75° to the right.

Draw lines 15° to the left.

NAME	INSTRUMENT DRAFTING	DATE	PROBLEM
			2—5

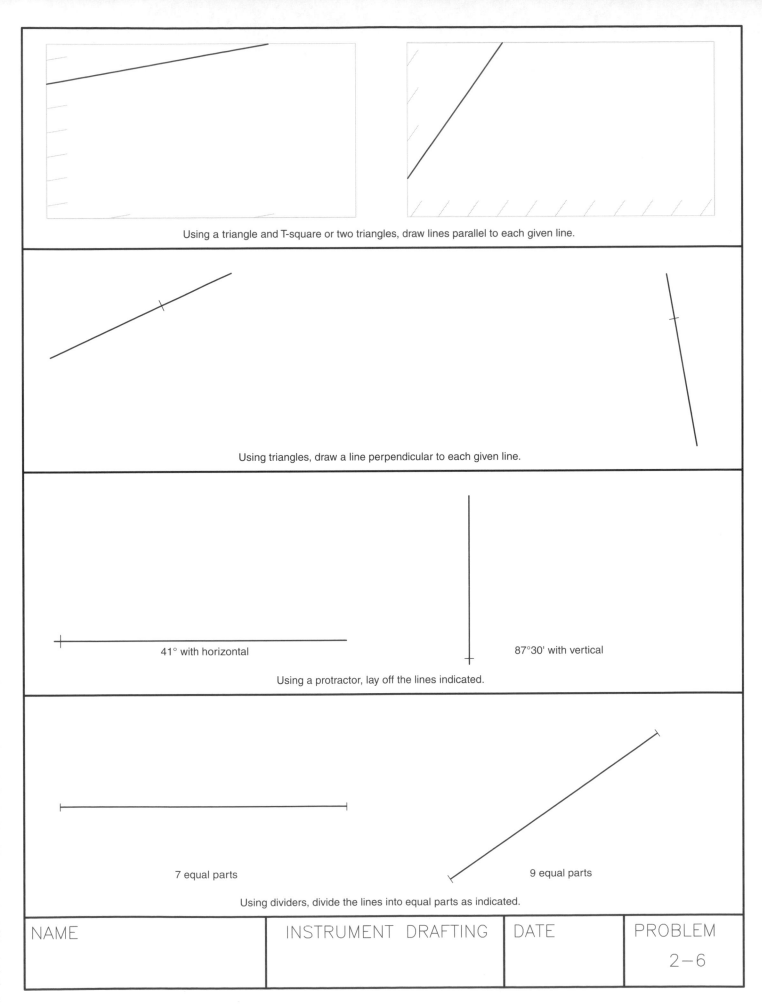

Using a triangle and T-square or two triangles, draw lines parallel to each given line.

Using triangles, draw a line perpendicular to each given line.

41° with horizontal

87°30' with vertical

Using a protractor, lay off the lines indicated.

7 equal parts

9 equal parts

Using dividers, divide the lines into equal parts as indicated.

NAME	INSTRUMENT DRAFTING	DATE	PROBLEM 2−6

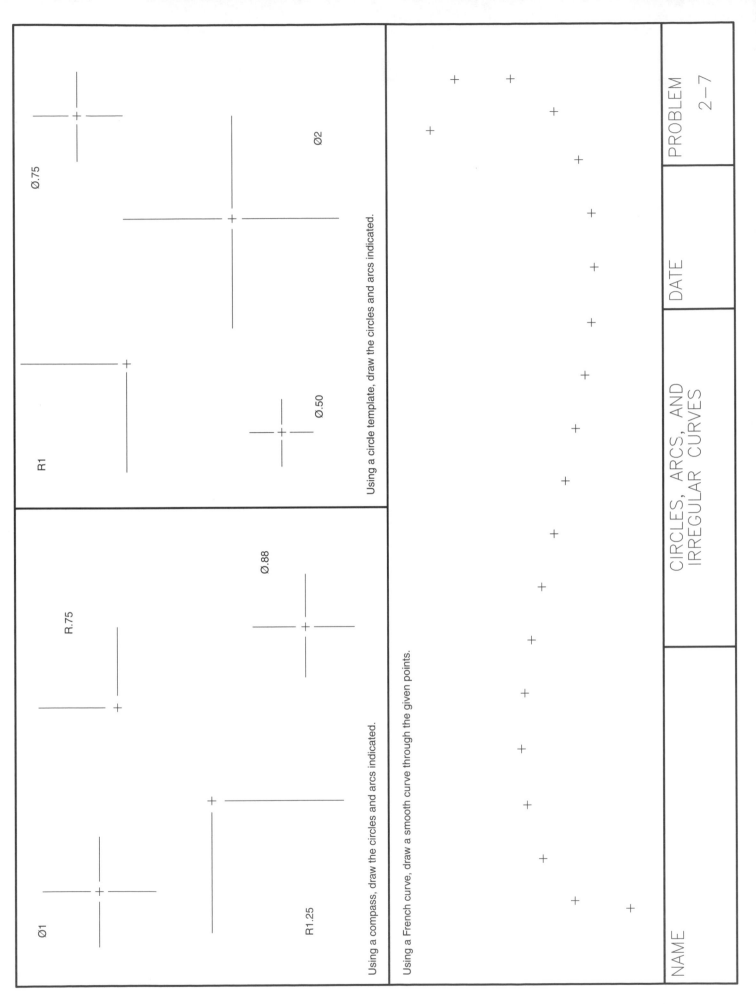

Ø.75

R1

Ø2

Using a circle template, draw the circles and arcs indicated.

Ø.50

R.75

Ø.88

Ø1

R1.25

Using a compass, draw the circles and arcs indicated.

Using a French curve, draw a smooth curve through the given points.

NAME

DATE

PROBLEM
2–7

CIRCLES, ARCS, AND
IRREGULAR CURVES

DRAW EACH PART TO THE SCALE SHOWN. DO NOT DIMENSION.

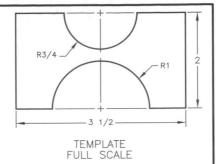

TEMPLATE
FULL SCALE

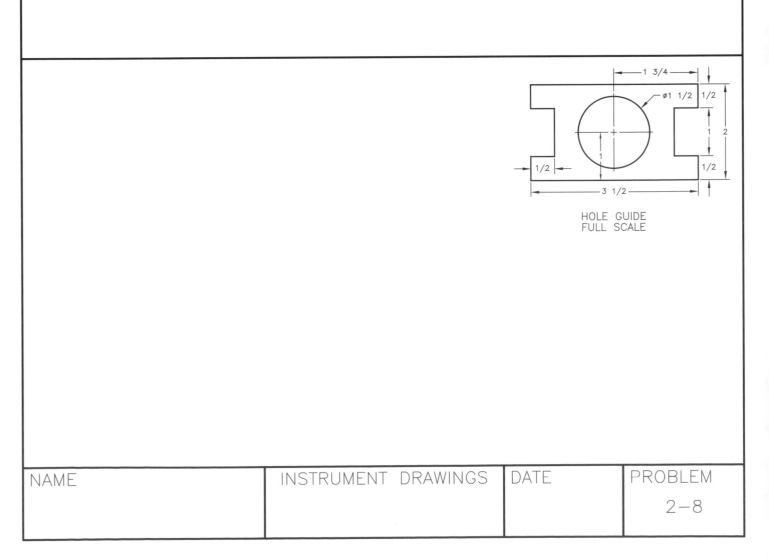

HOLE GUIDE
FULL SCALE

NAME	INSTRUMENT DRAWINGS	DATE	PROBLEM 2-8

DRAW EACH PART TO THE SCALE SHOWN. DO NOT DIMENSION.

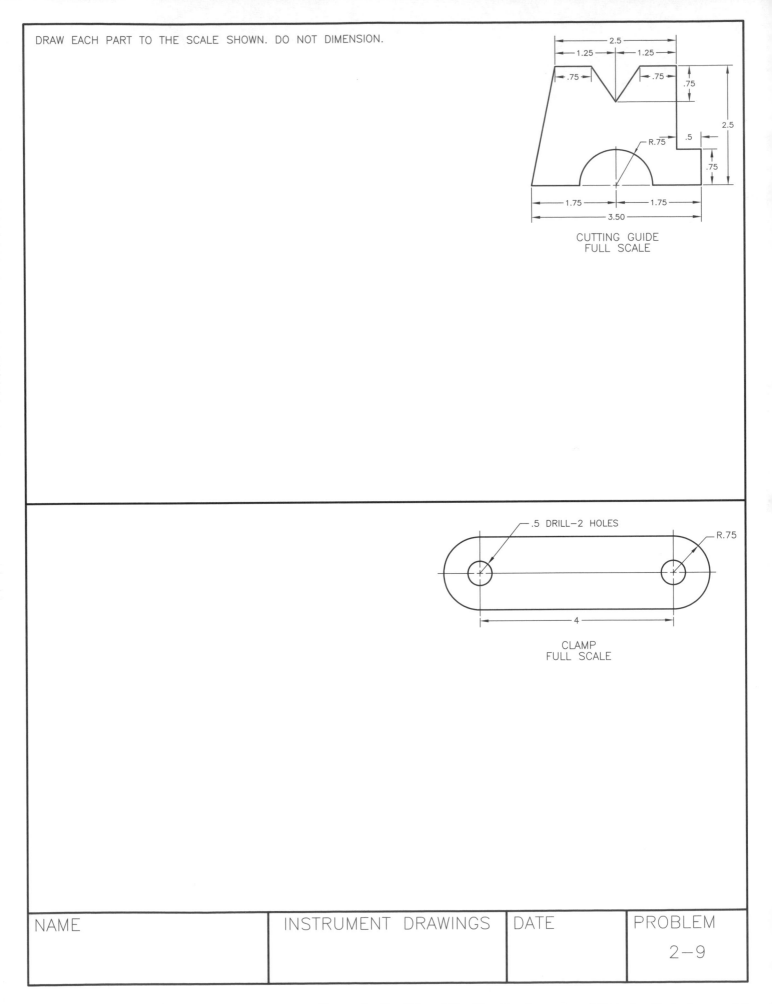

CUTTING GUIDE
FULL SCALE

CLAMP
FULL SCALE

NAME	INSTRUMENT DRAWINGS	DATE	PROBLEM
			2-9

DRAW EACH PART TO THE SCALE SHOWN. DO NOT DIMENSION.

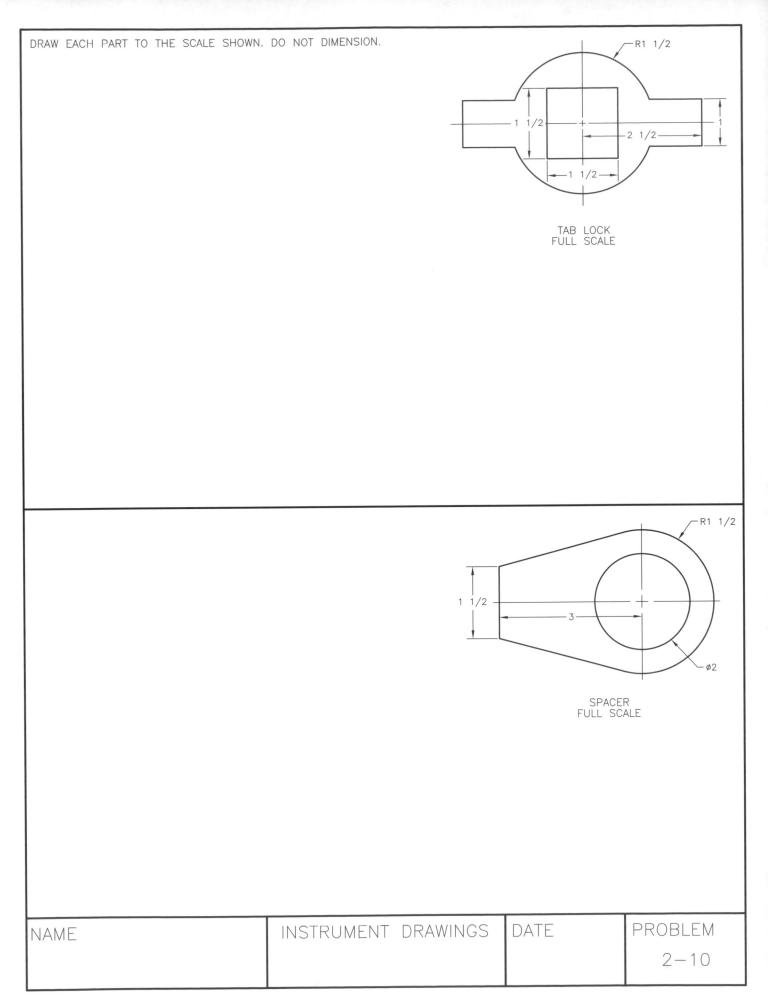

TAB LOCK
FULL SCALE

SPACER
FULL SCALE

NAME	INSTRUMENT DRAWINGS	DATE	PROBLEM
			2–10

DRAW EACH PART TO THE SCALE SHOWN. DO NOT DIMENSION.

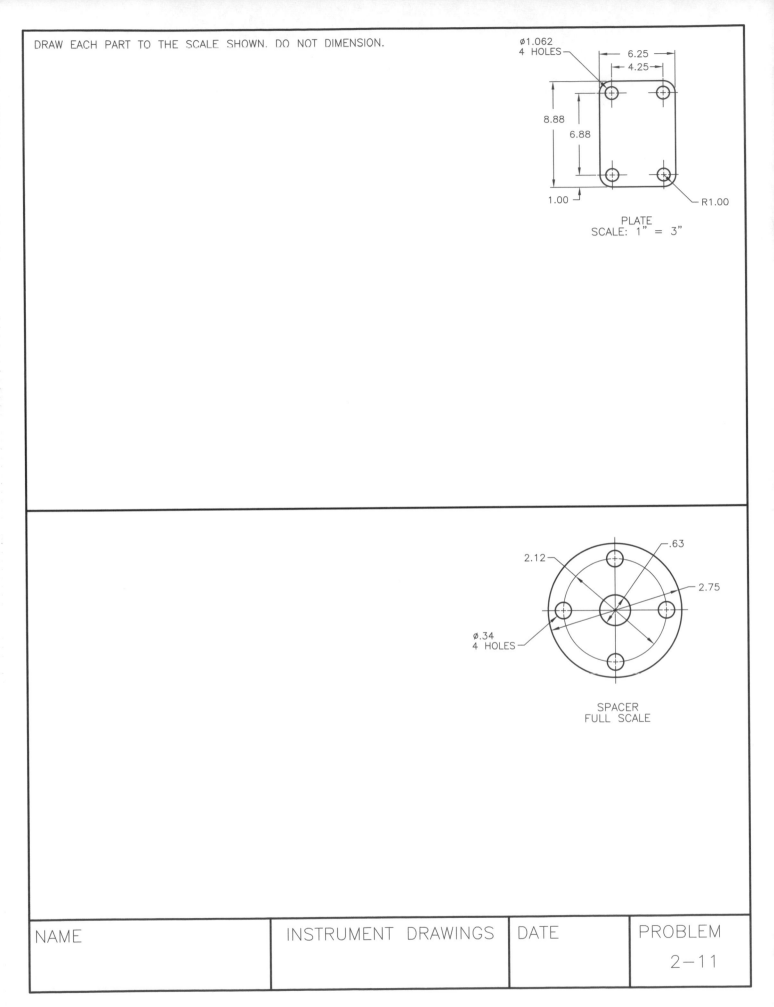

Ø1.062
4 HOLES

6.25
4.25

8.88

6.88

1.00

R1.00

PLATE
SCALE: 1" = 3"

.63

2.12

2.75

Ø.34
4 HOLES

SPACER
FULL SCALE

NAME	INSTRUMENT DRAWINGS	DATE	PROBLEM
			2-11

DRAW THE PART TO FULL SCALE. DO NOT DIMENSION.

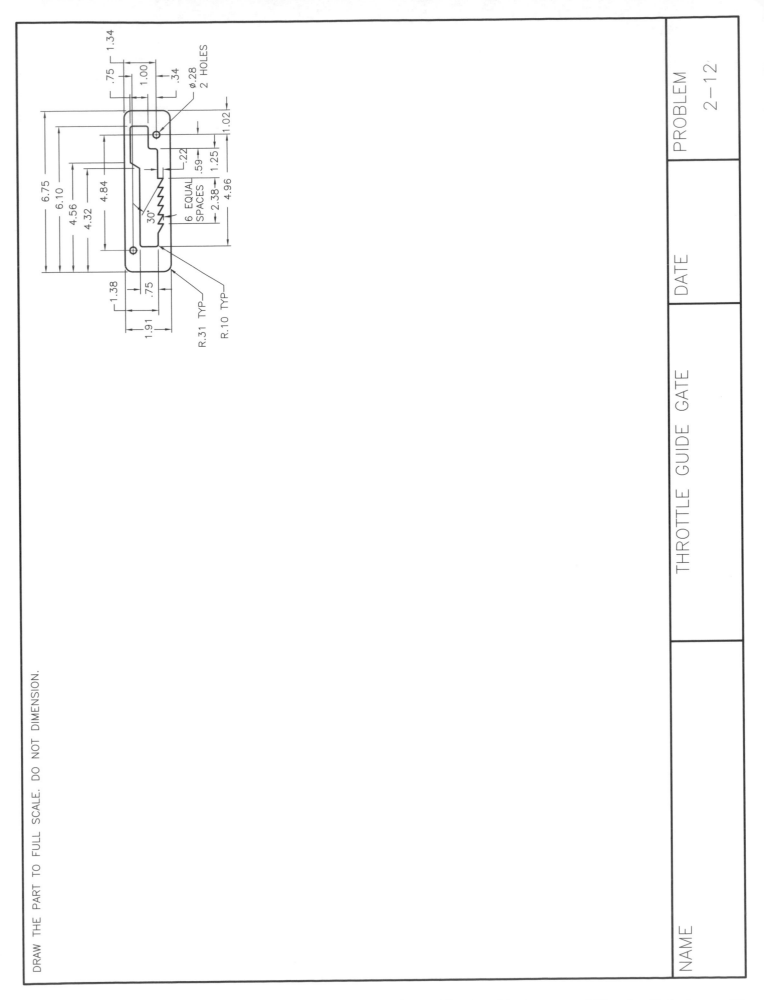

NAME

THROTTLE GUIDE GATE

DATE

PROBLEM

2-12

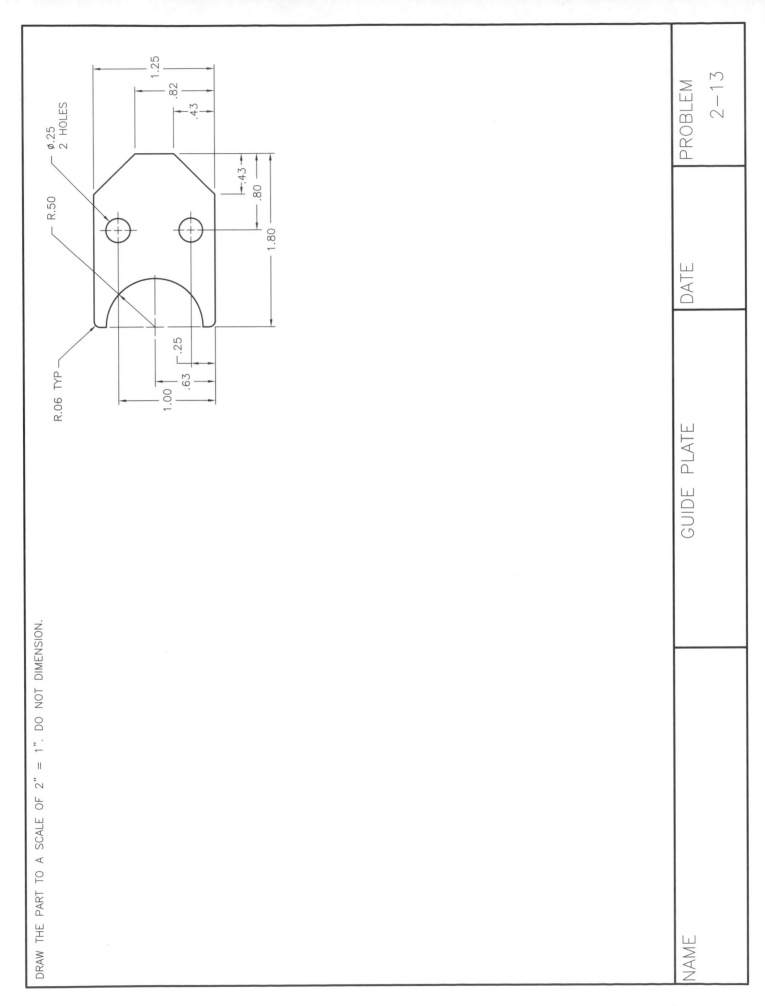

DRAW THE PART TO A SCALE OF 2" = 1". DO NOT DIMENSION.

1.25
.82
.43
Ø.25
2 HOLES
R.50
.43
.80
1.80
R.06 TYP
.25
.63
1.00

NAME

GUIDE PLATE

DATE

PROBLEM
2–13

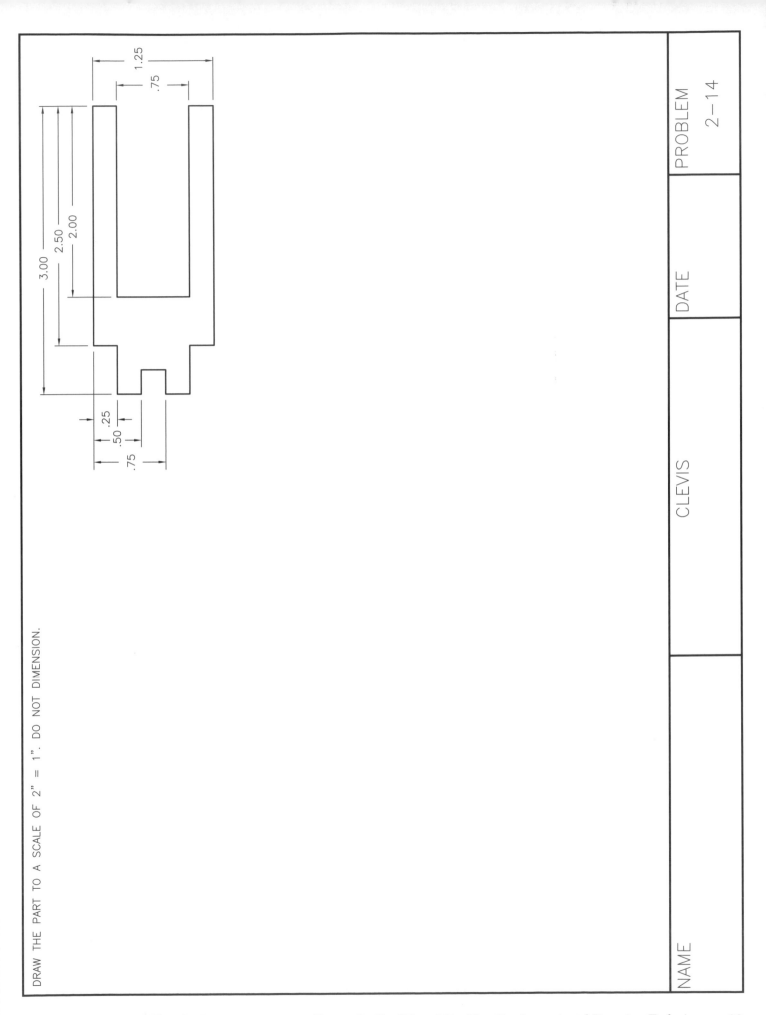

DRAW THE PART TO A SCALE OF 2" = 1". DO NOT DIMENSION.

1.25
.75

3.00
2.50
2.00

.25
.50
.75

NAME

CLEVIS

DATE

PROBLEM
2–14

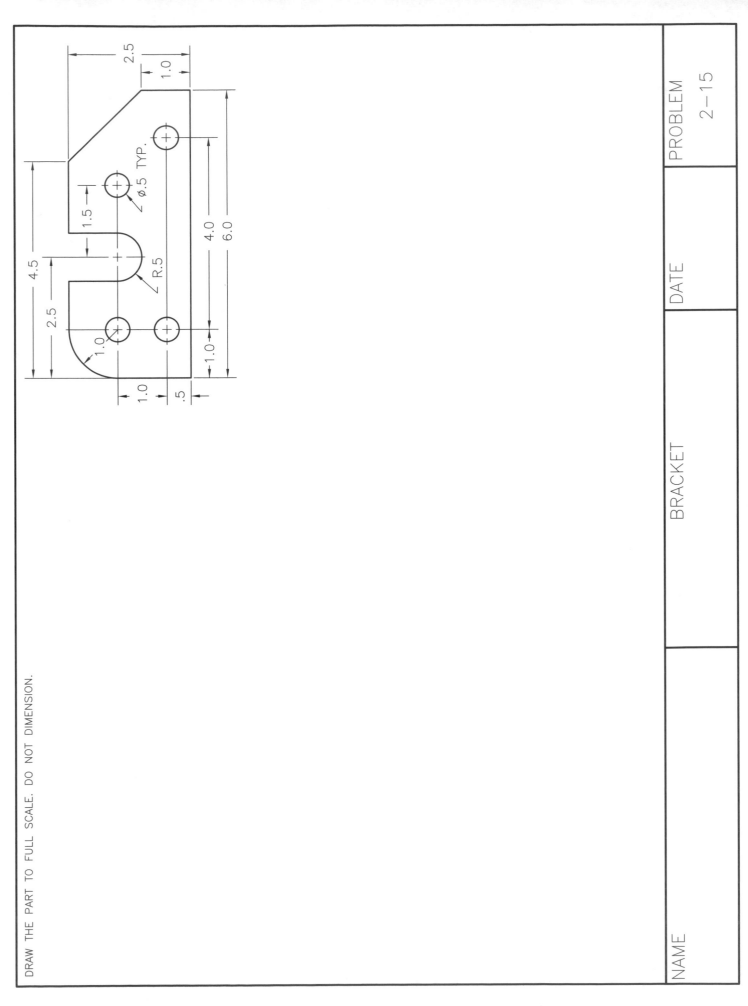

DRAW THE PART TO FULL SCALE. DO NOT DIMENSION.

NAME

BRACKET

DATE

PROBLEM
2–15

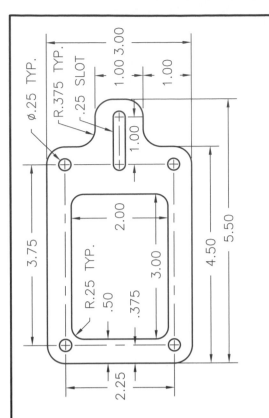

DRAW THE PART TO FULL SCALE. DO NOT DIMENSION.

Ø.25 TYP.

R.375 TYP.

.25 SLOT

1.00 3.00

1.00

1.00

3.75

R.25 TYP.

2.00

.50

.375

3.00

4.50

5.50

2.25

NAME	GASKET	DATE	PROBLEM
			2–16

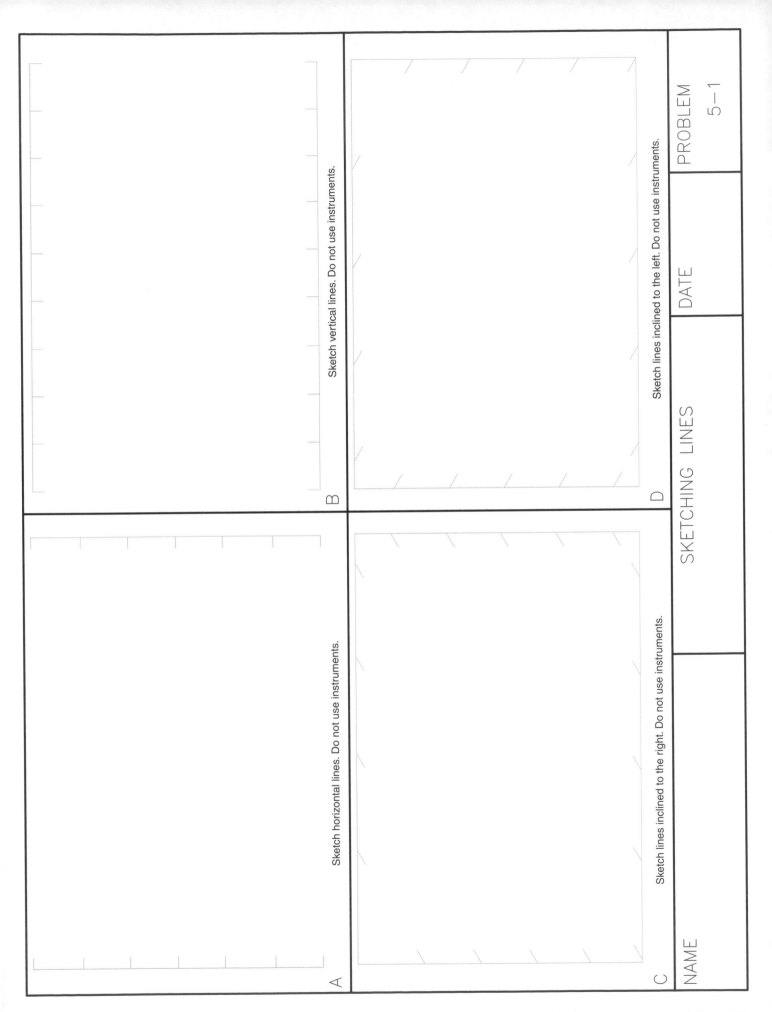

B

Sketch vertical lines. Do not use instruments.

D

Sketch lines inclined to the left. Do not use instruments.

A

Sketch horizontal lines. Do not use instruments.

C

Sketch lines inclined to the right. Do not use instruments.

PROBLEM
5–1

DATE

SKETCHING LINES

NAME

A   Sketch 75° angles. Do not use instruments.

B   Sketch 20° angles. Do not use instruments.

C   Sketch 45° angles. Do not use instruments.

D   Sketch 60° angles. Do not use instruments.

SKETCHING ANGLES

PROBLEM 5-2

DATE

NAME

A. Sketch a 2.5" circle using the centerline method. Darken finished work but do not erase construction lines.

B. Sketch a circle using the enclosing square method. Darken finished lines but do not erase construction lines.

C. Sketch a 2" circle using the free-circle method. Darken finished work but do not erase construction lines.

D. Sketch the arcs indicated. Darken finished work but do not erase construction lines.

R1.5

R1

R.75

R.5

NAME	SKETCHING CIRCLES AND ARCS	DATE	PROBLEM
			5-3

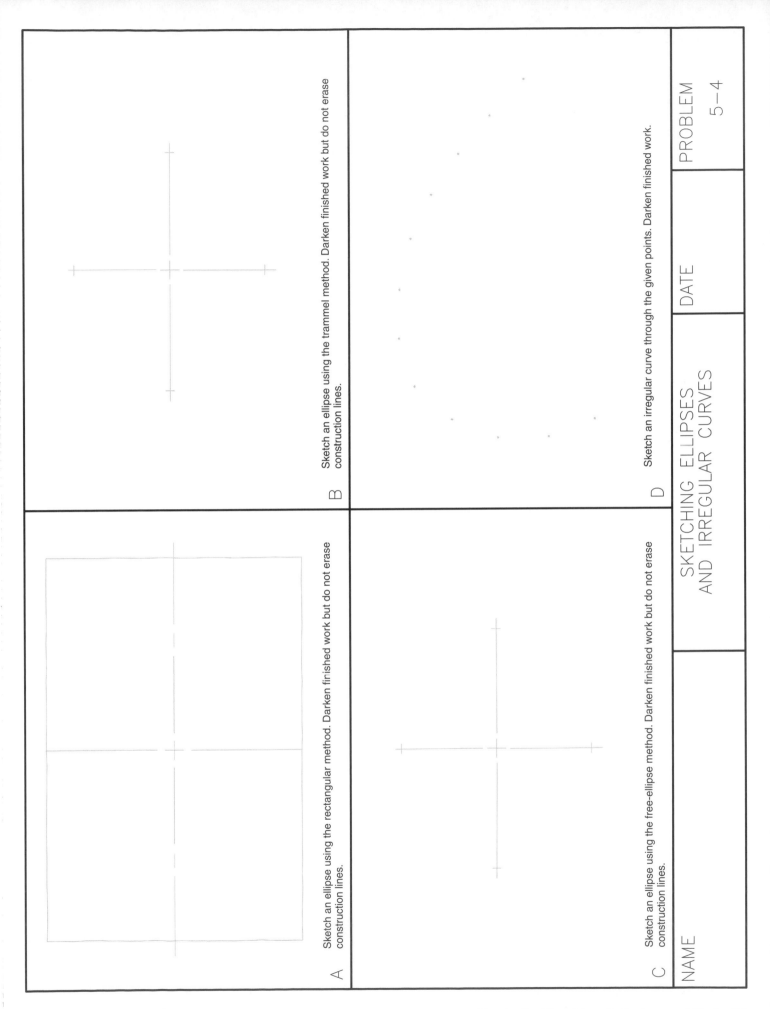

A   Sketch an ellipse using the rectangular method. Darken finished work but do not erase construction lines.

B   Sketch an ellipse using the trammel method. Darken finished work but do not erase construction lines.

C   Sketch an ellipse using the free-ellipse method. Darken finished work but do not erase construction lines.

D   Sketch an irregular curve through the given points. Darken finished work.

SKETCHING ELLIPSES
AND IRREGULAR CURVES

NAME

DATE

PROBLEM
5–4

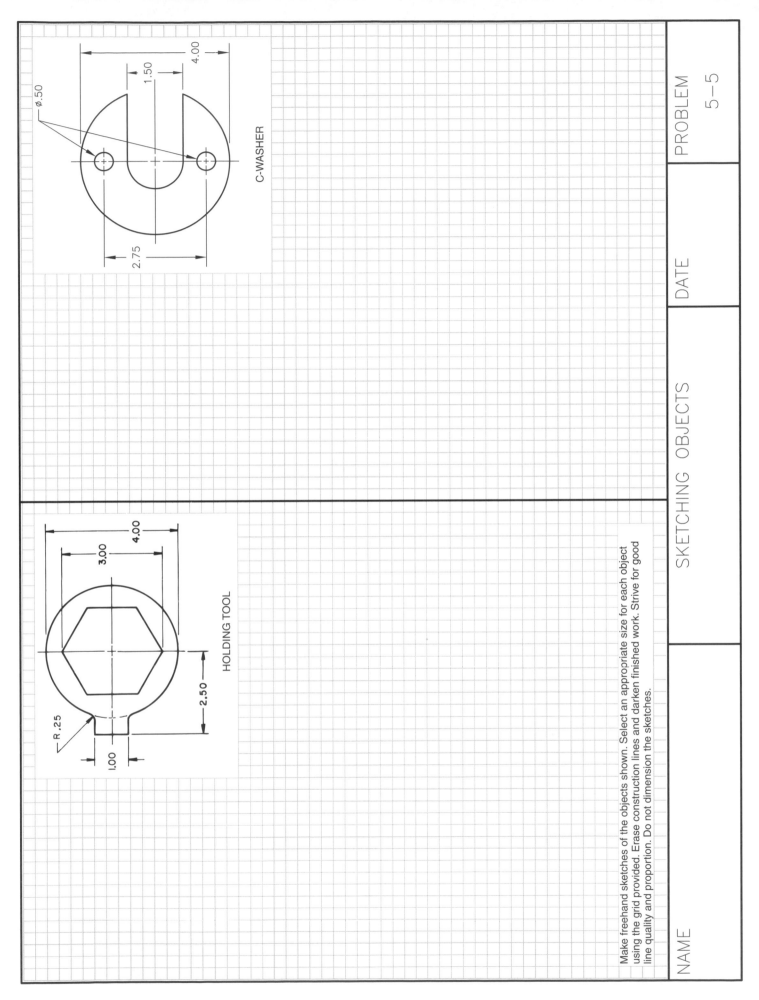

Ø.50

4.00

1.50

2.75

C-WASHER

4.00

3.00

R .25

1.00

2.50

HOLDING TOOL

Make freehand sketches of the objects shown. Select an appropriate size for each object using the grid provided. Erase construction lines and darken finished work. Strive for good line quality and proportion. Do not dimension the sketches.

PROBLEM
5–5

DATE

SKETCHING OBJECTS

NAME

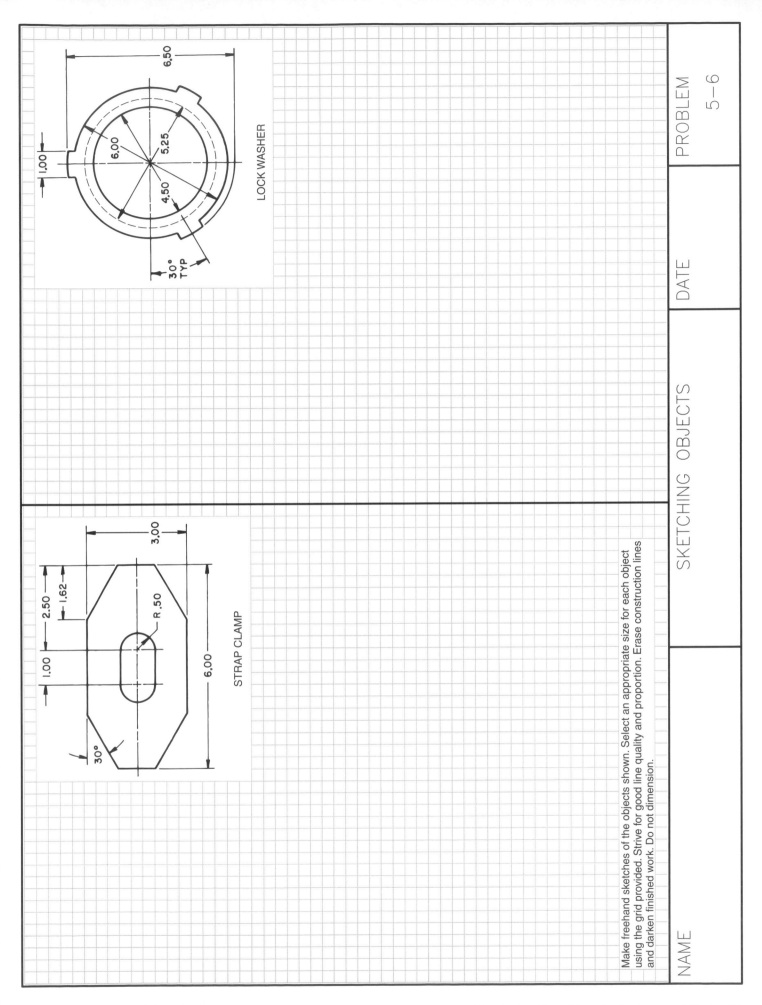

LOCK WASHER

6.50

6.00

5.25

4.50

1.00

30° TYP

STRAP CLAMP

3.00

2.50

1.62

1.00

R.50

6.00

30°

Make freehand sketches of the objects shown. Select an appropriate size for each object using the grid provided. Strive for good line quality and proportion. Erase construction lines and darken finished work. Do not dimension.

NAME

DATE

PROBLEM
5–6

SKETCHING OBJECTS

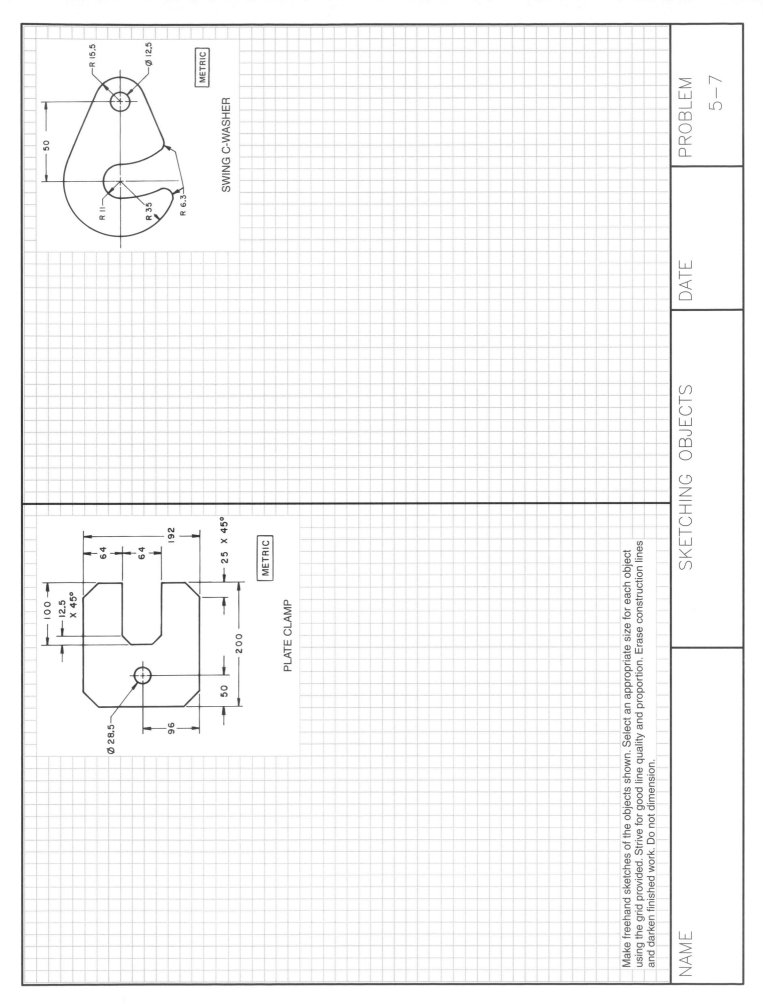

SWING C-WASHER

METRIC

R 15.5

Ø 12.5

50

R 11

R 35

R 6.3

PLATE CLAMP

METRIC

192

64

64

25 X 45°

100

12.5
X 45°

200

50

96

Ø 28.5

Make freehand sketches of the objects shown. Select an appropriate size for each object using the grid provided. Strive for good line quality and proportion. Erase construction lines and darken finished work. Do not dimension.

SKETCHING OBJECTS

NAME

PROBLEM

5–7

DATE

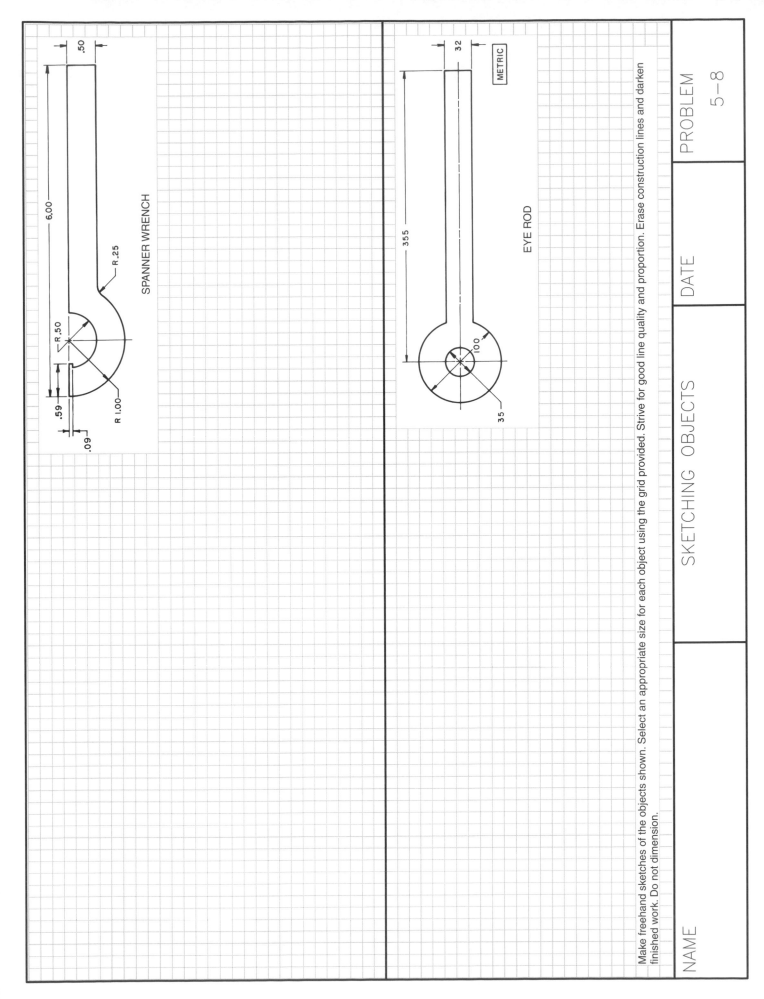

.50

6.00

R.25

R.50

.59

.60

R 1.00

SPANNER WRENCH

32

METRIC

355

100

35

EYE ROD

Make freehand sketches of the objects shown. Select an appropriate size for each object using the grid provided. Strive for good line quality and proportion. Erase construction lines and darken finished work. Do not dimension.

SKETCHING OBJECTS

NAME

DATE

PROBLEM

5-8

MAKE FREEHAND SKETCHES OF OBJECTS AS ASSIGNED BY YOUR INSTRUCTOR. STRIVE FOR GOOD LINE QUALITY AND PROPORTION.

SKETCHING OBJECTS

PROBLEM 5-9

DATE

NAME

ABCD

3/8" CAPITAL LETTERS AND NUMERALS

ABCD

1/8" CAPITAL LETTERS AND NUMERALS

abcd

1/8" LOWERCASE LETTERS AND NUMERALS

Refer to Figures 5-31 and 5-36 in the textbook and draw the lettering at the height indicated. Repeat each series as many times as space permits.

VERTICAL GOTHIC LETTERING

NAME

DATE

PROBLEM

5-10

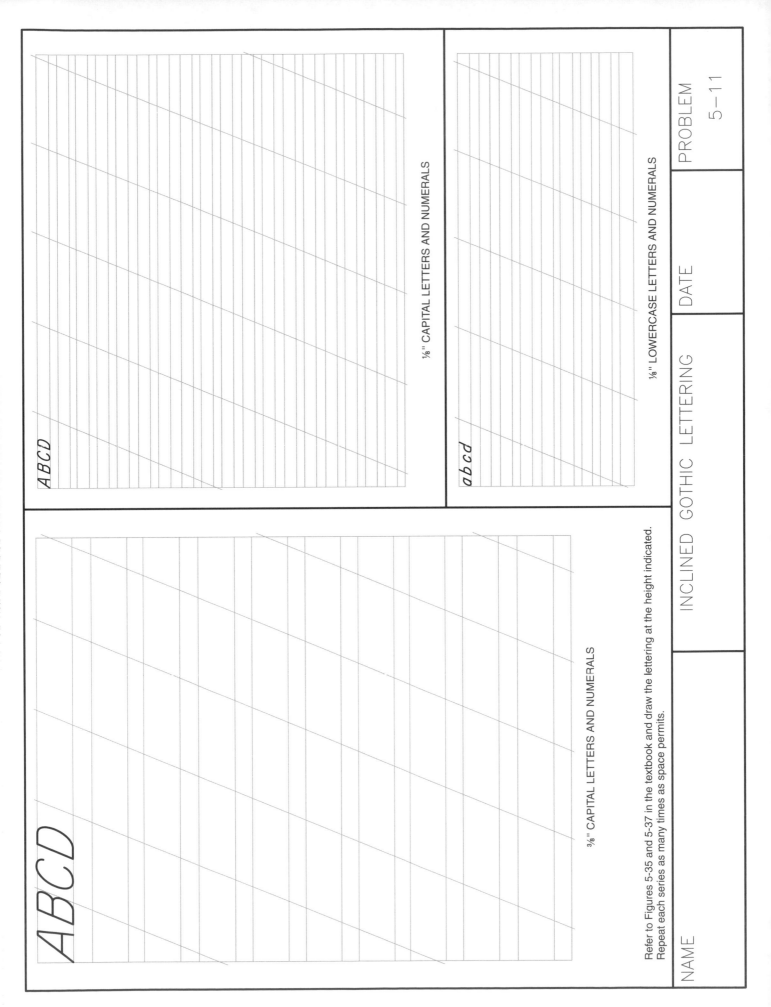

ABCD

ABCD

⅜" CAPITAL LETTERS AND NUMERALS

⅛" CAPITAL LETTERS AND NUMERALS

abcd

⅛" LOWERCASE LETTERS AND NUMERALS

Refer to Figures 5-35 and 5-37 in the textbook and draw the lettering at the height indicated. Repeat each series as many times as space permits.

INCLINED GOTHIC LETTERING

NAME

DATE

PROBLEM
5–11

SLOT MUST HAVE NO EXTERNAL BURRS.

.203 DIA. HOLE - PIERCE FROM BOTH SIDES - FOUR PLACES.

EMBOSS $\varnothing\frac{5}{16}$ $\overline{\downarrow}\frac{1}{16}$ - INSIDE ONLY - FOUR PLACES.

REMOVE BURRS AND SHARP EDGES.

DIMENSIONS THROUGHOUT ARE TO 90° BEND AS ASSEMBLED ON PRODUCT. PART SHOULD BE OVERBENT TO 91° FOR ADDITIONAL TENSION.

AN EASEMENT OF FOUR FEET ON EITHER SIDE OF THIS LINE IS RESERVED FOR UTILITY LINE THRU PROPERTIES.

DIMENSIONS, TOLERANCES AND SURFACE FINISH VALUES APPLY BEFORE THE APPLICATION OF THE FINISHES.

ROUTE MAIN HARNESS THROUGH EXISTING CLIP ON RIGHT SIDE OF PANEL ASSY, COWL TOP INNER FRONT.

FLAME DEPOSIT UNION CARBIDE'S CHROME OXIDE COATING LC-4 .002-.004 FINISH THICKNESS ON NOTED SURFACE.

FINISH AS FOLLOWS:
1. PAINT SYSTEM, ENAMEL, BLACK, M695476-110, (FNSH NO. 110) SPERRY SPEC M69771 AS NOTED. NO OVER SPRAY PERMISSIBLE.
2. PAINT SYSTEM, ENAMEL, WHITE, M695476-439, (FNSH NO. 439) SPERRY SPEC M692077 AS NOTED. NO OVER SPRAY PERMISSIBLE.

Using the guidelines provided, letter the notes at the heights indicated. Use vertical or inclined lettering as directed by your instructor. Strive for uniform and neat letter forms.

LETTERING NOTES

NAME

DATE

PROBLEM

5–12

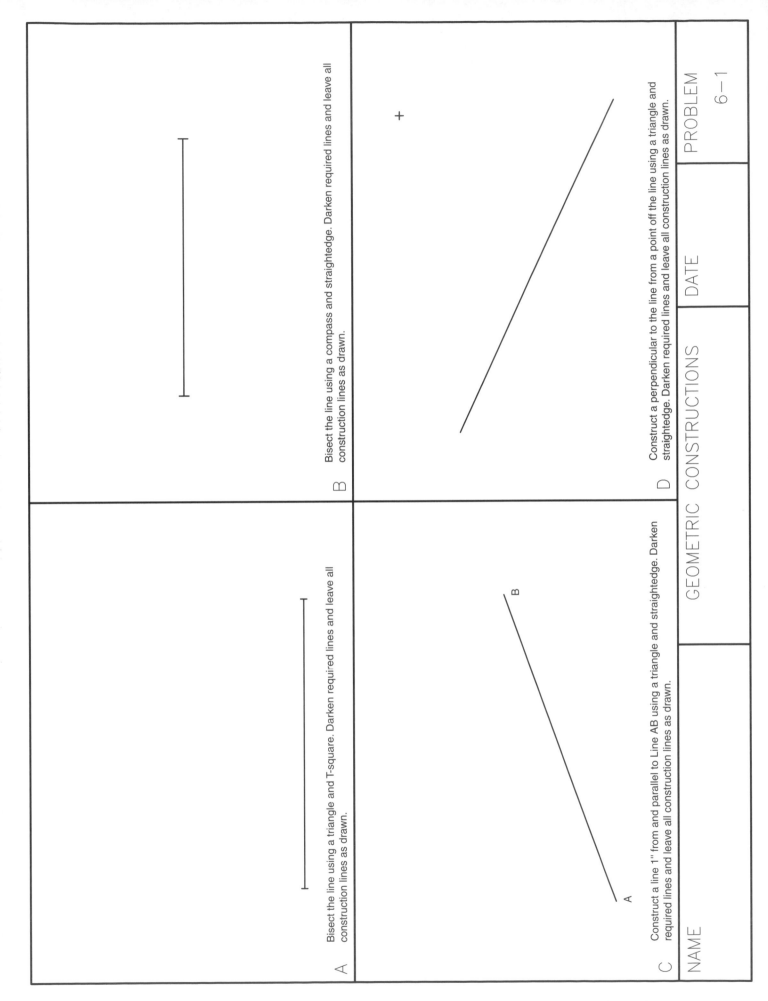

A Bisect the line using a triangle and T-square. Darken required lines and leave all construction lines as drawn.

B Bisect the line using a compass and straightedge. Darken required lines and leave all construction lines as drawn.

C Construct a line 1″ from and parallel to Line AB using a triangle and straightedge. Darken required lines and leave all construction lines as drawn.

D Construct a perpendicular to the line from a point off the line using a triangle and straightedge. Darken required lines and leave all construction lines as drawn.

NAME

GEOMETRIC CONSTRUCTIONS

DATE

PROBLEM

6–1

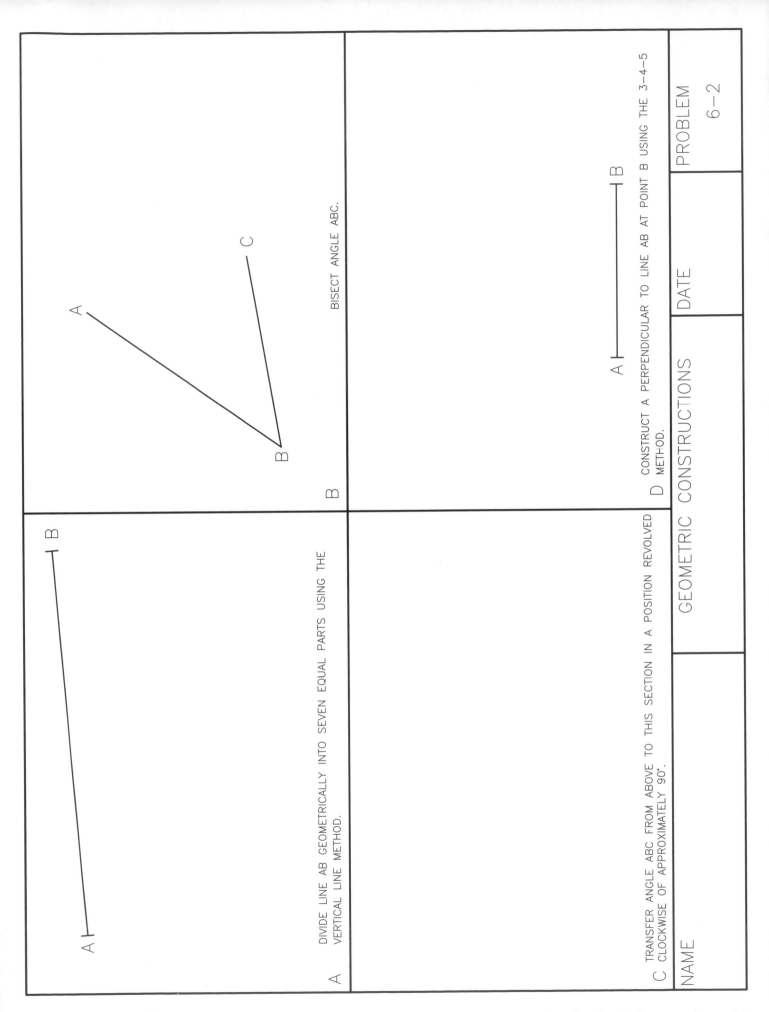

A DIVIDE LINE AB GEOMETRICALLY INTO SEVEN EQUAL PARTS USING THE VERTICAL LINE METHOD.

B BISECT ANGLE ABC.

C TRANSFER ANGLE ABC FROM ABOVE TO THIS SECTION IN A POSITION REVOLVED CLOCKWISE OF APPROXIMATELY 90°.

D CONSTRUCT A PERPENDICULAR TO LINE AB AT POINT B USING THE 3-4-5 METHOD.

NAME	GEOMETRIC CONSTRUCTIONS	DATE	PROBLEM
			6-2

A GIVEN SIDE AB, $\angle A = 37°$, AND $\angle B = 70°$, CONSTRUCT A TRIANGLE.

A —————— B

B GIVEN SIDES AB = 3, BC = $1\frac{1}{4}$, AND CA = $2\frac{1}{8}$, CONSTRUCT A TRIANGLE. MEASURE AND LABEL EACH ANGLE. PLACE SIDE AB HORIZONTALLY AT THE BOTTOM OF THE SPACE.

C GIVEN SIDE AB = $1\frac{1}{2}$, SIDE AC = 2, AND $\angle A = 30°$, CONSTRUCT A TRIANGLE. PLACE SIDE AB HORIZONTALLY AT THE BOTTOM OF THE SPACE.

D GIVEN SIDE AB = $2\frac{3}{4}$, CONSTRUCT AN EQUILATERAL TRIANGLE. PLACE SIDE AB HORIZONTALLY AT THE BOTTOM OF THE SPACE.

NAME		GEOMETRIC CONSTRUCTIONS	DATE	PROBLEM
				6-3

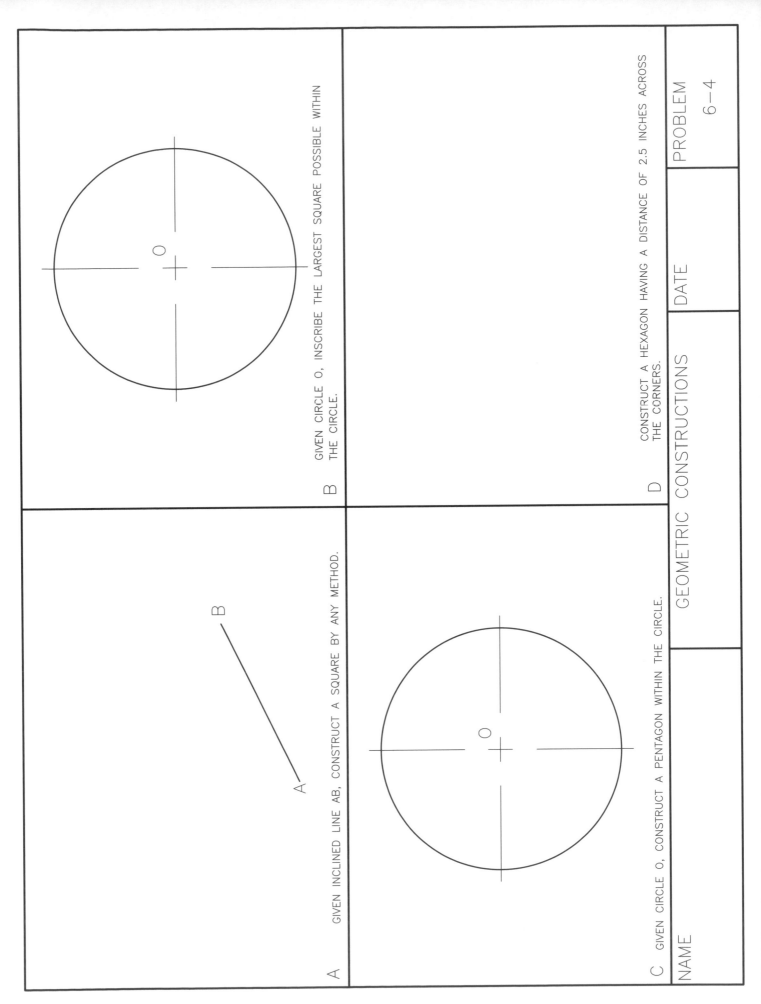

A   GIVEN INCLINED LINE AB, CONSTRUCT A SQUARE BY ANY METHOD.

B   GIVEN CIRCLE O, INSCRIBE THE LARGEST SQUARE POSSIBLE WITHIN THE CIRCLE.

C   GIVEN CIRCLE O, CONSTRUCT A PENTAGON WITHIN THE CIRCLE.

D   CONSTRUCT A HEXAGON HAVING A DISTANCE OF 2.5 INCHES ACROSS THE CORNERS.

GEOMETRIC CONSTRUCTIONS

NAME

DATE

PROBLEM
6-4

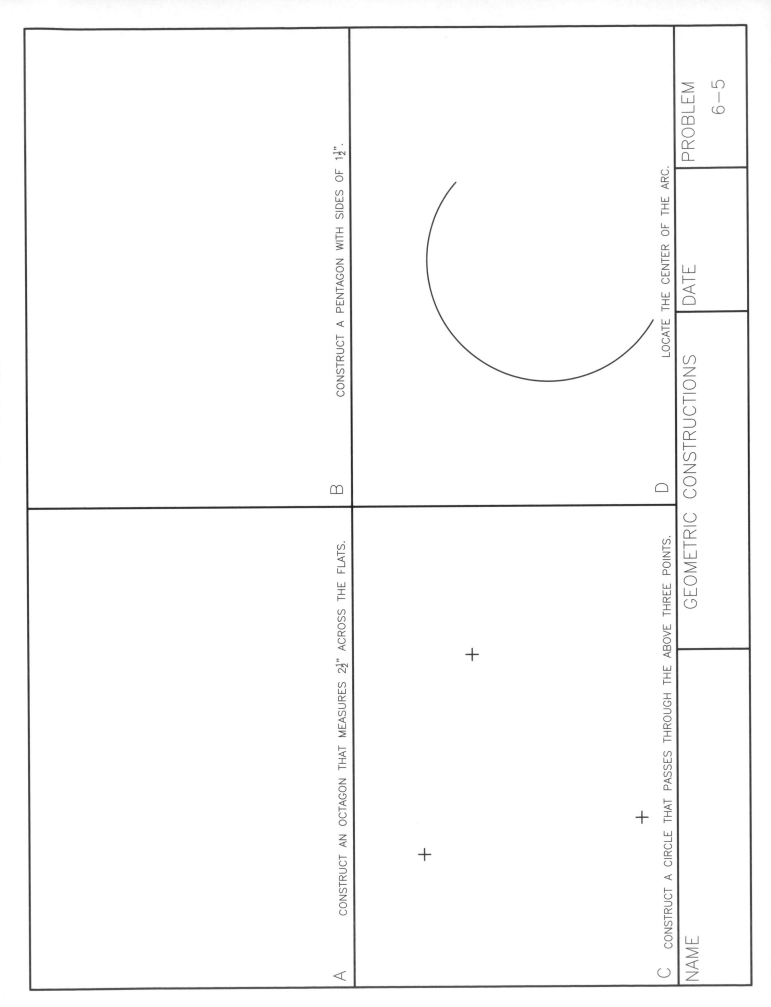

A   CONSTRUCT AN OCTAGON THAT MEASURES 2½" ACROSS THE FLATS.

B   CONSTRUCT A PENTAGON WITH SIDES OF 1¼".

C   CONSTRUCT A CIRCLE THAT PASSES THROUGH THE ABOVE THREE POINTS.

D   LOCATE THE CENTER OF THE ARC.

NAME _____

GEOMETRIC CONSTRUCTIONS

DATE _____

PROBLEM 6-5

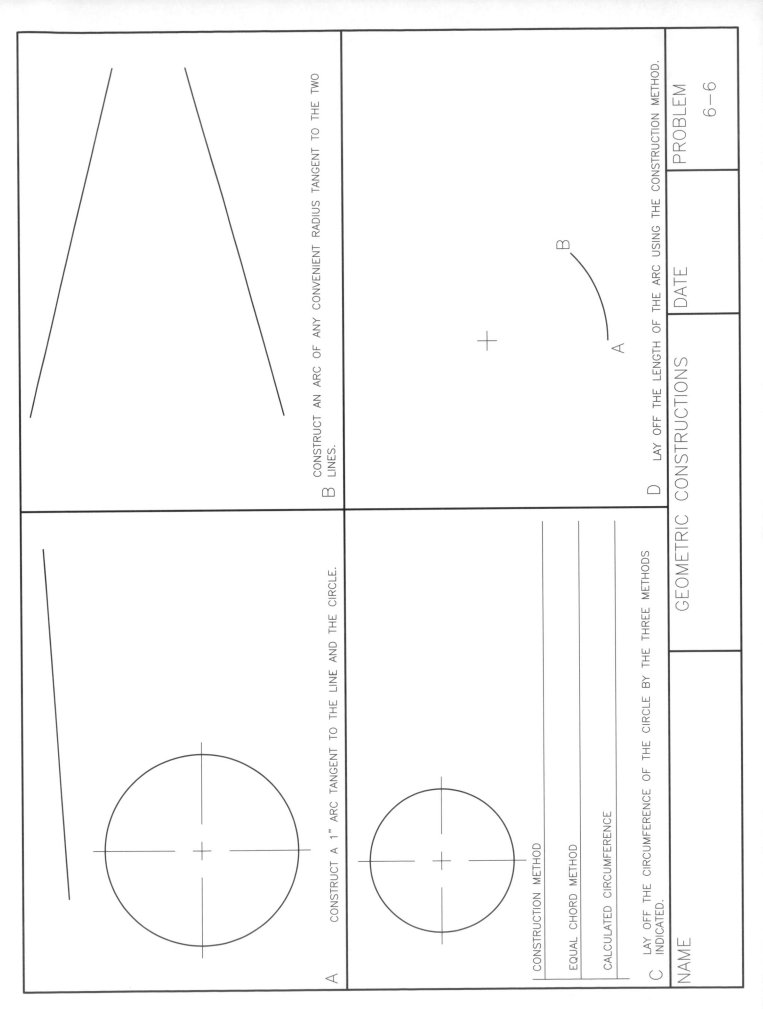

A   CONSTRUCT A 1" ARC TANGENT TO THE LINE AND THE CIRCLE.

B   CONSTRUCT AN ARC OF ANY CONVENIENT RADIUS TANGENT TO THE TWO LINES.

C   LAY OFF THE CIRCUMFERENCE OF THE CIRCLE BY THE THREE METHODS INDICATED.

CONSTRUCTION METHOD

EQUAL CHORD METHOD

CALCULATED CIRCUMFERENCE

D   LAY OFF THE LENGTH OF THE ARC USING THE CONSTRUCTION METHOD.

B

A

GEOMETRIC CONSTRUCTIONS

NAME

DATE

PROBLEM

6–6

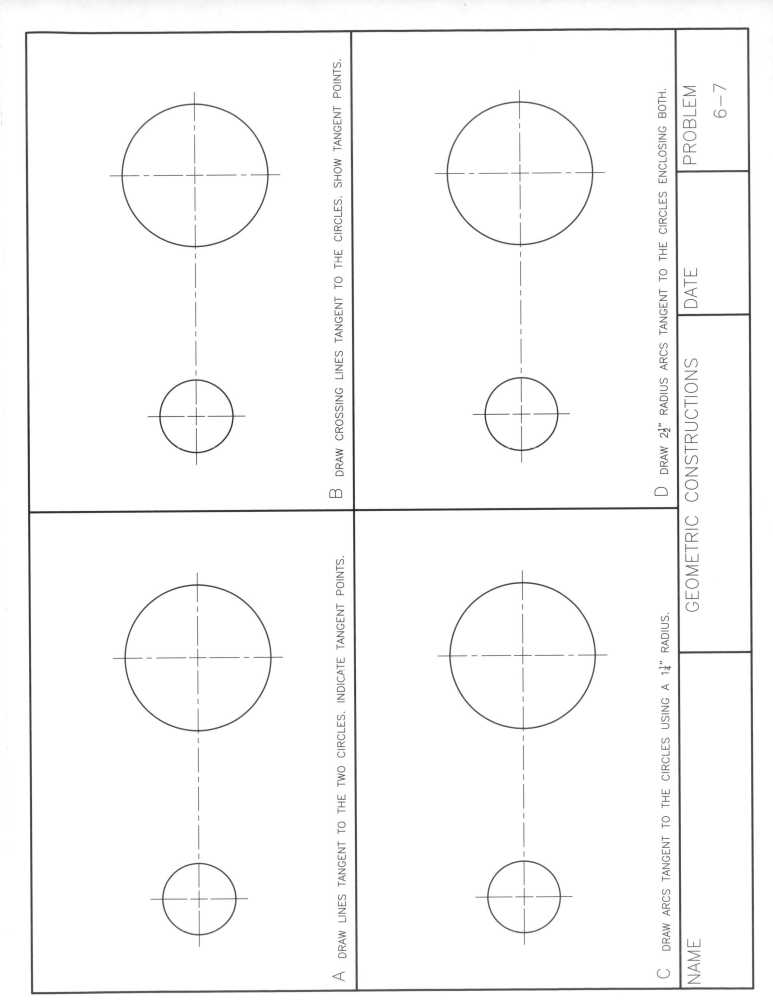

B DRAW CROSSING LINES TANGENT TO THE CIRCLES. SHOW TANGENT POINTS.

D DRAW 2½" RADIUS ARCS TANGENT TO THE CIRCLES ENCLOSING BOTH.

A DRAW LINES TANGENT TO THE TWO CIRCLES. INDICATE TANGENT POINTS.

C DRAW ARCS TANGENT TO THE CIRCLES USING A 1¼" RADIUS.

PROBLEM		
6–7		

DATE

GEOMETRIC CONSTRUCTIONS

NAME

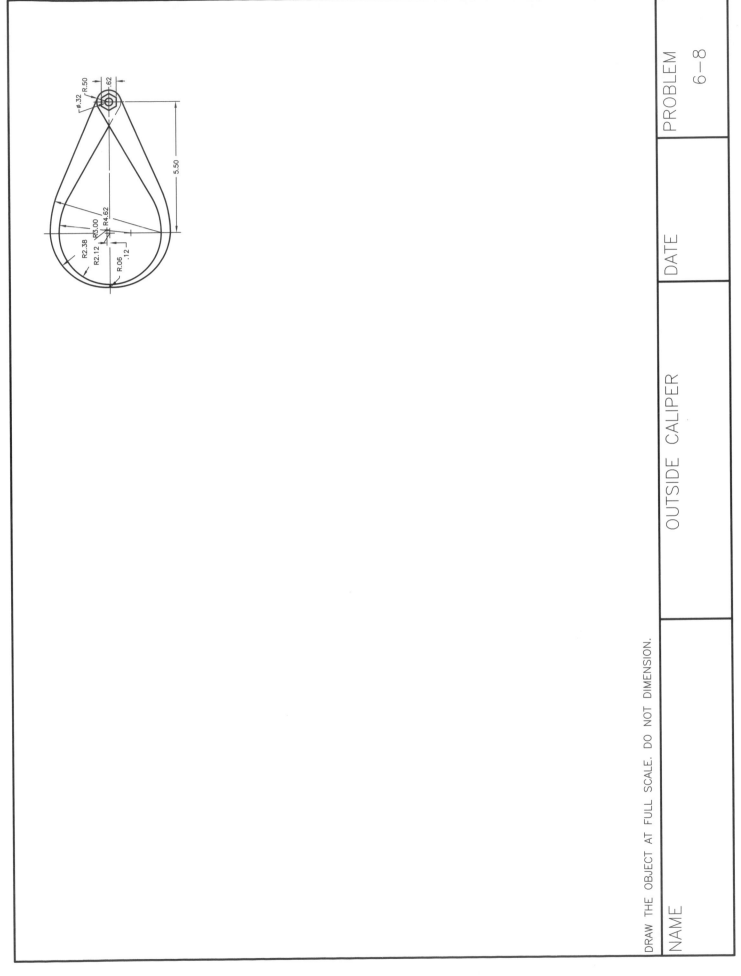

Chapter 6   Basic Geometric Constructions   **42**

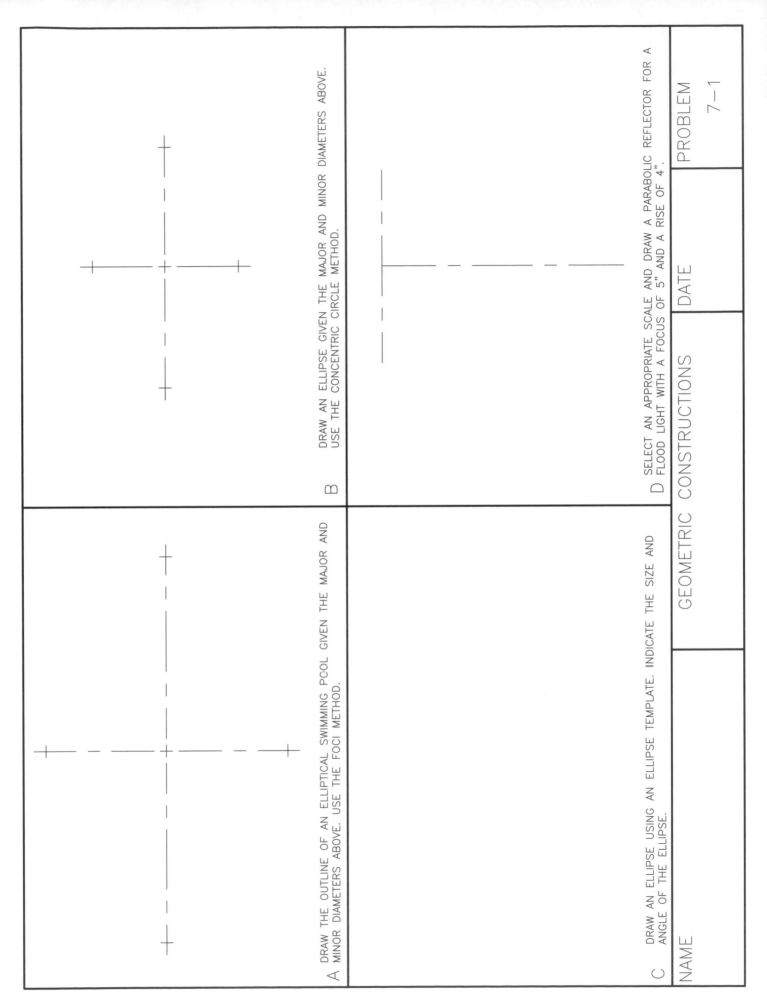

A   DRAW THE OUTLINE OF AN ELLIPTICAL SWIMMING POOL GIVEN THE MAJOR AND MINOR DIAMETERS ABOVE. USE THE FOCI METHOD.

B   DRAW AN ELLIPSE GIVEN THE MAJOR AND MINOR DIAMETERS ABOVE. USE THE CONCENTRIC CIRCLE METHOD.

C   DRAW AN ELLIPSE USING AN ELLIPSE TEMPLATE. INDICATE THE SIZE AND ANGLE OF THE ELLIPSE.

D   SELECT AN APPROPRIATE SCALE AND DRAW A PARABOLIC REFLECTOR FOR A FLOOD LIGHT WITH A FOCUS OF 5" AND A RISE OF 4".

NAME

GEOMETRIC CONSTRUCTIONS

DATE

PROBLEM
7-1

A   CONSTRUCT A HYPERBOLA AND ITS ASYMPTOTES GIVEN A HORIZONTAL
    TRANSVERSE AXIS OF .75" AND FOCI 1.25" APART. USE THE FOCI METHOD.

B   CONSTRUCT AN EQUILATERAL HYPERBOLA THRU POINT P.

    + P

C   DRAW ONE REVOLUTION OF A SPIRAL OF ARCHIMEDES WITH THE GENERATING
    POINT MOVING UNIFORMLY IN A COUNTERCLOCKWISE DIRECTION AND AWAY
    FROM THE CENTER AT THE RATE OF 1.25" PER REVOLUTION.

D   CONSTRUCT THE INVOLUTE OF A POINT STARTING AT THE APEX OF A .50"
    EQUILATERAL TRIANGLE FOR ONE REVOLUTION CLOCKWISE.

GEOMETRIC CONSTRUCTIONS

NAME   DATE

PROBLEM

7-2

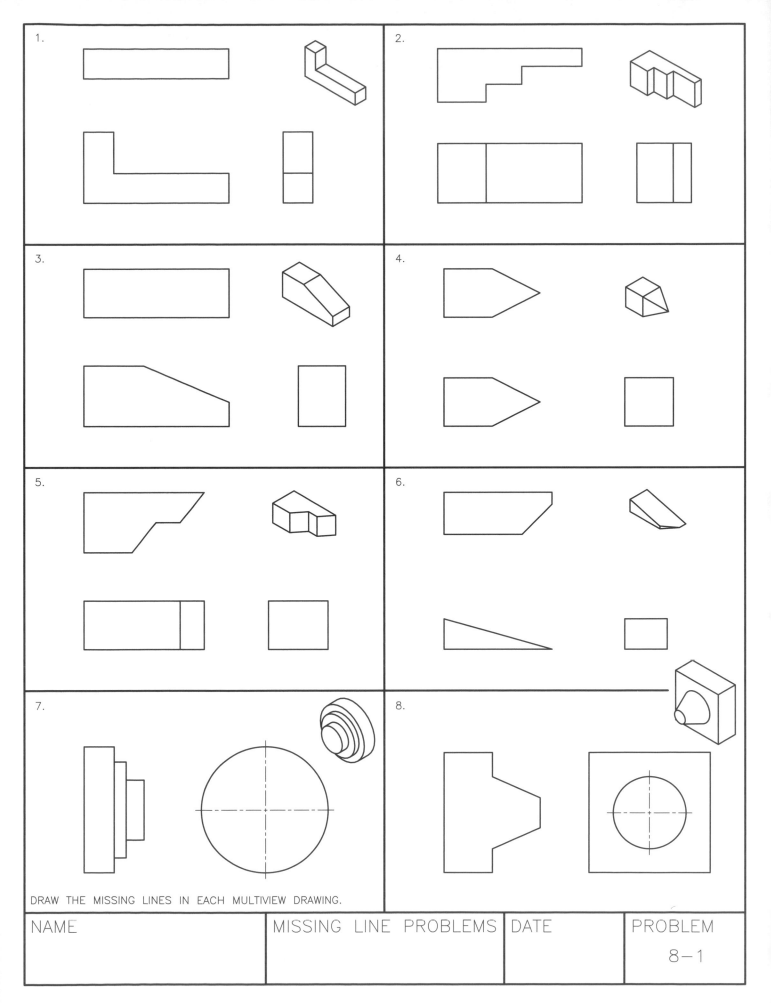

1.

2.

3.

4.

5.

6.

7.

8.

DRAW THE MISSING LINES IN EACH MULTIVIEW DRAWING.

| NAME | MISSING LINE PROBLEMS | DATE | PROBLEM |
| | | | 8−1 |

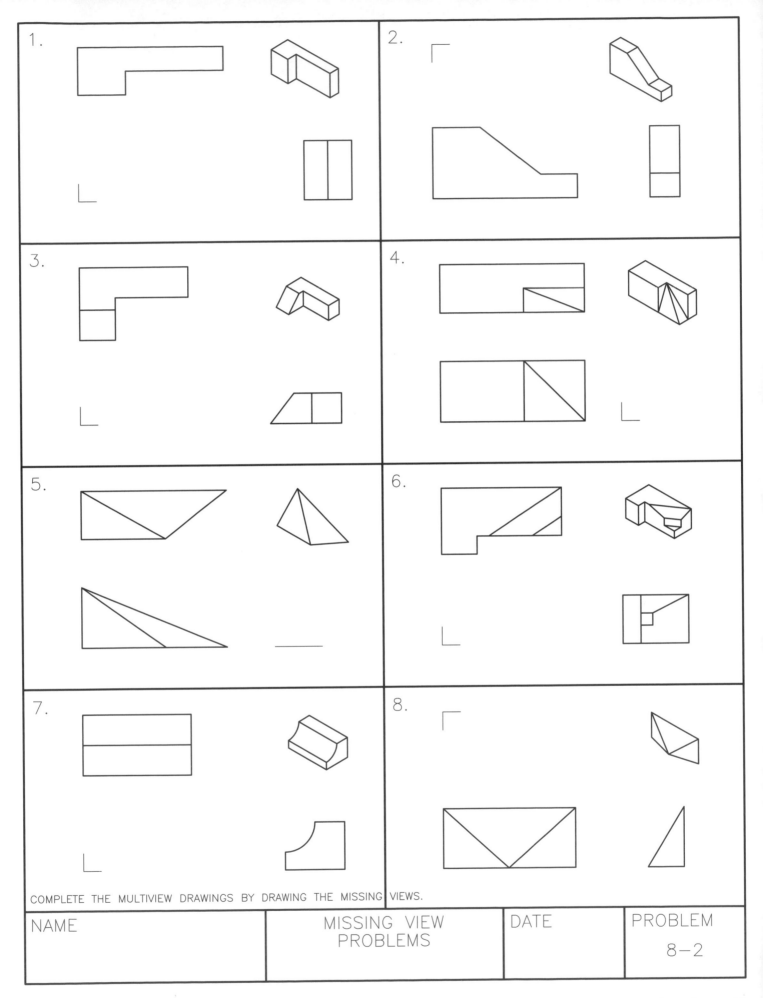

COMPLETE THE MULTIVIEW DRAWINGS BY DRAWING THE MISSING VIEWS.

NAME	MISSING VIEW PROBLEMS	DATE	PROBLEM 8–2

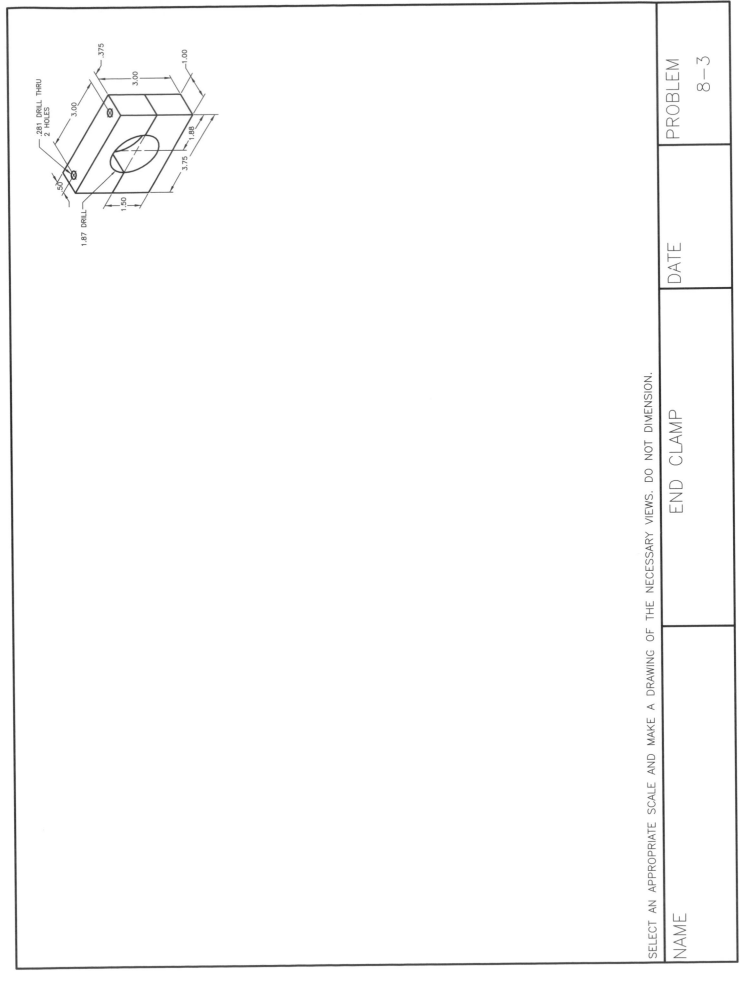

.375

3.00

1.00

.281 DRILL THRU
2 HOLES

3.00

1.88

3.75

.50

1.50

1.87 DRILL

NAME		END CLAMP	DATE	PROBLEM
				8–3

SELECT AN APPROPRIATE SCALE AND MAKE A DRAWING OF THE NECESSARY VIEWS. DO NOT DIMENSION.

NAME		STOP BLOCK	DATE	PROBLEM
				8–4

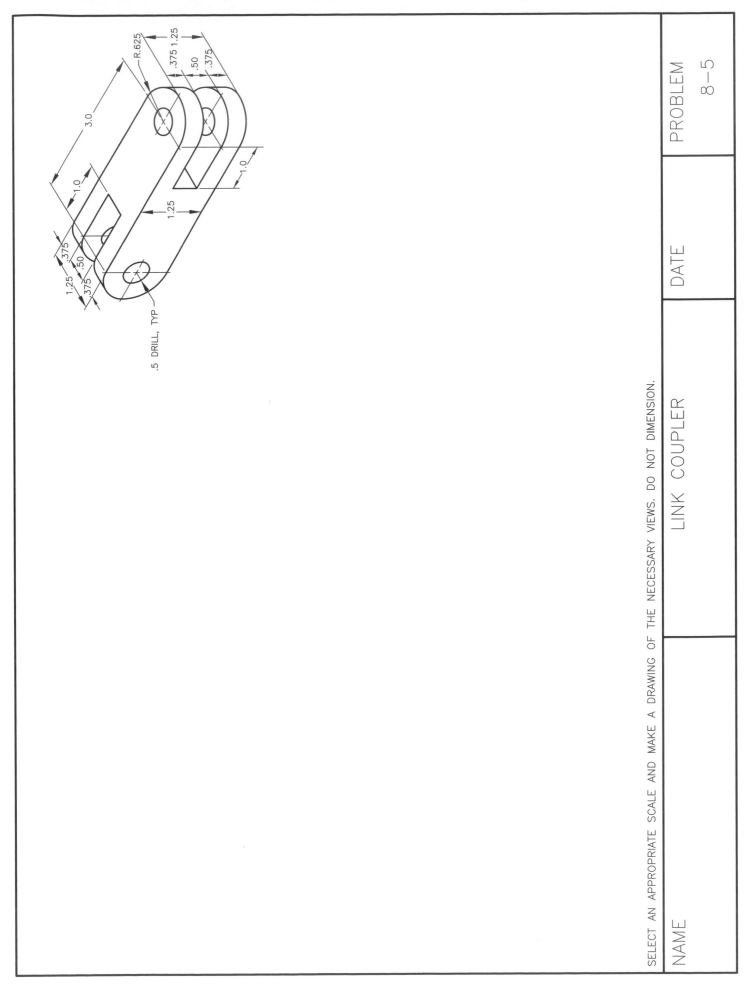

R.625

.375 1.25

.50

.375

3.0

1.0

1.25

1.0

.375

.50

.375

1.25

.5 DRILL, TYP

SELECT AN APPROPRIATE SCALE AND MAKE A DRAWING OF THE NECESSARY VIEWS. DO NOT DIMENSION.

NAME

LINK COUPLER

DATE

PROBLEM

8–5

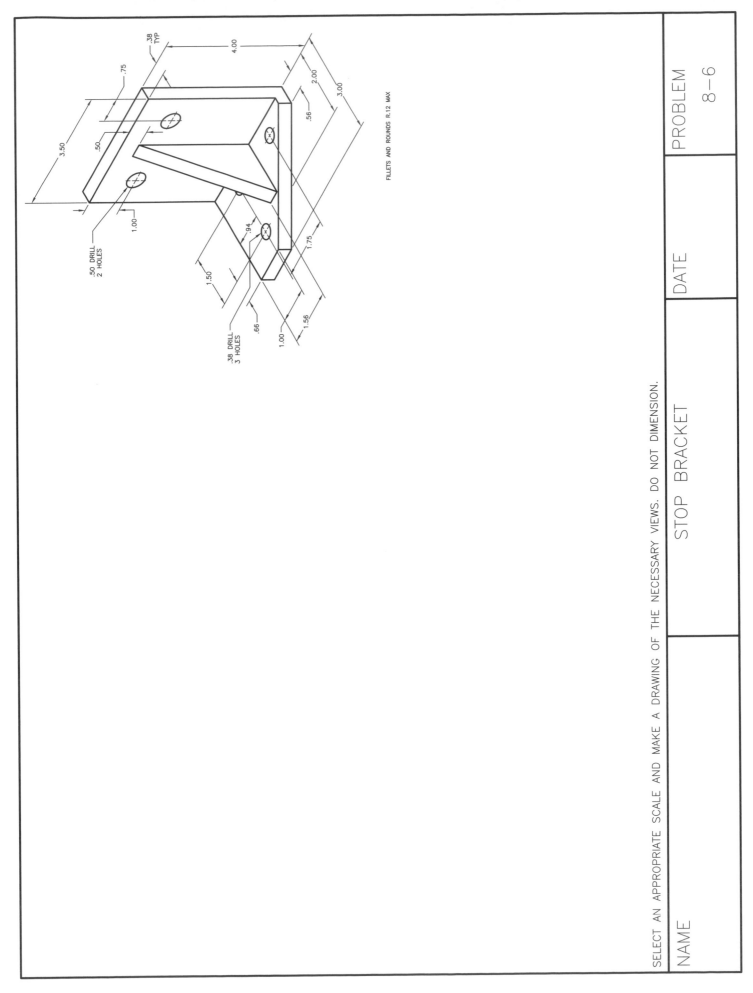

.38
TYP

4.00

.75

2.00

3.50

.56

.50

3.00

FILLETS AND ROUNDS R.12 MAX

1.00

.50 DRILL
2 HOLES

.94

1.75

1.50

.38 DRILL
3 HOLES

.66

1.00

1.56

SELECT AN APPROPRIATE SCALE AND MAKE A DRAWING OF THE NECESSARY VIEWS. DO NOT DIMENSION.

NAME

STOP BRACKET

DATE

PROBLEM

8–6

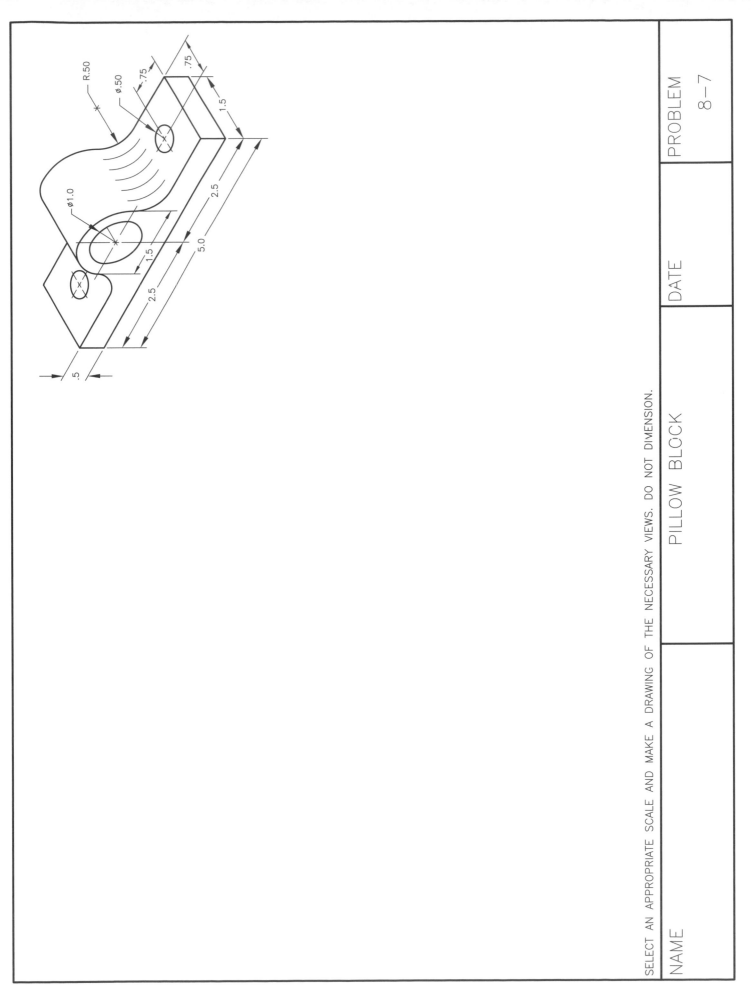

R.50

ø.50

.75

.75

1.5

ø1.0

2.5

5.0

1.5

2.5

.5

SELECT AN APPROPRIATE SCALE AND MAKE A DRAWING OF THE NECESSARY VIEWS. DO NOT DIMENSION.

NAME

DATE

PROBLEM

PILLOW BLOCK

8–7

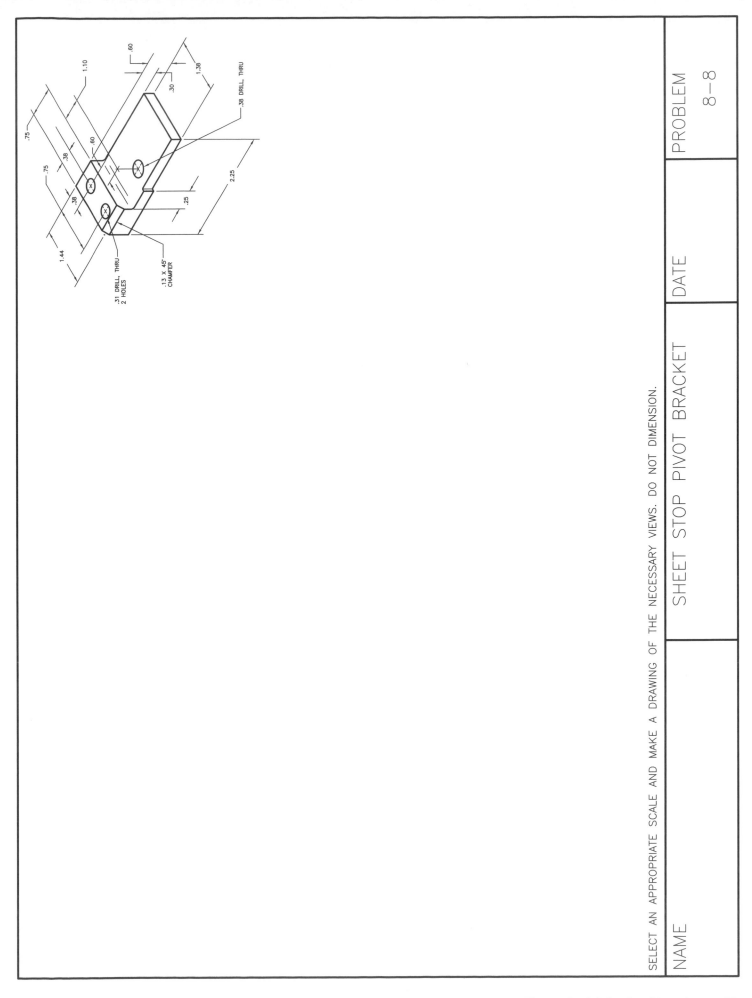

.60
1.10
.30
1.38
.75
.60
.38
.75
.38
.38 DRILL, THRU
2.25
.25
1.44
.31 DRILL, THRU
2 HOLES
.13 X 45°
CHAMFER

SELECT AN APPROPRIATE SCALE AND MAKE A DRAWING OF THE NECESSARY VIEWS. DO NOT DIMENSION.

NAME

SHEET STOP PIVOT BRACKET

DATE

PROBLEM

8-8

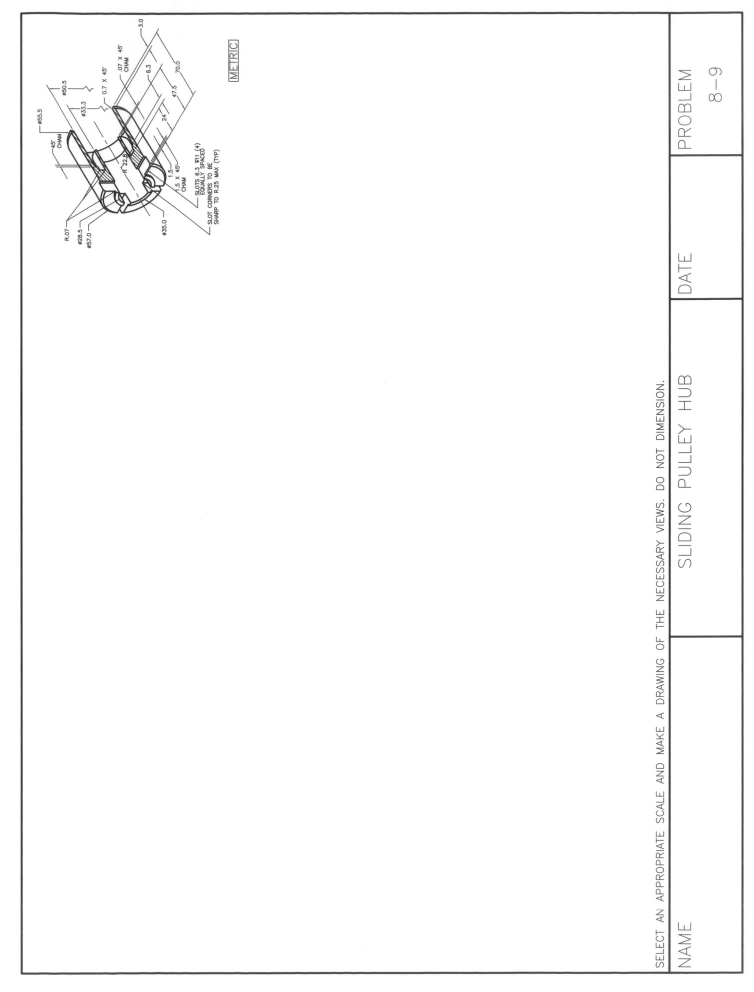

METRIC

Ø55.5
Ø50.5
Ø33.3
45° CHAM
0.7 X 45°
.07 X 45° CHAM
3.0
6.3
70.0
47.5
24
R 22.8
R.07
Ø28.5
Ø57.0
Ø35.0
1.5-
1.5 X 45° CHAM
SLOTS 6.3 ⊽11 (4) EQUALLY SPACED
SLOT CORNERS TO BE SHARP TO R.25 MAX (TYP)

SELECT AN APPROPRIATE SCALE AND MAKE A DRAWING OF THE NECESSARY VIEWS. DO NOT DIMENSION.

NAME

SLIDING PULLEY HUB

DATE

PROBLEM

8-9

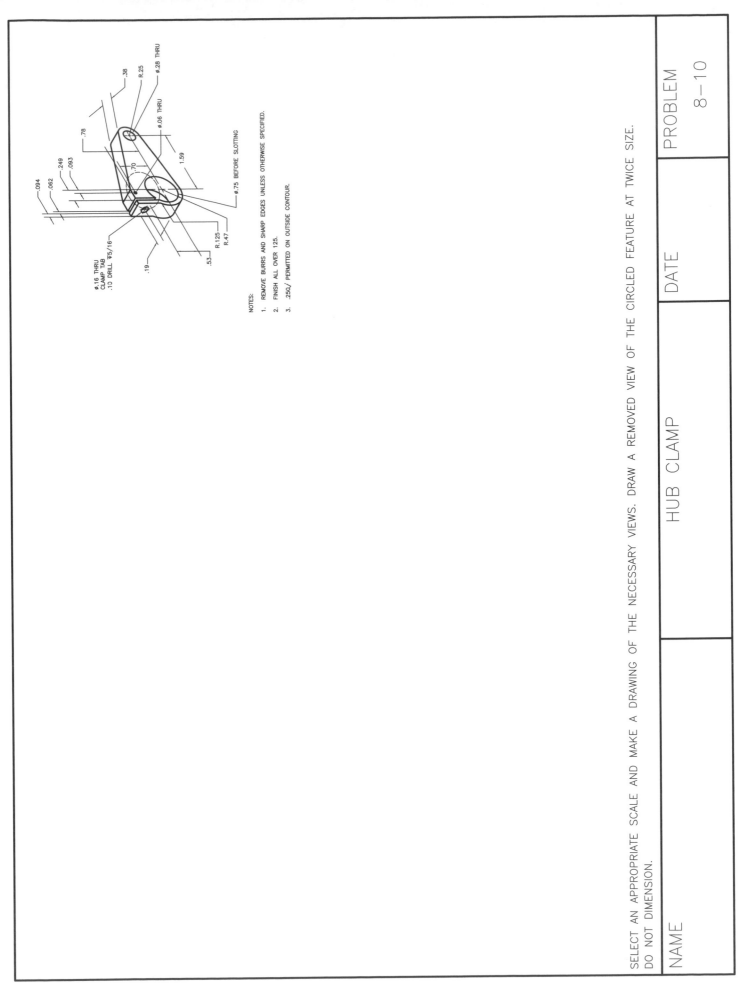

.094
.062
.249
.093

.78

.38
R.25
ø.28 THRU
ø.06 THRU

1.59

.70

ø.16 THRU
CLAMP TAB
.10 DRILL ⌴5/16

.19

.53

R.125
R.47

ø.75 BEFORE SLOTTING

NOTES:

1. REMOVE BURRS AND SHARP EDGES UNLESS OTHERWISE SPECIFIED.
2. FINISH ALL OVER 125.
3. .25√ PERMITTED ON OUTSIDE CONTOUR.

SELECT AN APPROPRIATE SCALE AND MAKE A DRAWING OF THE NECESSARY VIEWS. DRAW A REMOVED VIEW OF THE CIRCLED FEATURE AT TWICE SIZE. DO NOT DIMENSION.

NAME		DATE	PROBLEM
	HUB CLAMP		8–10

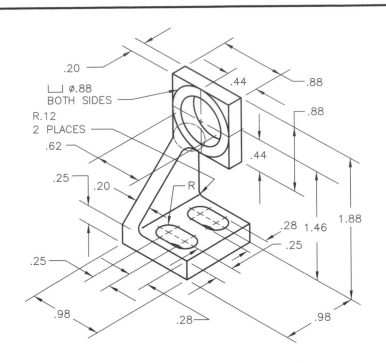

.20

⌴ ⌀.88
BOTH SIDES

R.12
2 PLACES

.62

.25

.20

R

.44

.88

.88

.44

.28 1.46

.25

1.88

.25

.98

.28

.98

SELECT AN APPROPRIATE SCALE AND MAKE A DRAWING OF THE NECESSARY VIEWS. DRAW A REMOVED VIEW OF THE CIRCLED FEATURE AT TWICE SIZE. DO NOT DIMENSION.

NAME	SINGLE BEARING HANGER	DATE	PROBLEM
			8-11

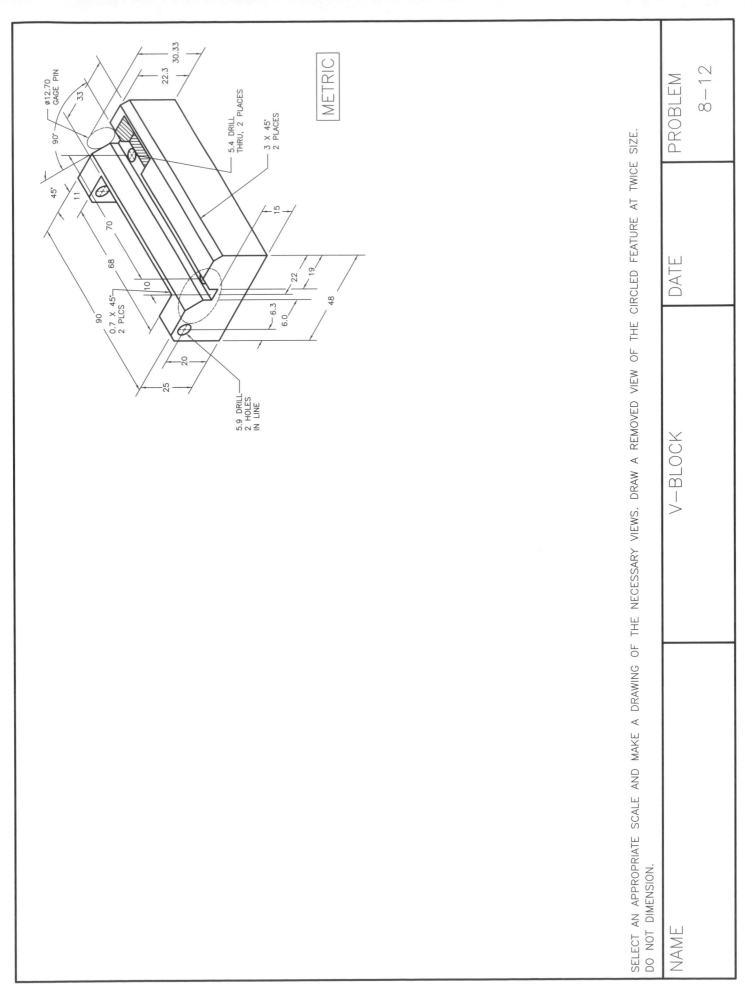

METRIC

ø12.70 GAGE PIN

30.33
22.3
33
90°
45°
11
70
68
110
90
0.7 X 45°
2 PLCS
20
25

5.4 DRILL
THRU, 2 PLACES

3 X 45°
2 PLACES

15
22
19
6.3
6.0
48

5.9 DRILL
2 HOLES
IN LINE

SELECT AN APPROPRIATE SCALE AND MAKE A DRAWING OF THE NECESSARY VIEWS. DRAW A REMOVED VIEW OF THE CIRCLED FEATURE AT TWICE SIZE.
DO NOT DIMENSION.

| NAME | V–BLOCK | DATE | PROBLEM |
| | | | 8–12 |

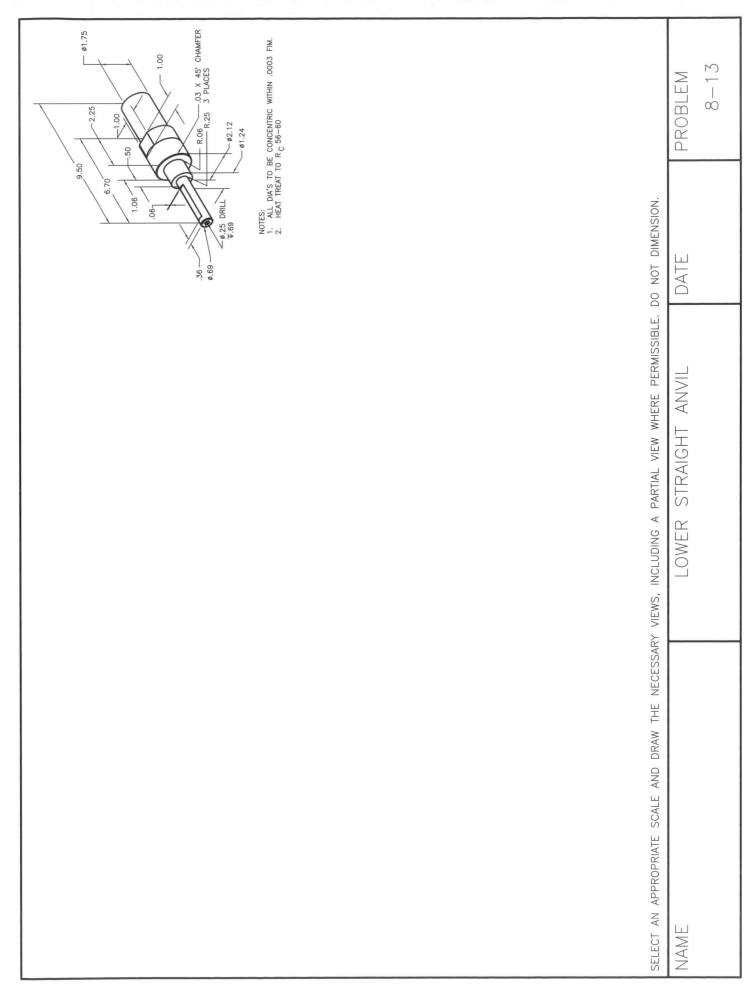

ø1.75

1.00

.03 X 45° CHAMFER
3 PLACES

2.25

1.00

R.06

R.25

ø2.12

ø1.24

.50

9.50

6.70

1.06

.06

ø.25 DRILL
▼.69

.36

ø.69

NOTES:
1. ALL DIA'S TO BE CONCENTRIC WITHIN .0003 FIM.
2. HEAT TREAT TO R$_C$ 56–60

SELECT AN APPROPRIATE SCALE AND DRAW THE NECESSARY VIEWS, INCLUDING A PARTIAL VIEW WHERE PERMISSIBLE. DO NOT DIMENSION.

NAME

LOWER STRAIGHT ANVIL

DATE

PROBLEM

8–13

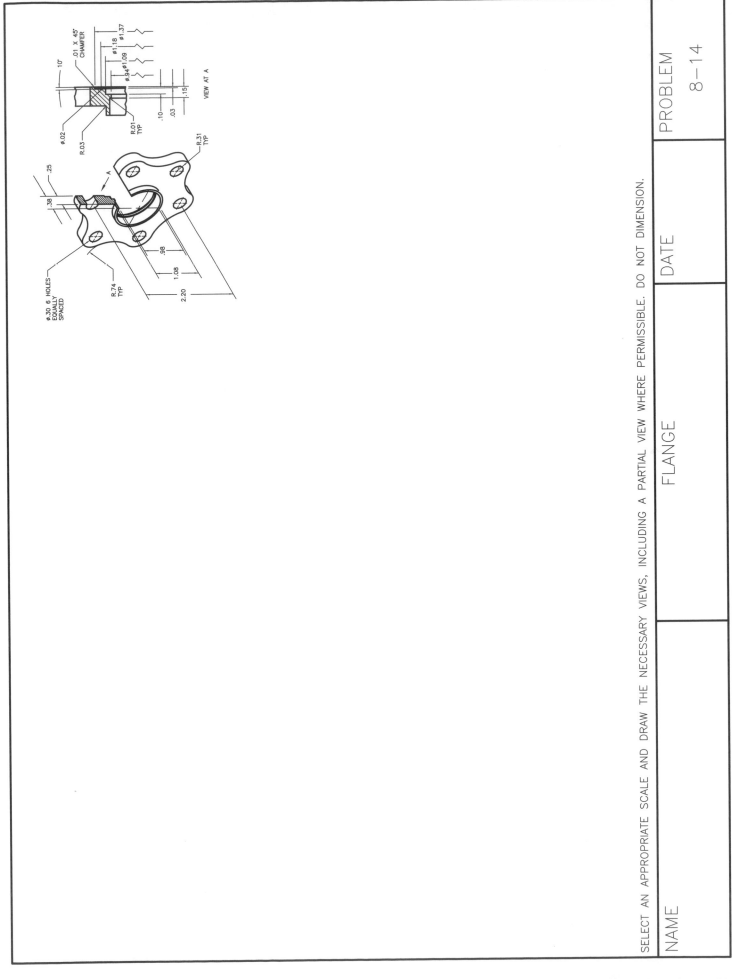

VIEW AT A

.01 X 45° CHAMFER

10°

⌀1.18
⌀1.37

⌀.94 ⌀1.09

R.01
TYP

⌀.02

R.03

.10

.03

.15

R.31
TYP

.25

A

.38

⌀.30 6 HOLES
EQUALLY
SPACED

R.74
TYP

.98

1.08

2.20

SELECT AN APPROPRIATE SCALE AND DRAW THE NECESSARY VIEWS, INCLUDING A PARTIAL VIEW WHERE PERMISSIBLE. DO NOT DIMENSION.

NAME

DATE

PROBLEM

8–14

FLANGE

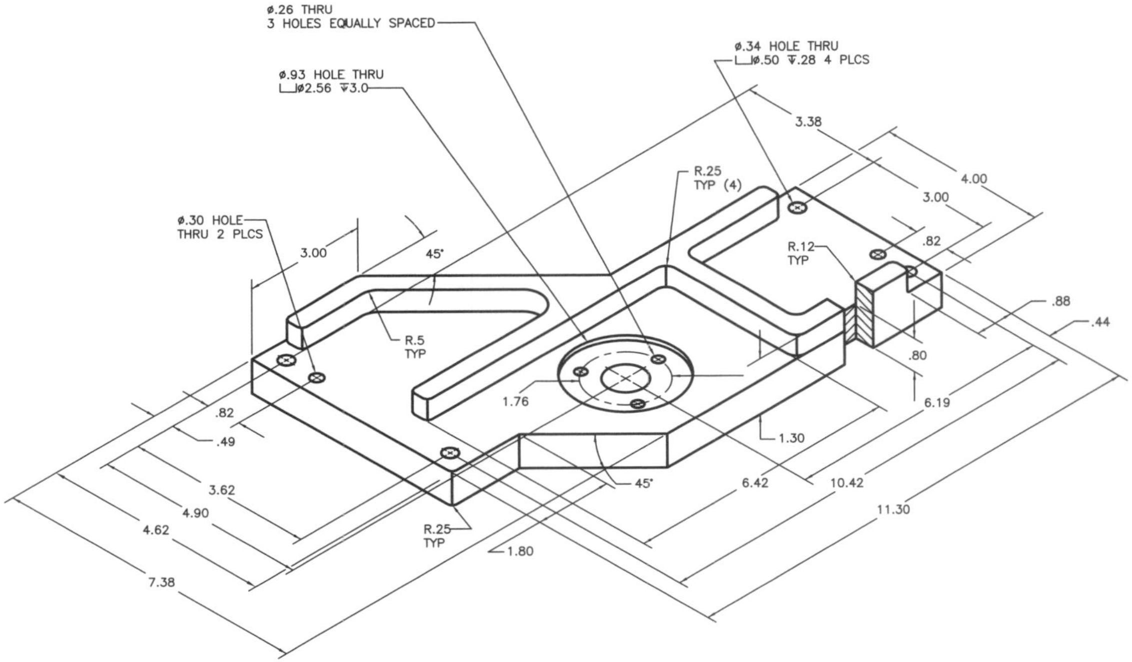
ø.26 THRU
3 HOLES EQUALLY SPACED
ø.93 HOLE THRU
⌴ø2.56 ↧3.0
ø.34 HOLE THRU
⌴ø.50 ↧.28 4 PLCS
ø.30 HOLE
THRU 2 PLCS
3.00
45°
R.5
TYP
R.25
TYP (4)
R.12
TYP
3.38
4.00
3.00
.82
.88
.44
.80
6.19
1.76
1.30
6.42
10.42
11.30
45°
1.80
R.25
TYP
.82
.49
3.62
4.90
4.62
7.38

RIB THICKNESS .5, FILLETS & ROUNDS R.12 UNLESS SHOWN OTHERWISE

SELECT AN APPROPRIATE SCALE AND DRAW THE NECESSARY VIEWS. USE CONVENTIONAL DRAFTING PRACTICES WHERE APPLICABLE. DO NOT DIMENSION.

NAME	VARIABLE GEAR COVER	DATE	PROBLEM 8–15

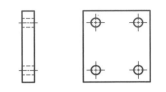

PRESSURE REGULATOR PLATE

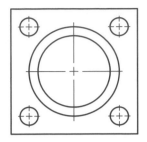
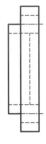

BEARING HOUSING

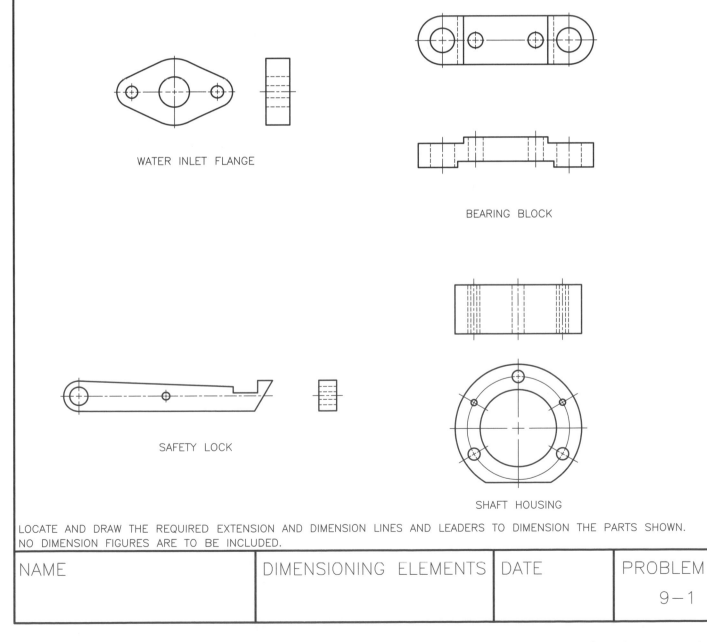

WATER INLET FLANGE

BEARING BLOCK

SAFETY LOCK

SHAFT HOUSING

LOCATE AND DRAW THE REQUIRED EXTENSION AND DIMENSION LINES AND LEADERS TO DIMENSION THE PARTS SHOWN. NO DIMENSION FIGURES ARE TO BE INCLUDED.

NAME	DIMENSIONING ELEMENTS	DATE	PROBLEM
			9–1

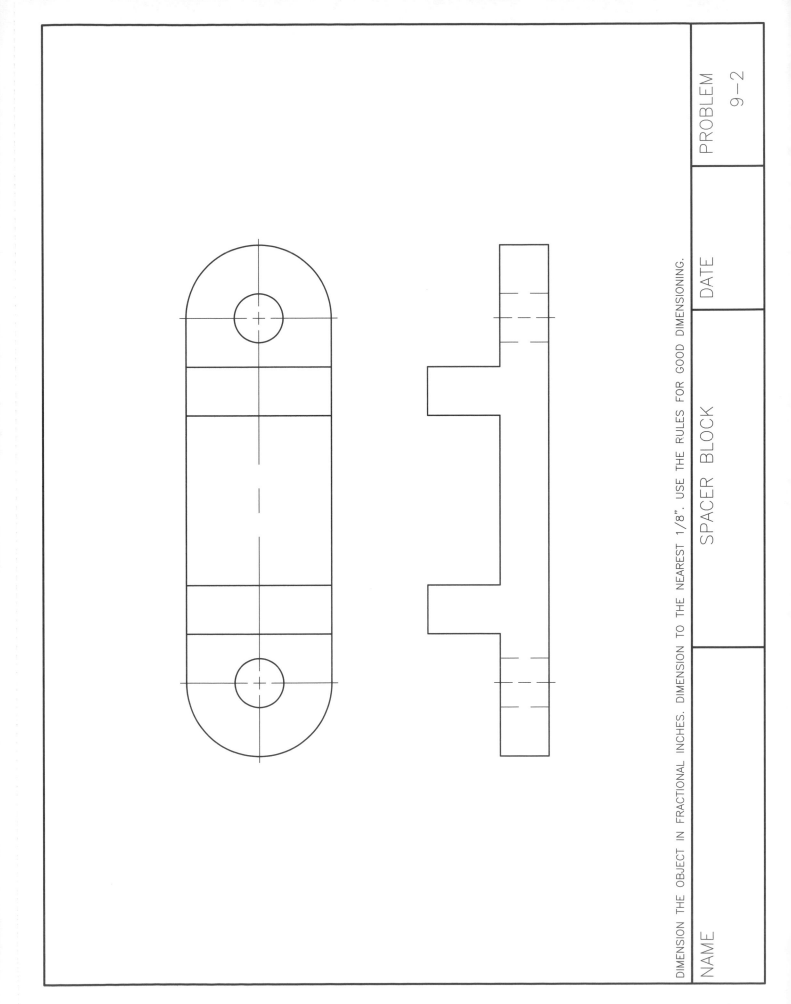

DIMENSION THE OBJECT IN FRACTIONAL INCHES. DIMENSION TO THE NEAREST 1/8". USE THE RULES FOR GOOD DIMENSIONING.

NAME

SPACER BLOCK

DATE

PROBLEM
9–2

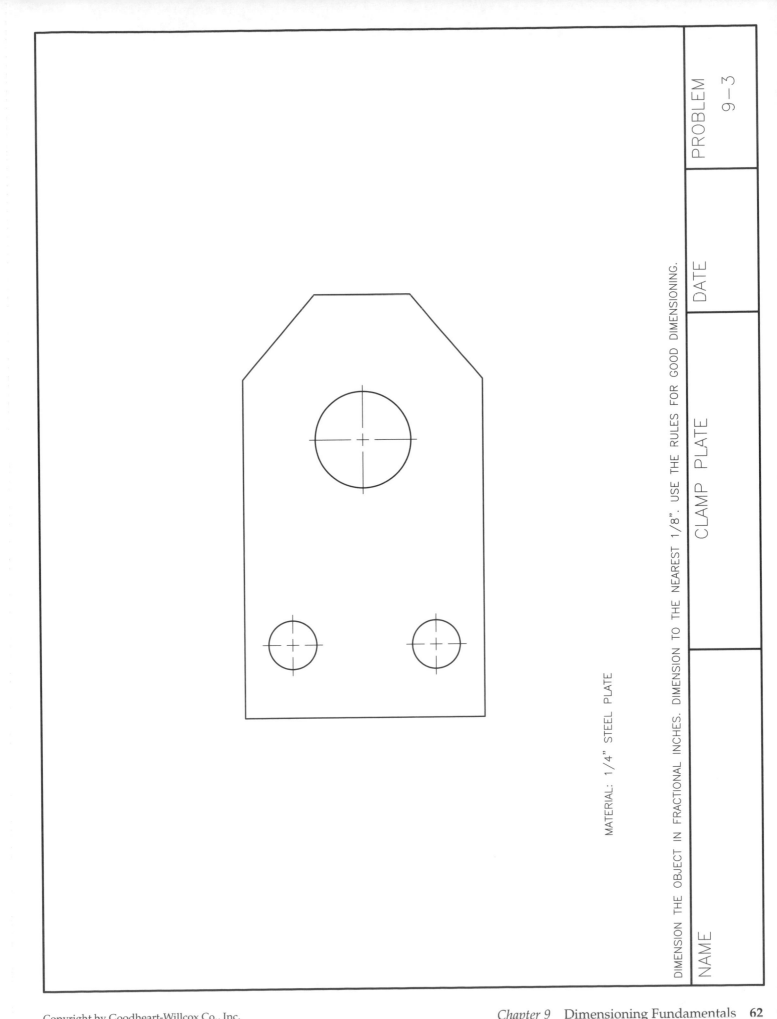

MATERIAL: 1/4" STEEL PLATE

DIMENSION THE OBJECT IN FRACTIONAL INCHES. DIMENSION TO THE NEAREST 1/8". USE THE RULES FOR GOOD DIMENSIONING.

NAME	CLAMP PLATE	DATE	PROBLEM
			9–3

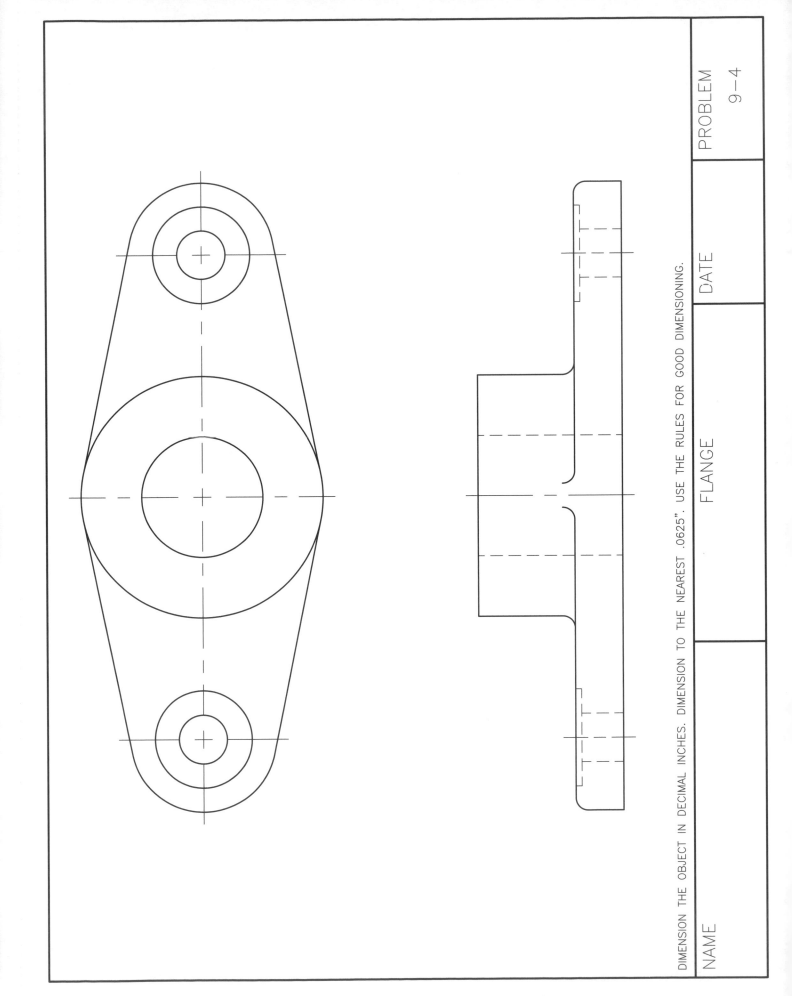

DIMENSION THE OBJECT IN DECIMAL INCHES. DIMENSION TO THE NEAREST .0625". USE THE RULES FOR GOOD DIMENSIONING.

NAME

DATE

PROBLEM
9-4

FLANGE

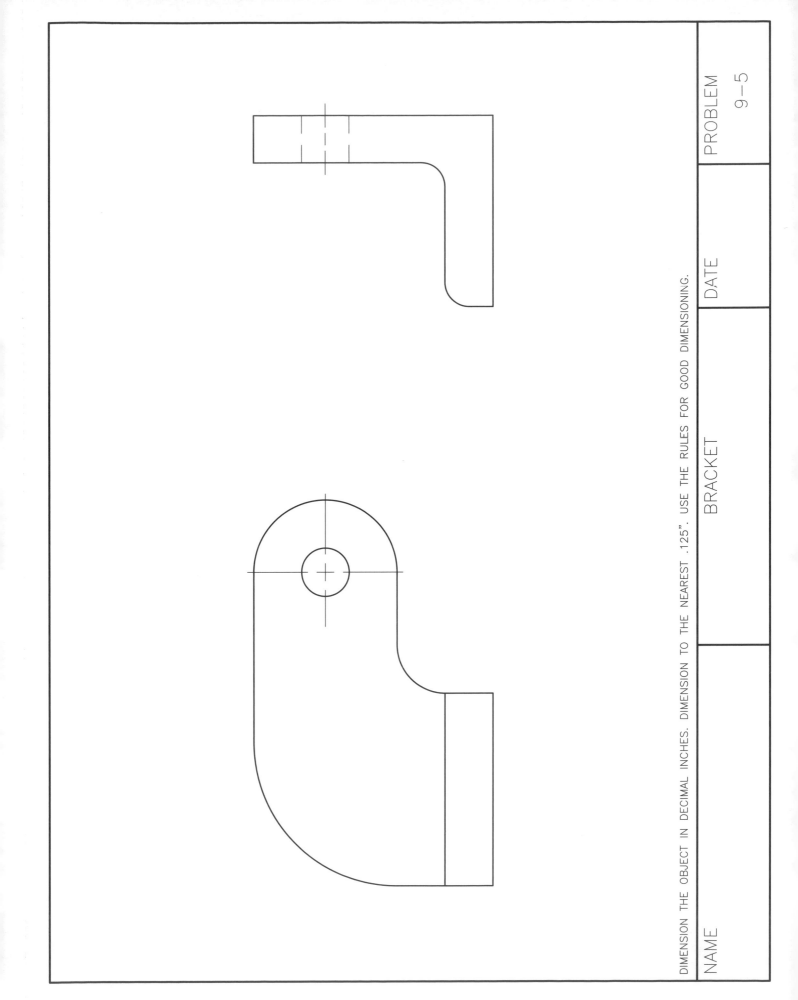

DIMENSION THE OBJECT IN DECIMAL INCHES. DIMENSION TO THE NEAREST .125". USE THE RULES FOR GOOD DIMENSIONING.

NAME

BRACKET

DATE

PROBLEM

9-5

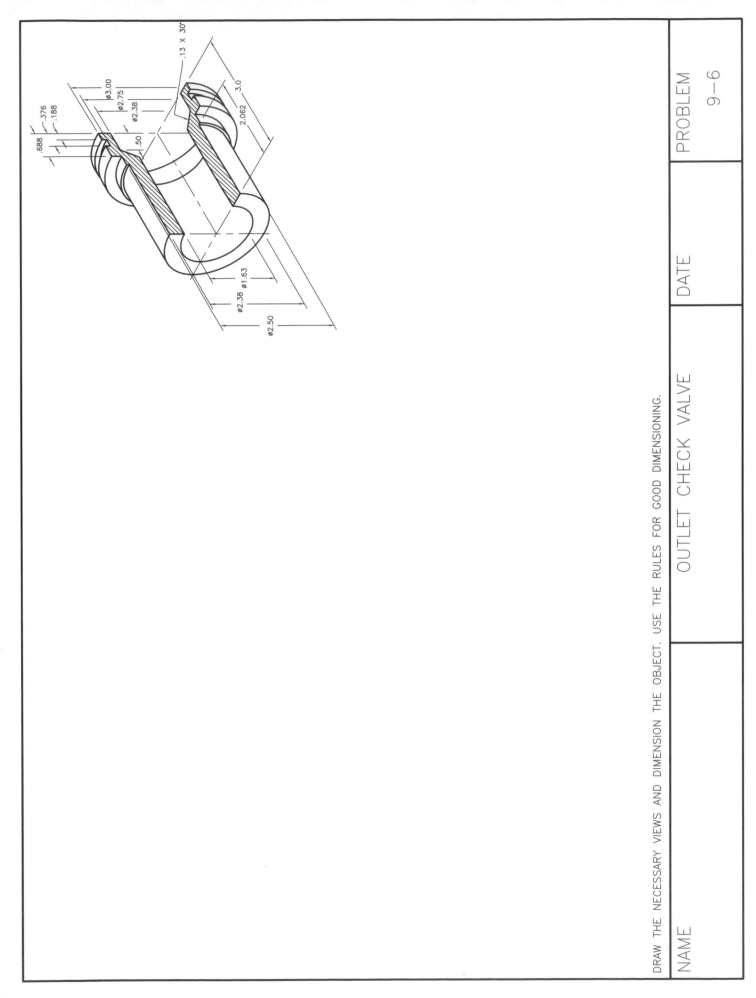

.13 X 30°

Ø3.00
Ø2.75
Ø2.38

.376
.188

.688

.50

3.0

2.062

Ø2.38 Ø1.63

Ø2.50

PROBLEM

9-6

DATE

OUTLET CHECK VALVE

DRAW THE NECESSARY VIEWS AND DIMENSION THE OBJECT. USE THE RULES FOR GOOD DIMENSIONING.

NAME

Copyright by Goodheart-Willcox Co., Inc.

Chapter 9   Dimensioning Fundamentals   **65**

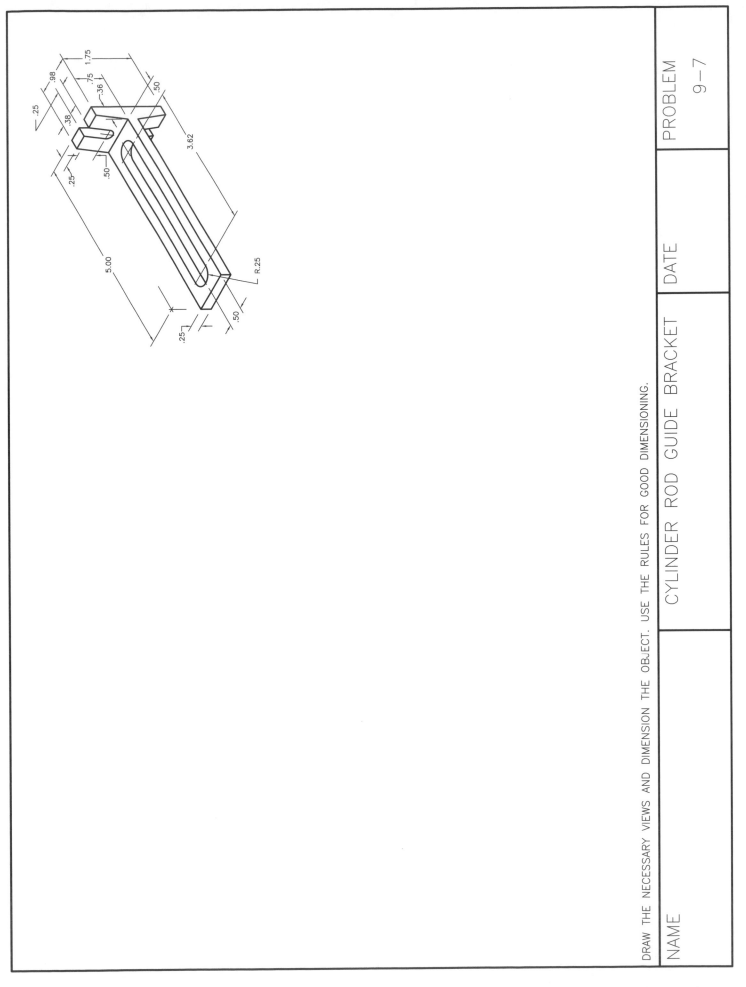

.25

.98

1.75

.75

.36

.50

.38

.25

3.62

.50

5.00

R.25

.25

.50

DRAW THE NECESSARY VIEWS AND DIMENSION THE OBJECT. USE THE RULES FOR GOOD DIMENSIONING.

NAME	CYLINDER ROD GUIDE BRACKET	DATE	PROBLEM
			9–7

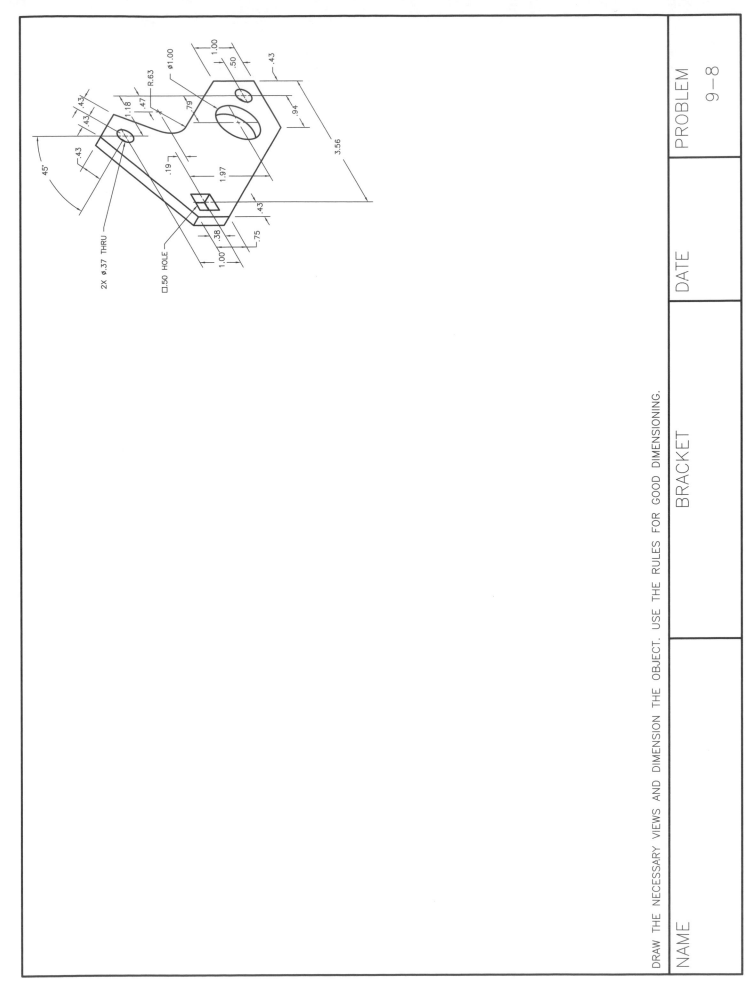

Chapter 9 Dimensioning Fundamentals **67**

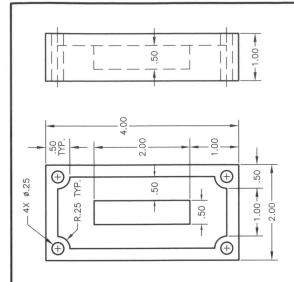

.50

1.00

4.00

.50 TYP.

2.00

1.00

4X ⌀.25

R.25 TYP.

.50

.50

.50

1.00

2.00

1.00

DRAW AND DIMENSION THE NECESSARY VIEWS OF THE OBJECT, INCLUDING A FULL SECTION.

NAME

BOX END CAP

DATE

PROBLEM
10-1

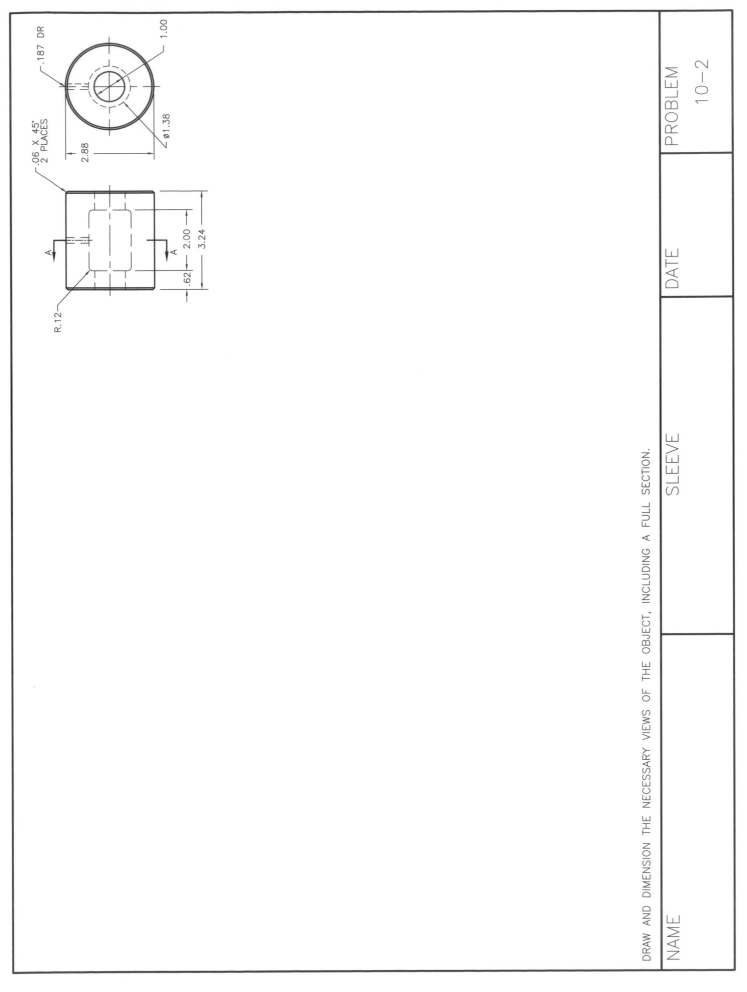

.187 DR

1.00

.06 X 45°
2 PLACES

2.88

Ø1.38

R.12

A

A

3.24

2.00

.62

DRAW AND DIMENSION THE NECESSARY VIEWS OF THE OBJECT, INCLUDING A FULL SECTION.

NAME

SLEEVE

DATE

PROBLEM
10–2

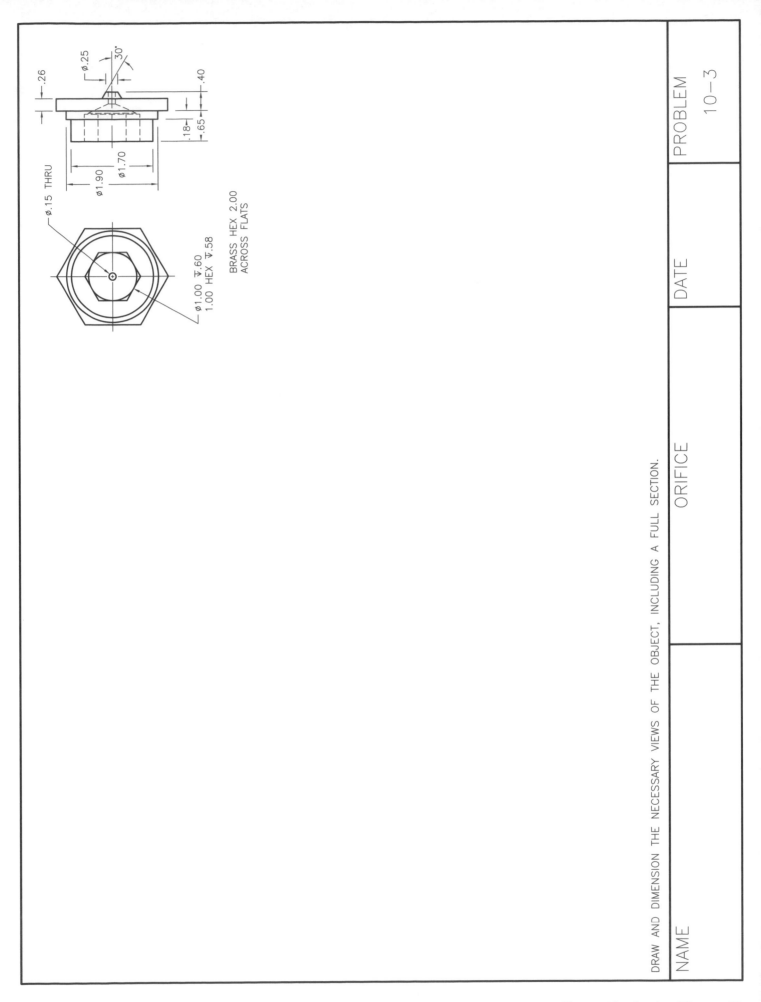

Ø.26

Ø.25

30°

.40

.18

.65

Ø.15 THRU

Ø1.70

Ø1.90

Ø1.00 ⌴.60
1.00 HEX ⌴.58

BRASS HEX 2.00
ACROSS FLATS

DRAW AND DIMENSION THE NECESSARY VIEWS OF THE OBJECT, INCLUDING A FULL SECTION.

PROBLEM

10-3

DATE

ORIFICE

NAME

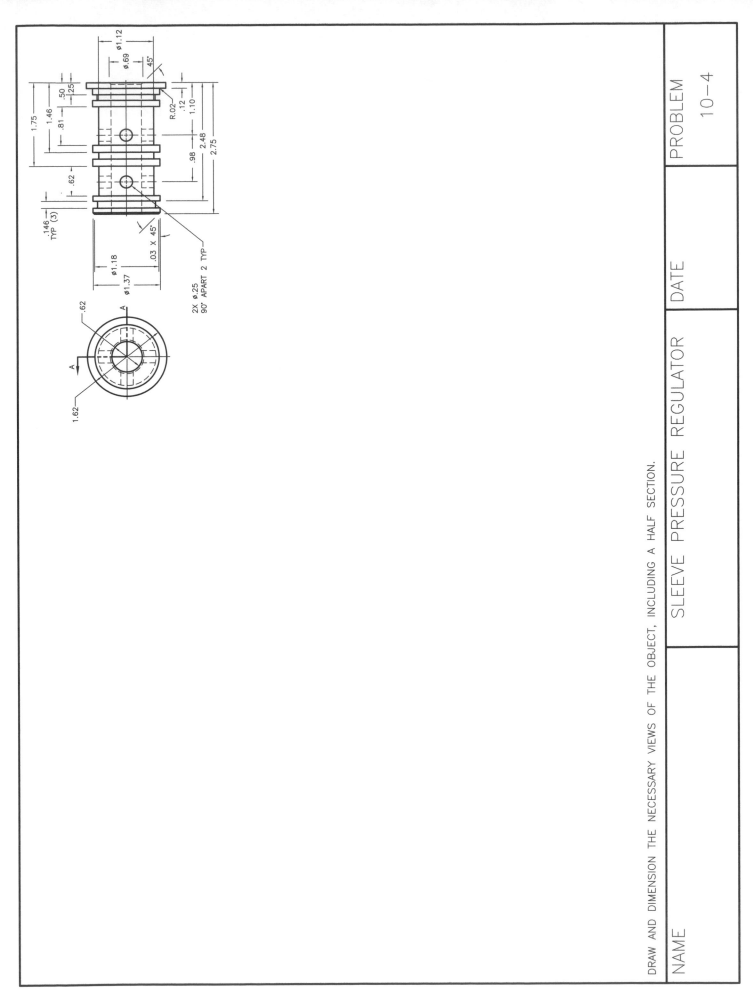

2X ∅.25
90° APART 2 TYP

DRAW AND DIMENSION THE NECESSARY VIEWS OF THE OBJECT, INCLUDING A HALF SECTION.

NAME

SLEEVE PRESSURE REGULATOR

DATE

PROBLEM

10-4

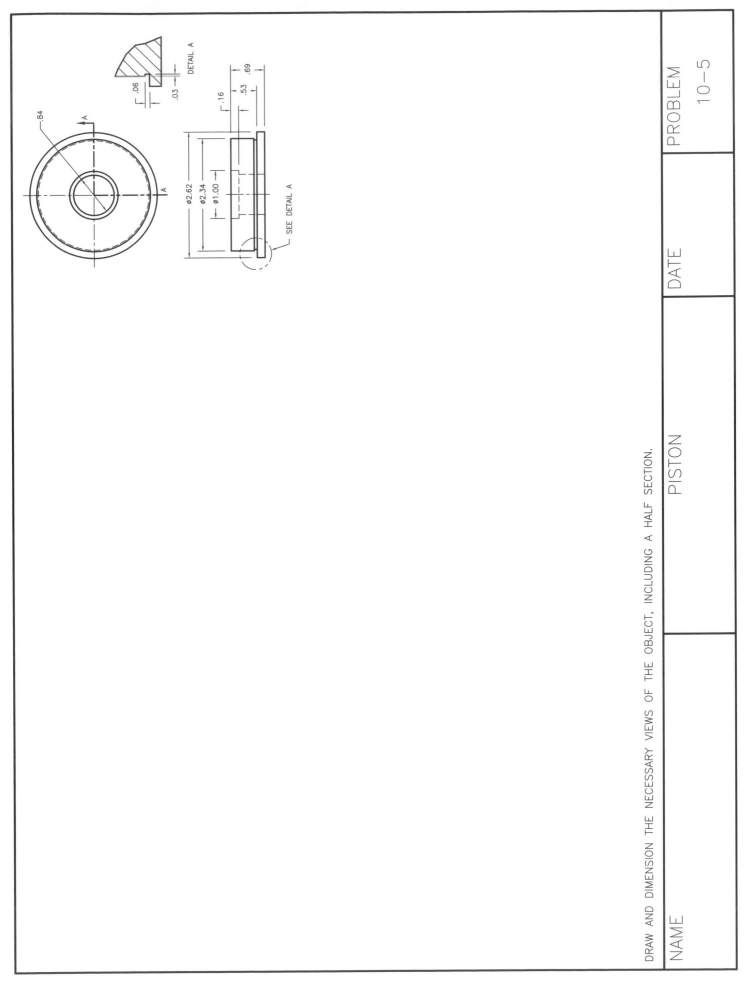

DETAIL A

.06
.03

.84

A

A

Ø2.62
Ø2.34
Ø1.00

.16
.53
.69

SEE DETAIL A

DRAW AND DIMENSION THE NECESSARY VIEWS OF THE OBJECT, INCLUDING A HALF SECTION.

NAME

PISTON

DATE

PROBLEM

10—5

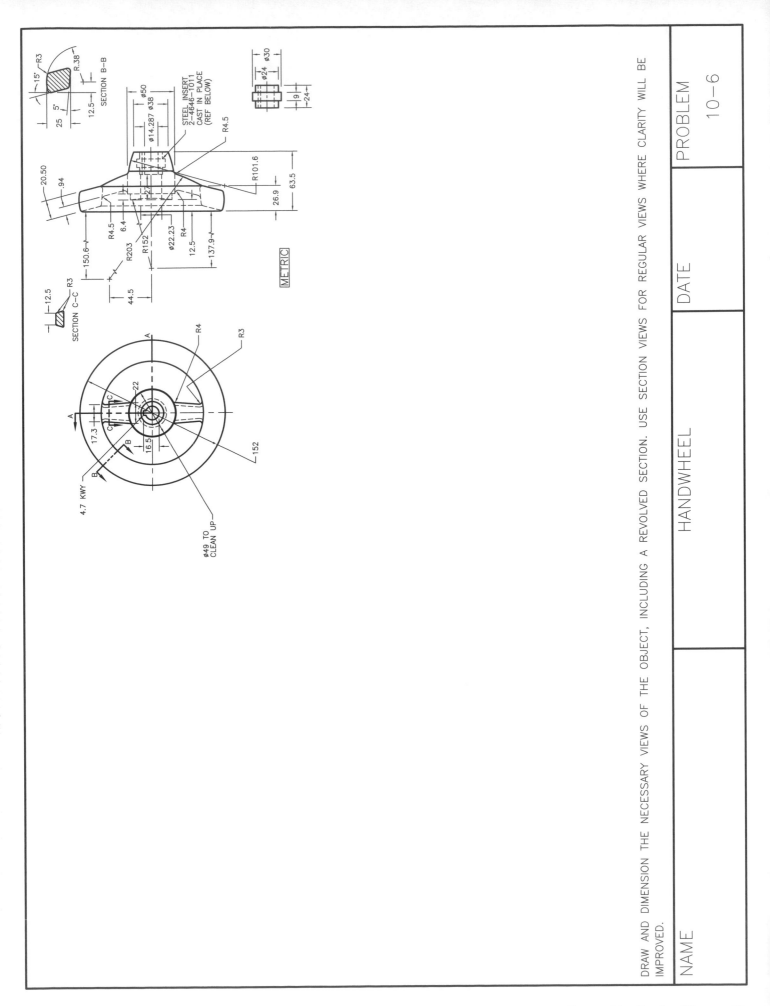

SECTION B–B

R3
R.38
15°
5°
25
12.5

SECTION C–C
R3
12.5

20.50
.94

Ø50
Ø38
Ø14.287
STEEL INSERT
2-4646-1011
CAST IN PLACE
(REF BELOW)
R4.5

R4.5
6.4
R203
Ø22.23
R4
12.5
R152
137.9
150.6
44.5

R101.6
63.5
26.9

METRIC

Ø24
Ø30
9
24

A
R4
R3

22
C
C
A
17.3
B
16.5
B
4.7 KWY
152
Ø49 TO
CLEAN UP

DRAW AND DIMENSION THE NECESSARY VIEWS OF THE OBJECT, INCLUDING A REVOLVED SECTION. USE SECTION VIEWS FOR REGULAR VIEWS WHERE CLARITY WILL BE IMPROVED.

NAME

HANDWHEEL

DATE

PROBLEM
10–6

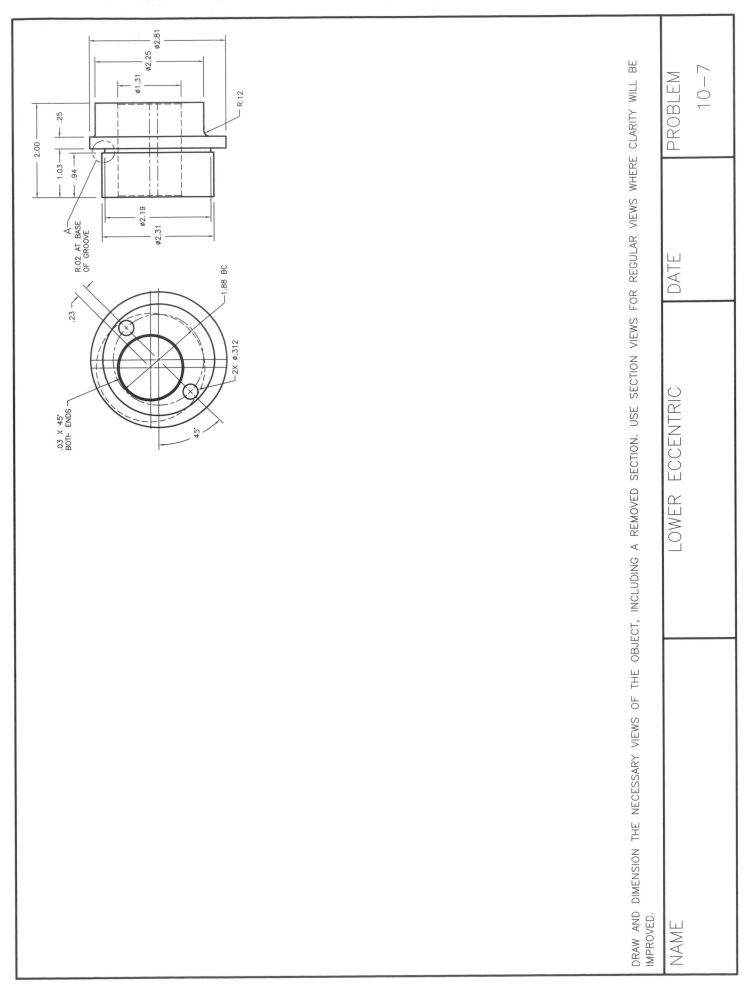

Ø2.81
Ø2.25
Ø1.31
R.12
.25
2.00
1.03
.94
A
R.02 AT BASE
OF GROOVE
Ø2.19
Ø2.31

1.88 BC
.23
Ø.312
2X Ø.312
45°
.03 X 45°
BOTH ENDS

DRAW AND DIMENSION THE NECESSARY VIEWS OF THE OBJECT, INCLUDING A REMOVED SECTION. USE SECTION VIEWS FOR REGULAR VIEWS WHERE CLARITY WILL BE IMPROVED.

NAME	LOWER ECCENTRIC	DATE	PROBLEM 10–7

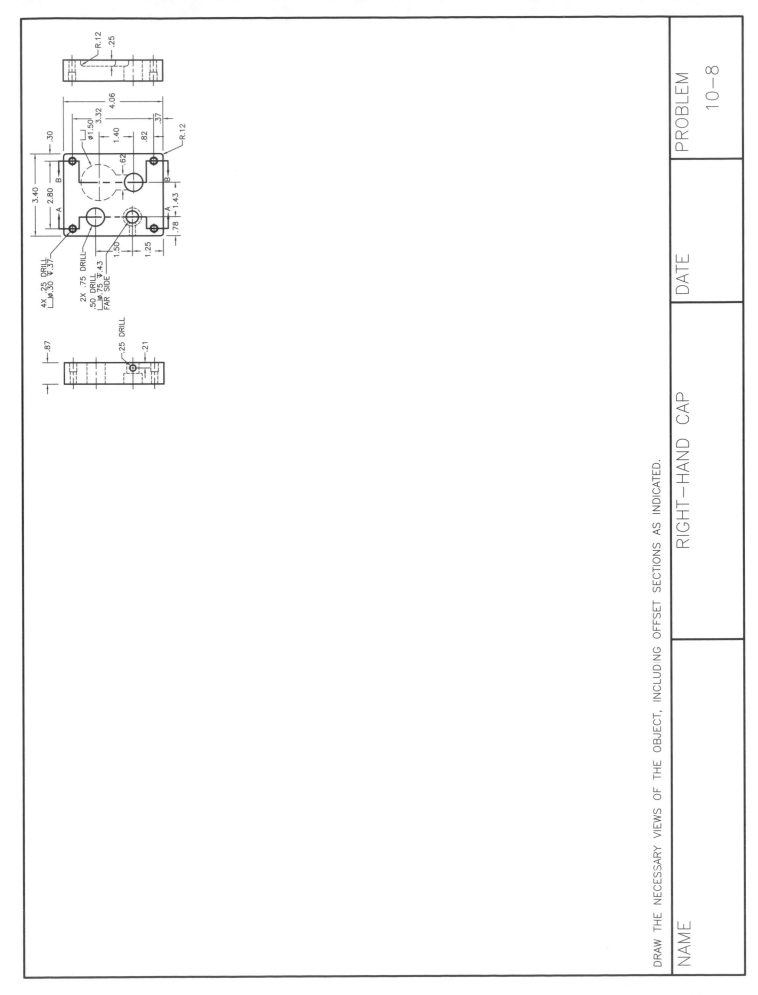

DRAW THE NECESSARY VIEWS OF THE OBJECT, INCLUDING OFFSET SECTIONS AS INDICATED.

NAME

RIGHT—HAND CAP

DATE

PROBLEM

10—8

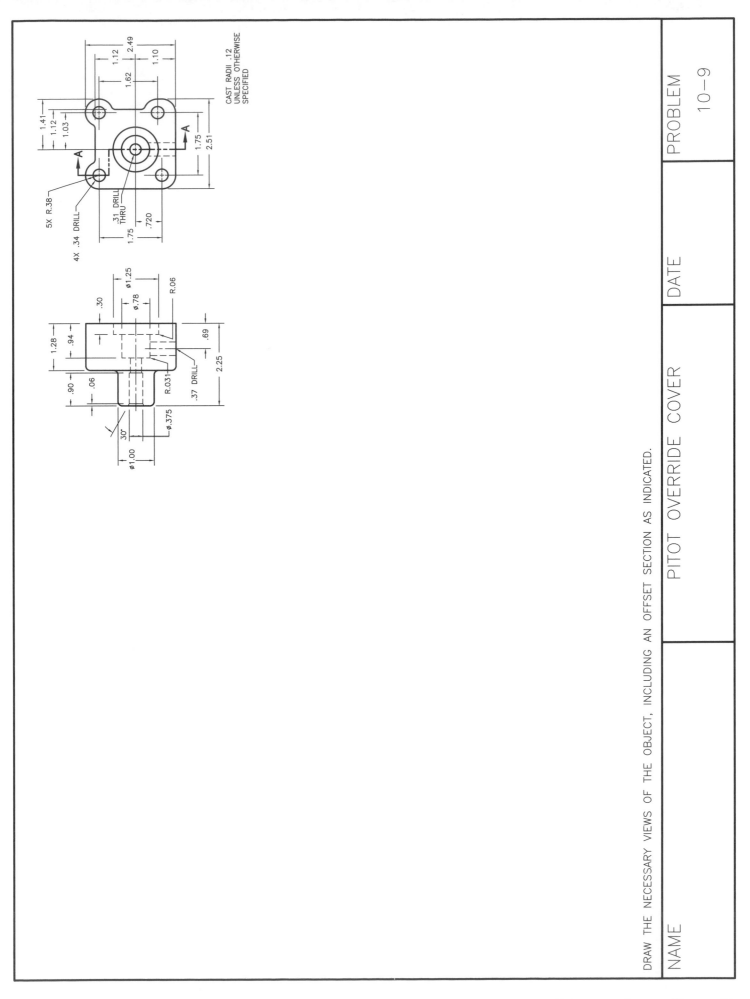

CAST RADII .12
UNLESS OTHERWISE
SPECIFIED

1.12
2.49
1.10
1.62
1.41
1.12
1.03
A
A
1.75
2.51
5X R.38
4X .34 DRILL
.31 DRILL THRU
.720
1.75

Ø1.25
.30
Ø.78
R.06
1.28
.94
.69
2.25
.90
.06
R.031
.37 DRILL
30°
Ø.375
Ø1.00

DRAW THE NECESSARY VIEWS OF THE OBJECT, INCLUDING AN OFFSET SECTION AS INDICATED.

NAME

PITOT OVERRIDE COVER

DATE

PROBLEM
10-9

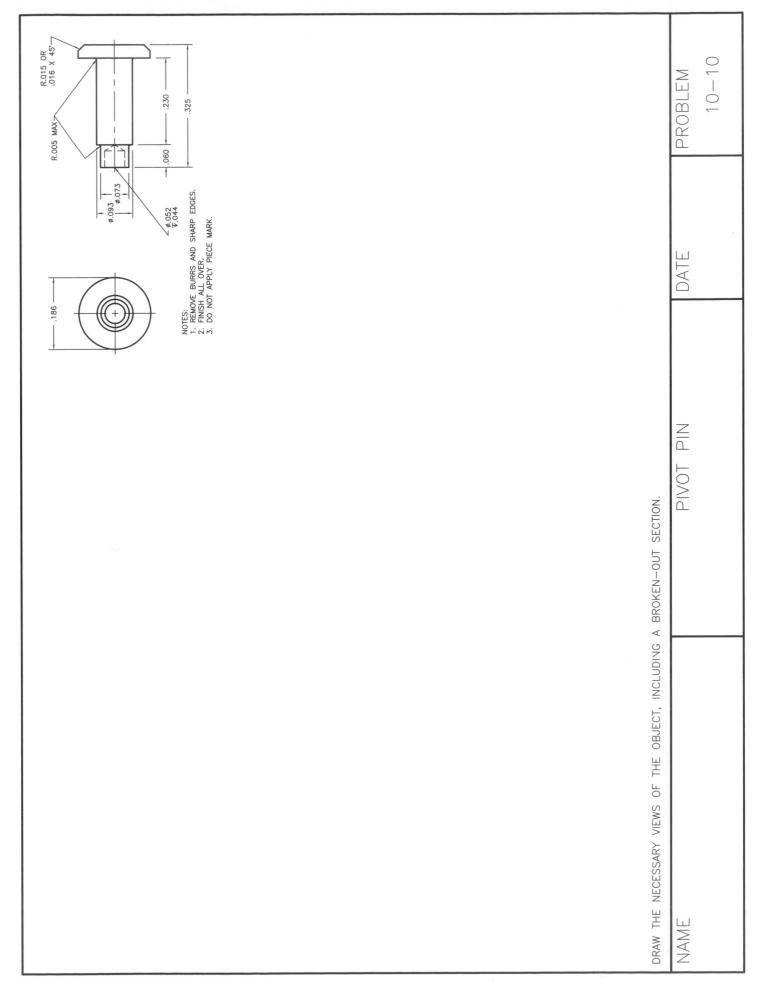

R.015 OR
.016 X 45°

R.005 MAX

.230

.325

.060

ø.093

ø.073

ø.052
⌴.044

NOTES:
1. REMOVE BURRS AND SHARP EDGES.
2. FINISH ALL OVER.
3. DO NOT APPLY PIECE MARK.

.186

DRAW THE NECESSARY VIEWS OF THE OBJECT, INCLUDING A BROKEN–OUT SECTION.

PROBLEM
10–10

DATE

PIVOT PIN

NAME

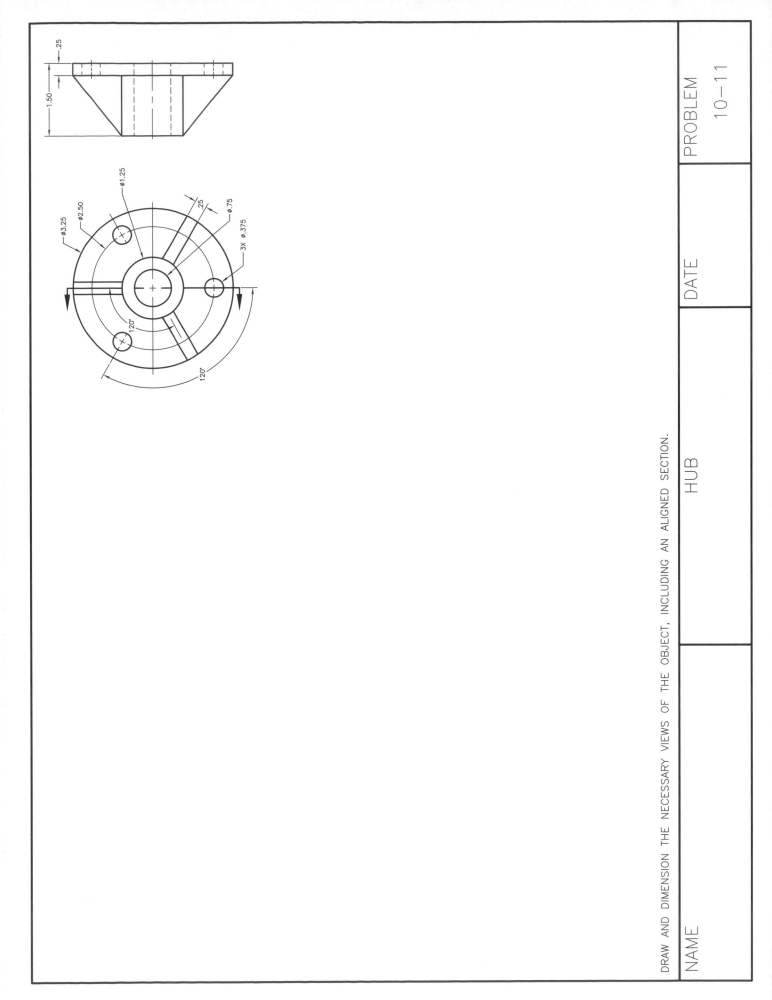

DRAW AND DIMENSION THE NECESSARY VIEWS OF THE OBJECT, INCLUDING AN ALIGNED SECTION.

NAME

HUB

DATE

PROBLEM
10–11

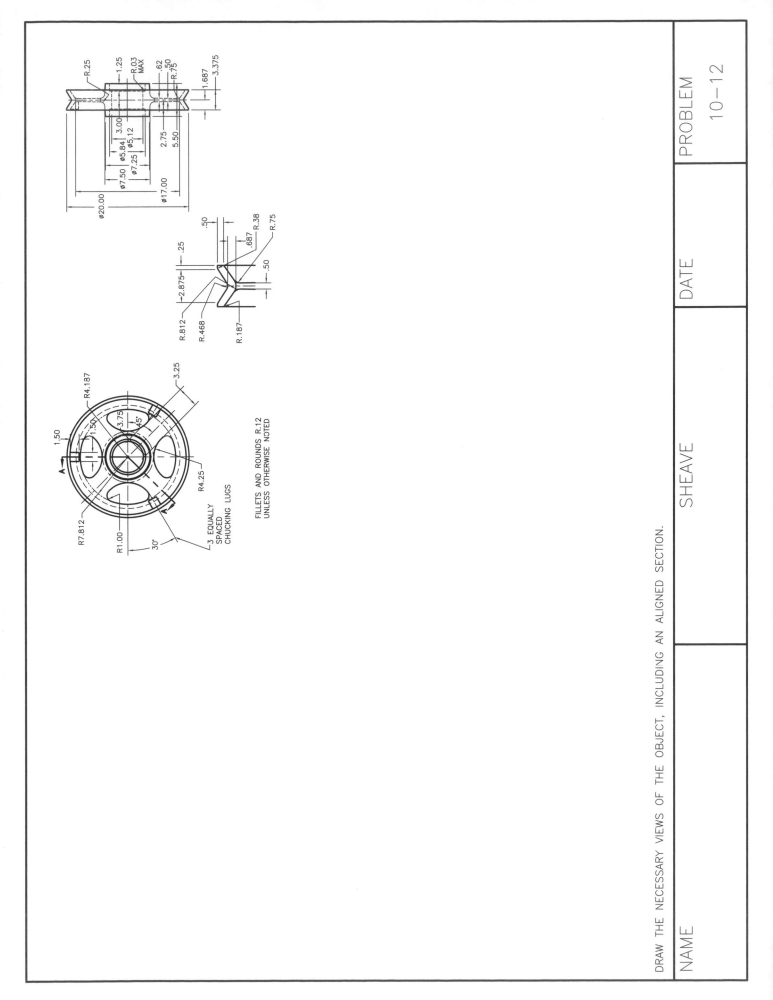

R.25
1.25
R.03 MAX
.62
.50
R.75
1.687
3.375

3.00
Ø5.84
Ø5.12
2.75
5.50

Ø7.50
Ø7.25
17.00

Ø20.00

.50
.25
.687
R.38
R.75
2.875
.50

R.812
R.468
R.187

3.25
R4.187
1.50
3.75
45°
R4.25
1.50
A
R7.812
R1.00
30°
3 EQUALLY SPACED CHUCKING LUGS

FILLETS AND ROUNDS R.12 UNLESS OTHERWISE NOTED

DRAW THE NECESSARY VIEWS OF THE OBJECT, INCLUDING AN ALIGNED SECTION.

NAME

SHEAVE

DATE

PROBLEM
10-12

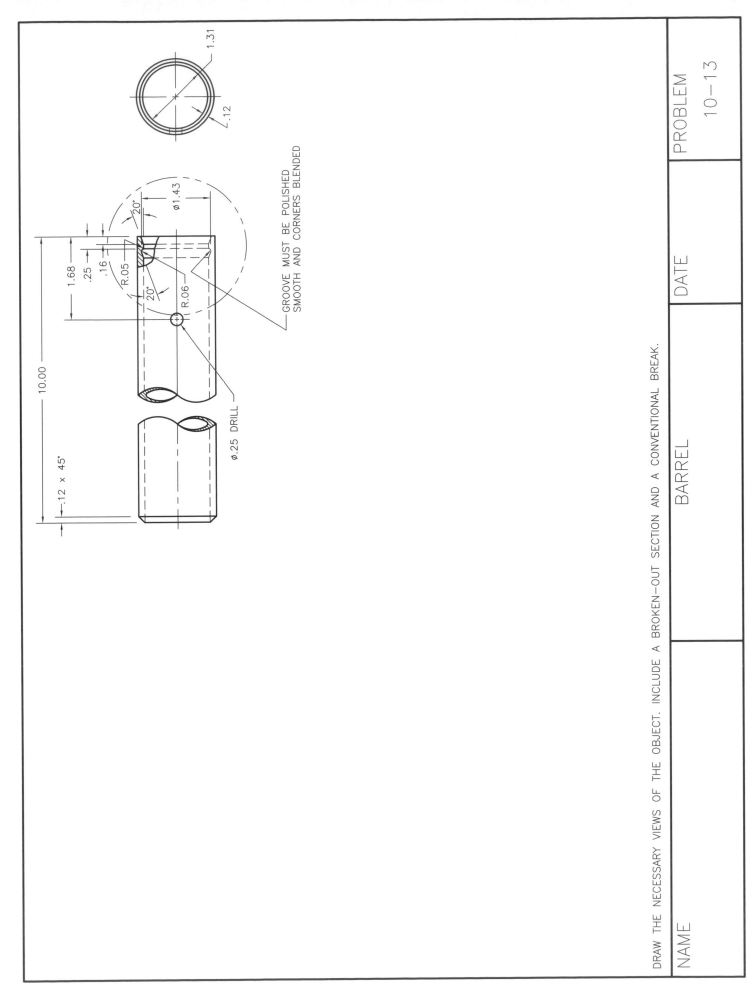

1.31

⌀.12

1.43

20°

1.68

.25

.16

R.05

20°

R.06

GROOVE MUST BE POLISHED
SMOOTH AND CORNERS BLENDED

⌀.25 DRILL

10.00

.12 × 45°

DRAW THE NECESSARY VIEWS OF THE OBJECT. INCLUDE A BROKEN–OUT SECTION AND A CONVENTIONAL BREAK.

NAME		BARREL	DATE	PROBLEM
				10–13

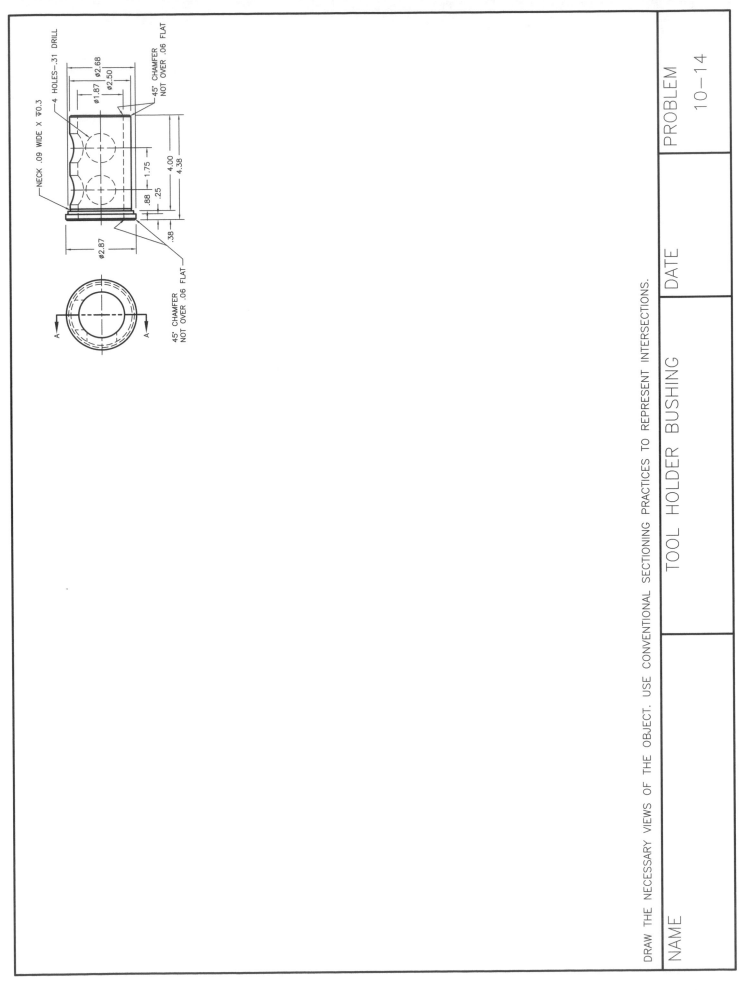

NECK .09 WIDE X ⊽0.3

4 HOLES—.31 DRILL

ø2.68
ø2.50
ø1.87

45° CHAMFER
NOT OVER .06 FLAT

4.38
4.00
1.75
.88
.25

ø2.87

.38

45° CHAMFER
NOT OVER .06 FLAT

A — A

DRAW THE NECESSARY VIEWS OF THE OBJECT. USE CONVENTIONAL SECTIONING PRACTICES TO REPRESENT INTERSECTIONS.

NAME		DATE	PROBLEM
	TOOL HOLDER BUSHING		10–14

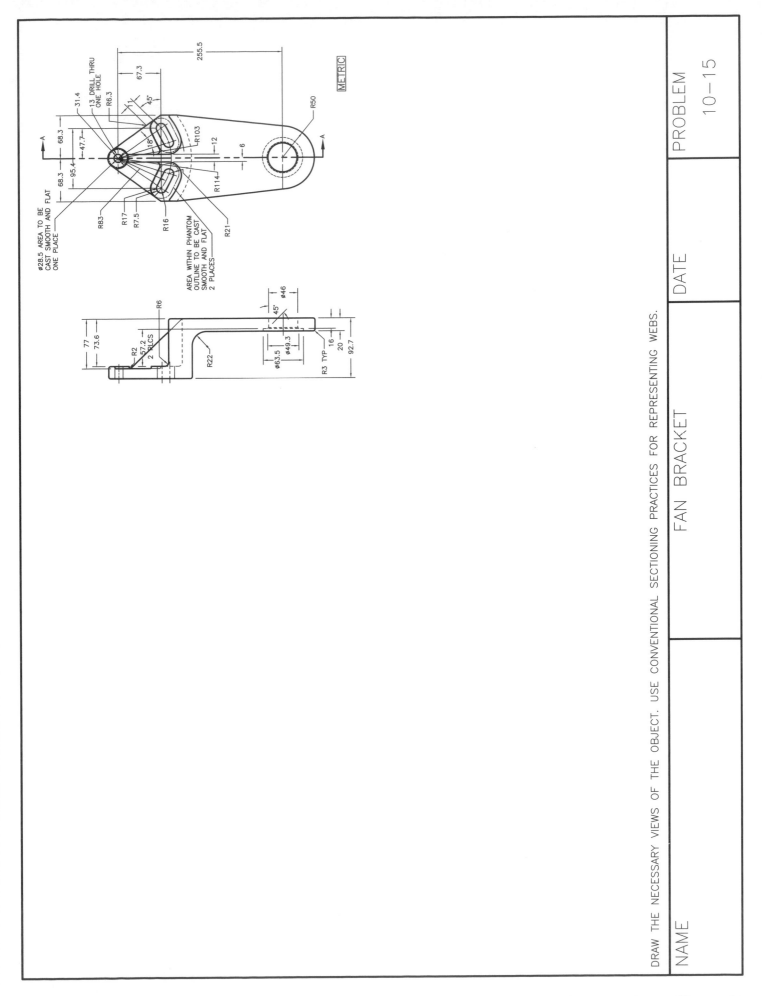

METRIC

R50

255.5

67.3

45°

.13 DRILL THRU
ONE HOLE

R6.3

31.4

R103

18°

R114

R12

6

68.3

47.7

95.4

68.3

A

A

Ø28.5 AREA TO BE
CAST SMOOTH AND FLAT
ONE PLACE

R83

R17

R7.5

R16

R21

AREA WITHIN PHANTOM
OUTLINE TO BE CAST
SMOOTH AND FLAT
2 PLACES

R6

Ø46

45°

77

73.6

R2

57.2

2 PLCS

R22

Ø63.5

Ø49.3

16

20

92.7

R3 TYP

DRAW THE NECESSARY VIEWS OF THE OBJECT. USE CONVENTIONAL SECTIONING PRACTICES FOR REPRESENTING WEBS.

NAME

FAN BRACKET

DATE

PROBLEM
10–15

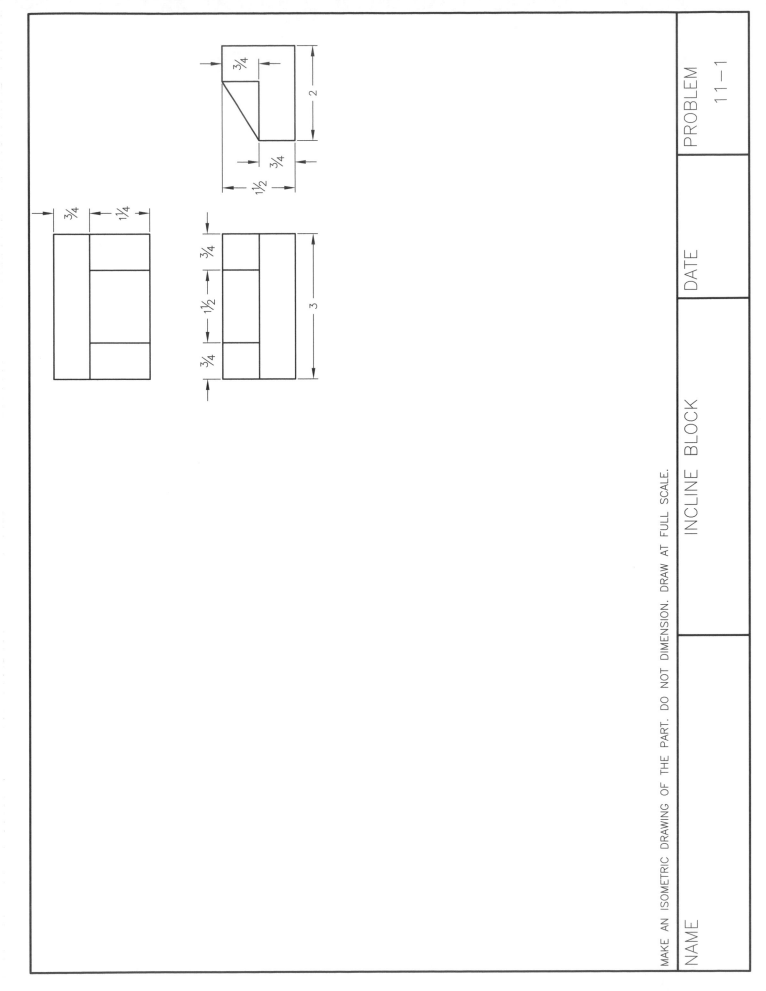

MAKE AN ISOMETRIC DRAWING OF THE PART. DO NOT DIMENSION. DRAW AT FULL SCALE.

NAME	INCLINE BLOCK	DATE	PROBLEM
			11–1

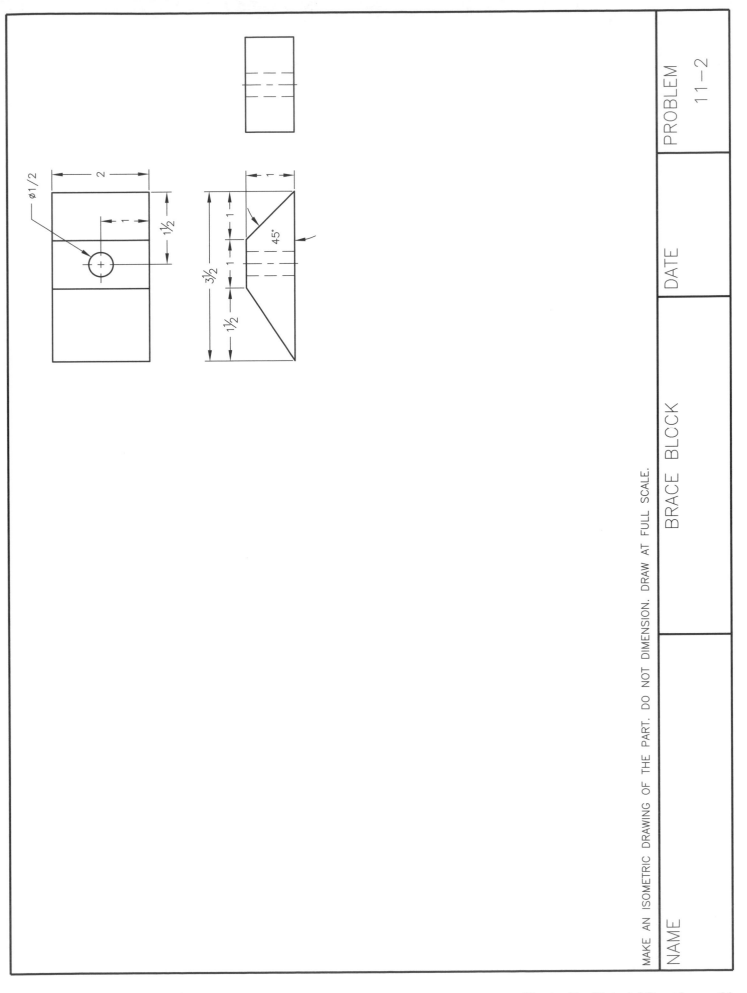

MAKE AN ISOMETRIC DRAWING OF THE PART. DO NOT DIMENSION. DRAW AT FULL SCALE.

NAME		DATE	PROBLEM
	BRACE BLOCK		11-2

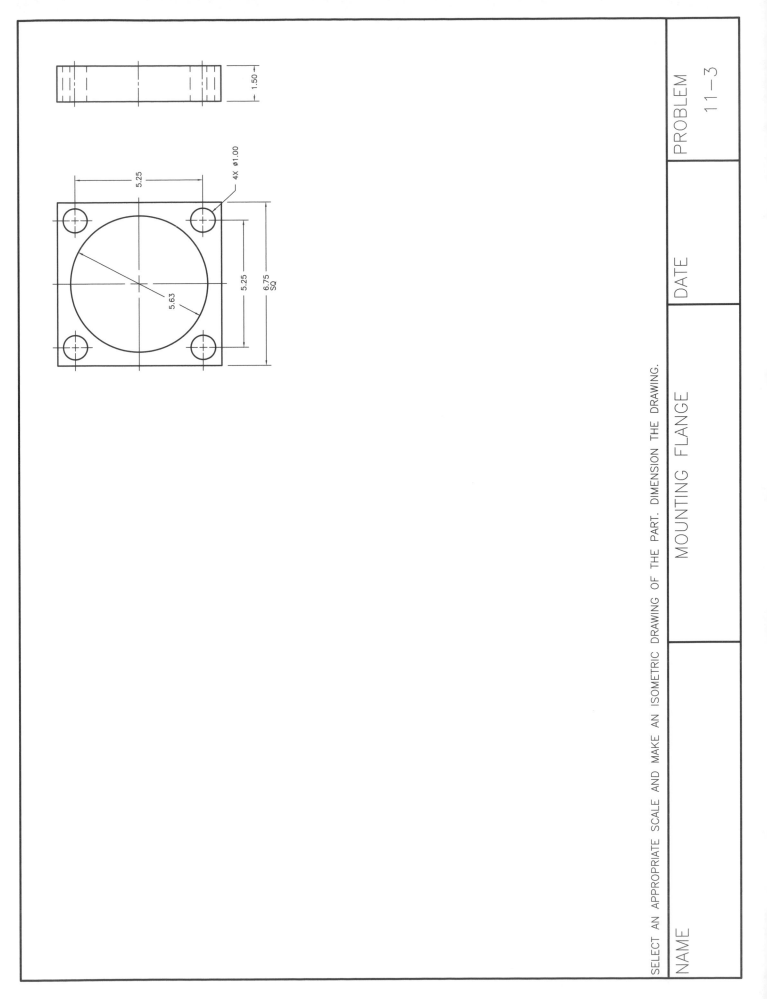

4X ⌀1.00

5.25

5.25

6.75
SQ

5.63

1.50

SELECT AN APPROPRIATE SCALE AND MAKE AN ISOMETRIC DRAWING OF THE PART. DIMENSION THE DRAWING.

NAME

MOUNTING FLANGE

DATE

PROBLEM
11–3

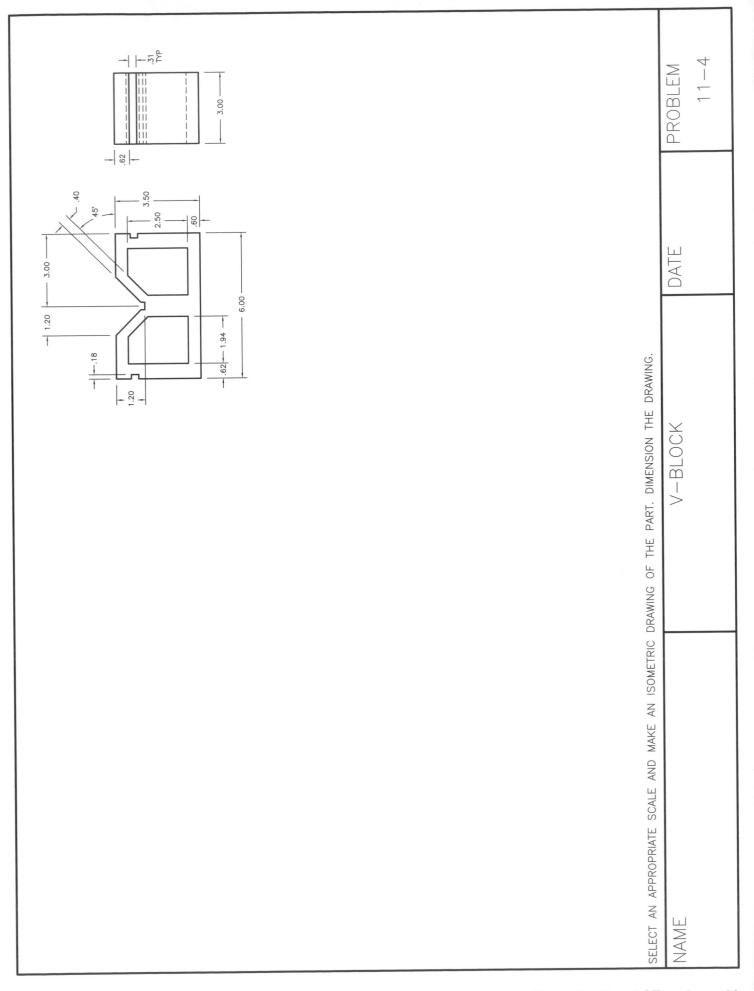

.31
TYP

3.00

.62

.40

45°

3.50

2.50

.60

3.00

1.20

6.00

.18

1.94

.62

1.20

SELECT AN APPROPRIATE SCALE AND MAKE AN ISOMETRIC DRAWING OF THE PART. DIMENSION THE DRAWING.

NAME

V–BLOCK

DATE

PROBLEM
11–4

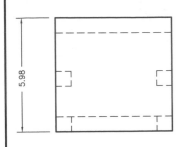

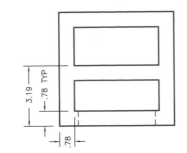

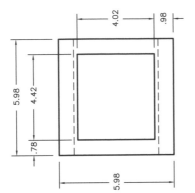

MAKE AN ISOMETRIC DRAWING OF THE PART. DIMENSION THE DRAWING. DRAW AT A SCALE OF 1" = 3" OR 3/8" = 1".

BOX ANGLE

NAME

DATE

PROBLEM
11-5

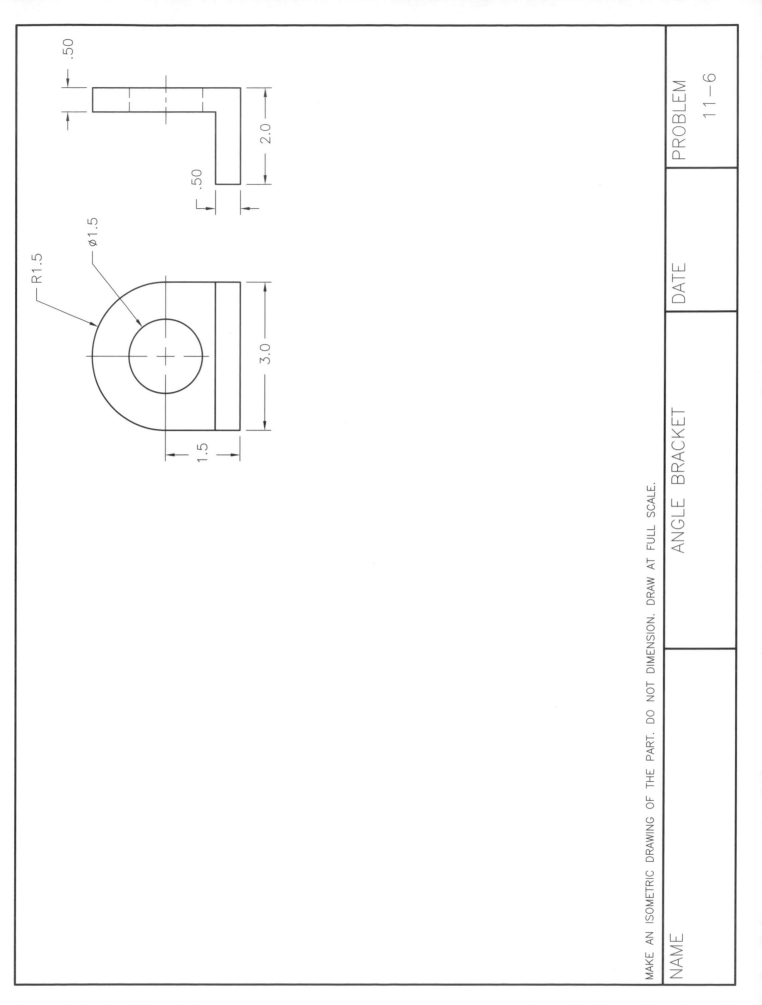

.50

2.0

.50

R1.5

Ø1.5

3.0

1.5

MAKE AN ISOMETRIC DRAWING OF THE PART. DO NOT DIMENSION. DRAW AT FULL SCALE.

NAME

ANGLE BRACKET

DATE

PROBLEM

11—6

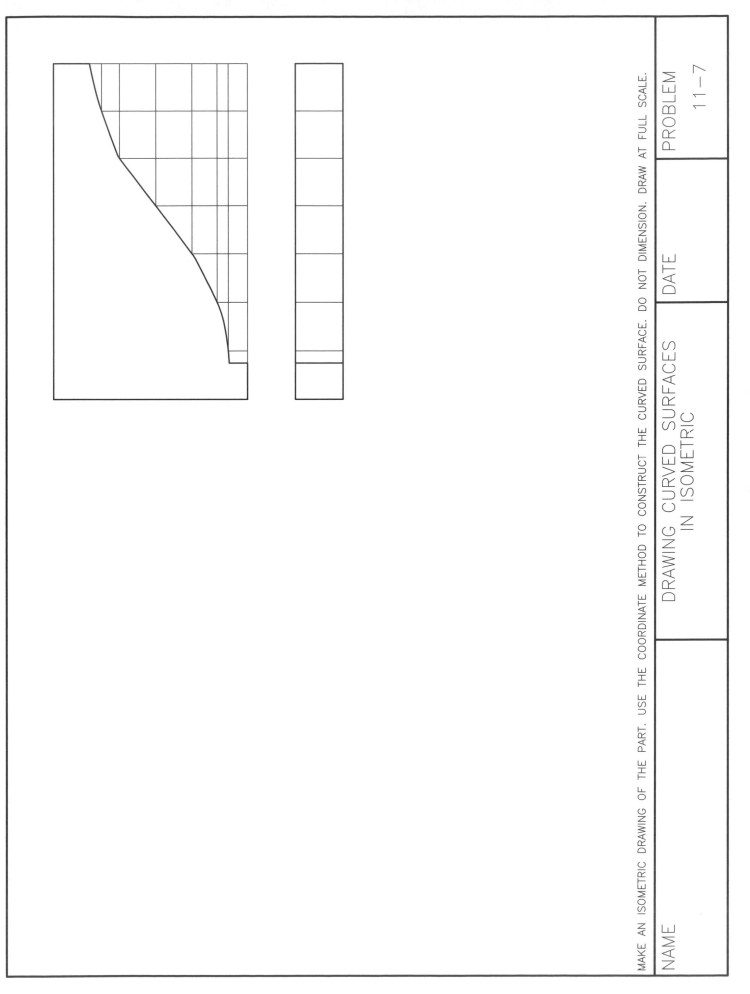

NAME	DATE	PROBLEM
DRAWING CURVED SURFACES IN ISOMETRIC		11–7

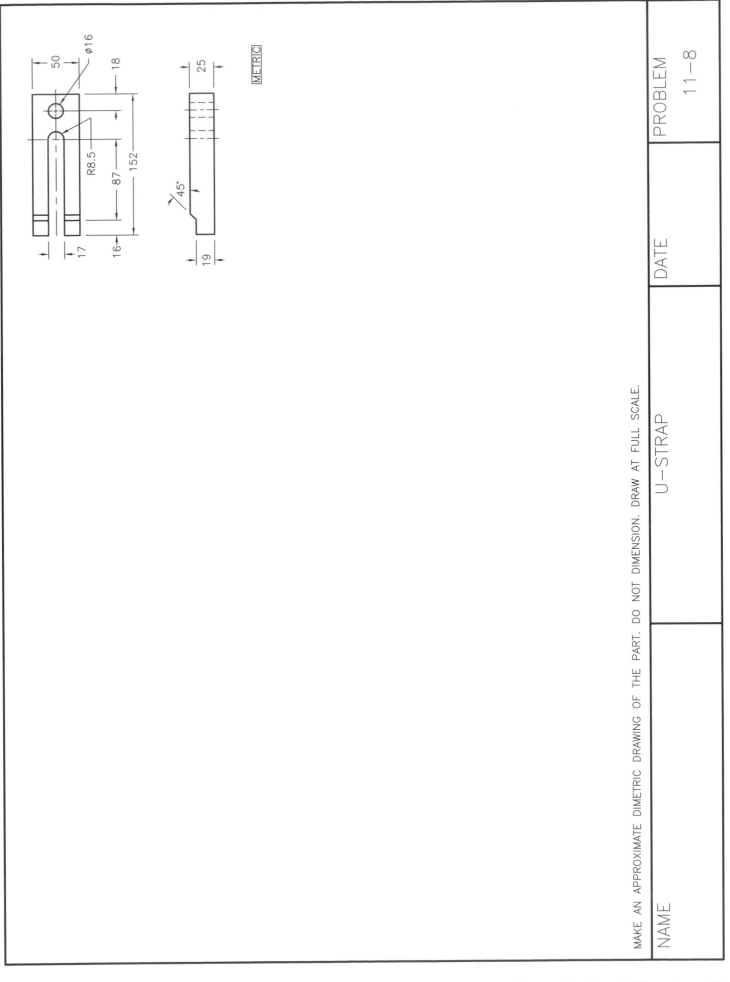

50

Ø16

18

R8.5

87

152

17

16

25

45°

19

METRIC

MAKE AN APPROXIMATE DIMETRIC DRAWING OF THE PART. DO NOT DIMENSION. DRAW AT FULL SCALE.

| NAME | | U–STRAP | DATE | PROBLEM 11–8 |

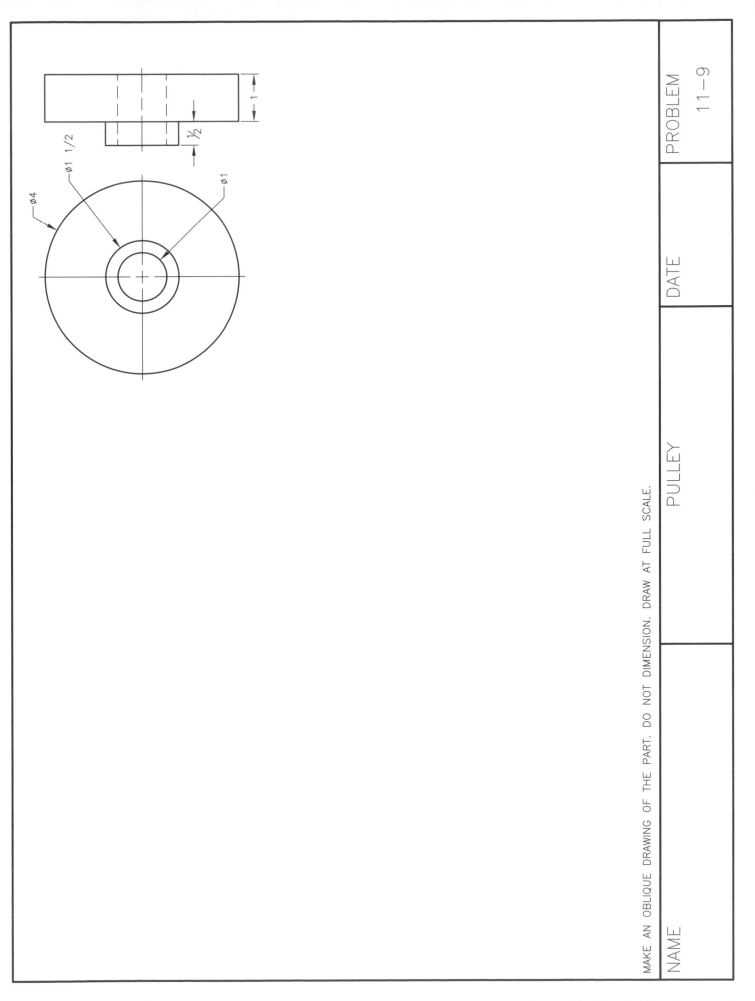

ⱷ4

ⱷ1 1/2

ⱷ1

1

1/2

MAKE AN OBLIQUE DRAWING OF THE PART. DO NOT DIMENSION. DRAW AT FULL SCALE.

NAME

PULLEY

DATE

PROBLEM
11–9

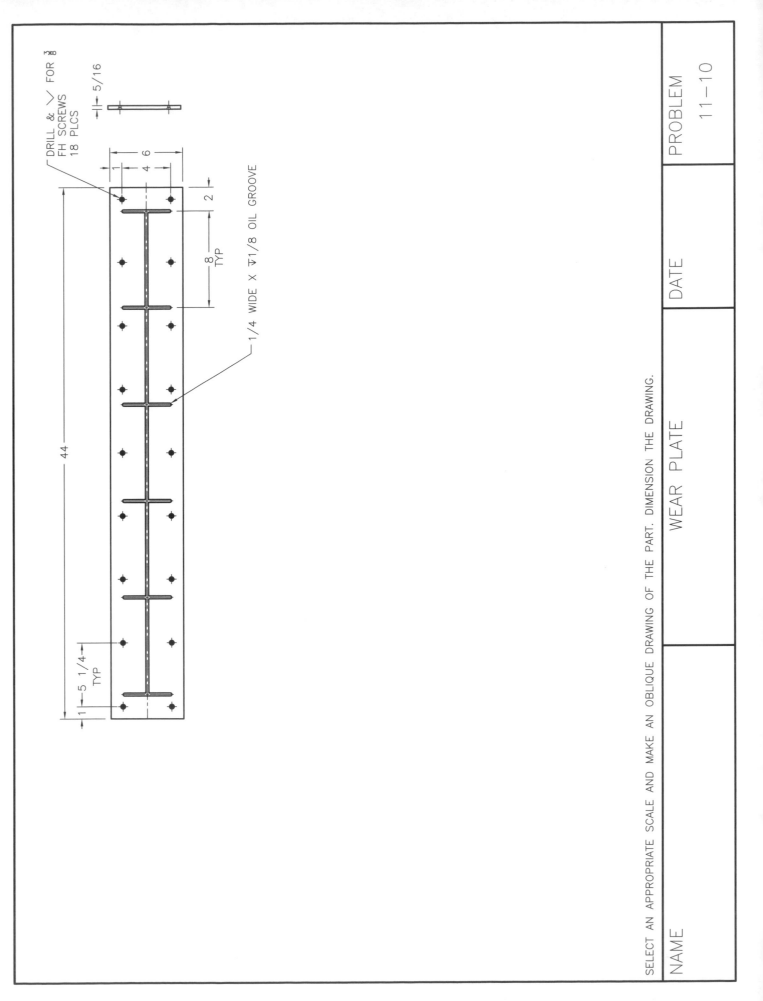

DRILL & ⌵ FOR
FH SCREWS
18 PLCS

⌀3×8

5/16

6

1

4

2

8
TYP

44

1/4 WIDE X ⊽1/8 OIL GROOVE

5 1/4
TYP

1

SELECT AN APPROPRIATE SCALE AND MAKE AN OBLIQUE DRAWING OF THE PART. DIMENSION THE DRAWING.

NAME

WEAR PLATE

DATE

PROBLEM
11-10

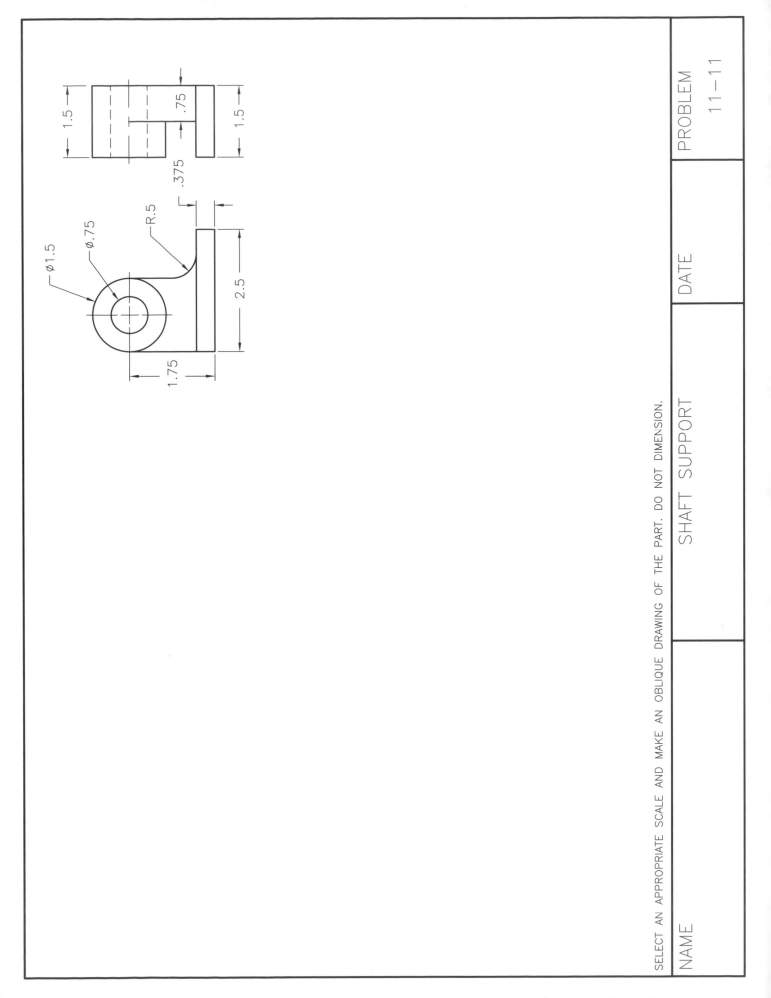

1.5

.75

1.5

.375

R.5

⌀.75

⌀1.5

2.5

1.75

SELECT AN APPROPRIATE SCALE AND MAKE AN OBLIQUE DRAWING OF THE PART. DO NOT DIMENSION.

NAME

SHAFT SUPPORT

DATE

PROBLEM
11−11

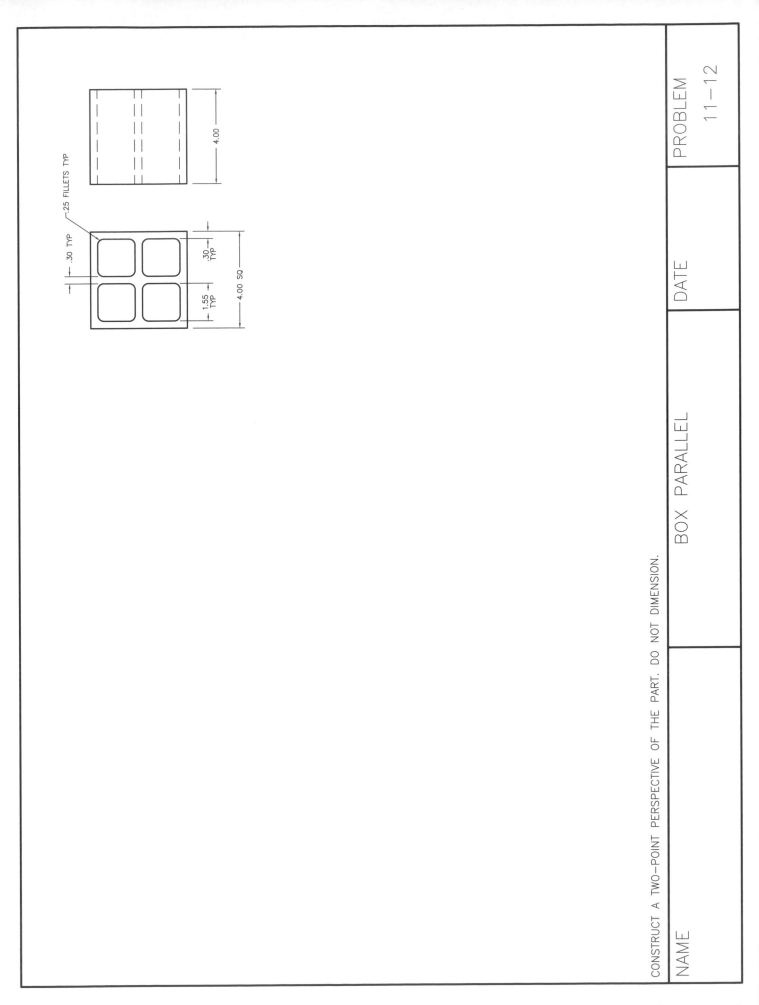

.25 FILLETS TYP

.30 TYP

4.00

.30 TYP

1.55 TYP

4.00 SQ

CONSTRUCT A TWO-POINT PERSPECTIVE OF THE PART. DO NOT DIMENSION.

NAME

BOX PARALLEL

DATE

PROBLEM 11-12

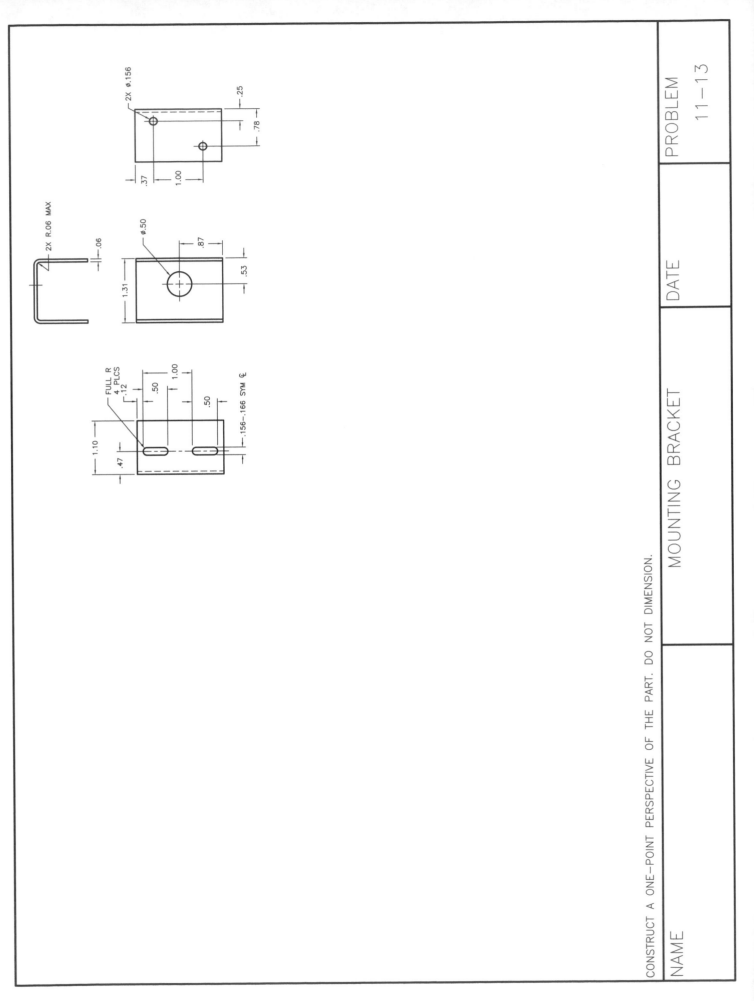

2X ⌀.156

.25

.78

.37

1.00

2X R.06 MAX

.06

⌀.50

.87

1.31

.53

FULL R
4 PLCS

.12

.50

1.00

.50

1.10

.47

.156-.166 SYM ℄

CONSTRUCT A ONE-POINT PERSPECTIVE OF THE PART. DO NOT DIMENSION.

NAME

MOUNTING BRACKET

DATE

PROBLEM

11-13

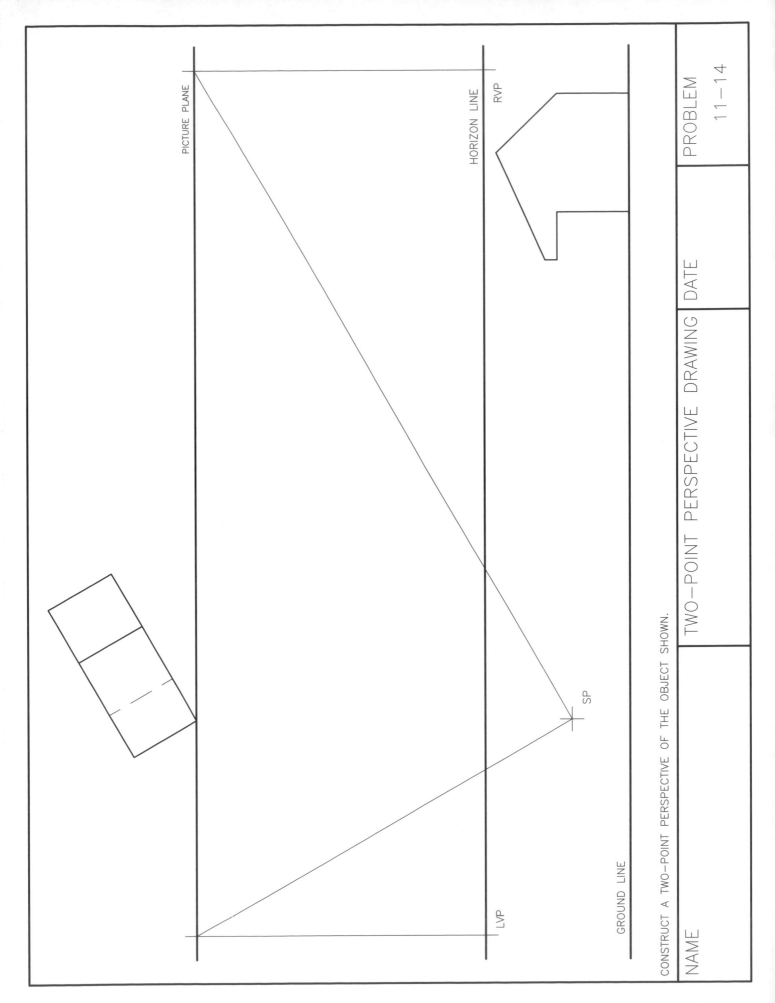

PICTURE PLANE

HORIZON LINE

RVP

SP

LVP

GROUND LINE

CONSTRUCT A TWO-POINT PERSPECTIVE OF THE OBJECT SHOWN.

NAME		TWO-POINT PERSPECTIVE DRAWING	DATE	PROBLEM
				11-14

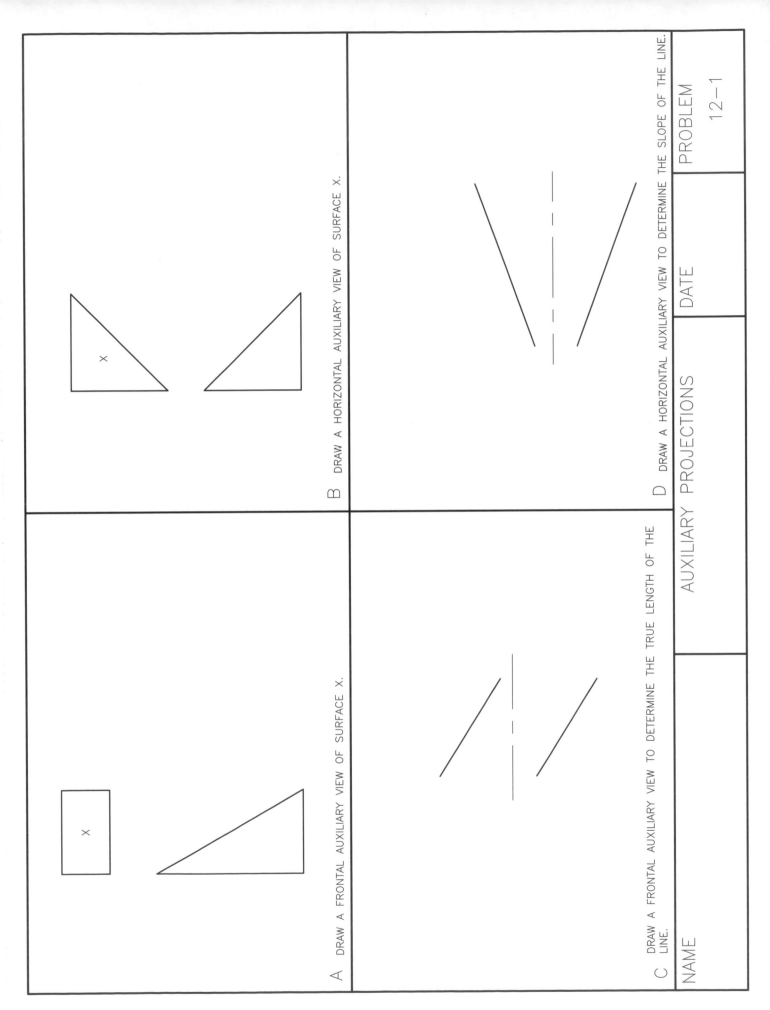

A DRAW A FRONTAL AUXILIARY VIEW OF SURFACE X.

B DRAW A HORIZONTAL AUXILIARY VIEW OF SURFACE X.

C DRAW A FRONTAL AUXILIARY VIEW TO DETERMINE THE TRUE LENGTH OF THE LINE.

D DRAW A HORIZONTAL AUXILIARY VIEW TO DETERMINE THE SLOPE OF THE LINE.

NAME

AUXILIARY PROJECTIONS

DATE

PROBLEM
12–1

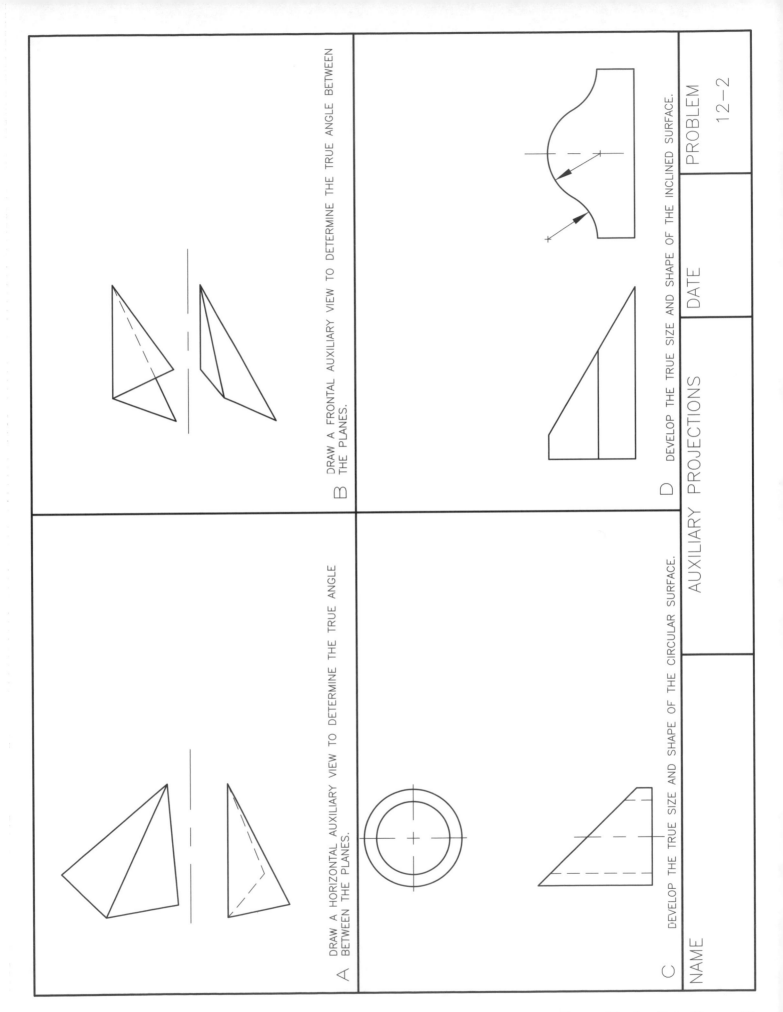

A DRAW A HORIZONTAL AUXILIARY VIEW TO DETERMINE THE TRUE ANGLE BETWEEN THE PLANES.

B DRAW A FRONTAL AUXILIARY VIEW TO DETERMINE THE TRUE ANGLE BETWEEN THE PLANES.

C DEVELOP THE TRUE SIZE AND SHAPE OF THE CIRCULAR SURFACE.

D DEVELOP THE TRUE SIZE AND SHAPE OF THE INCLINED SURFACE.

NAME

DATE

PROBLEM
12–2

AUXILIARY PROJECTIONS

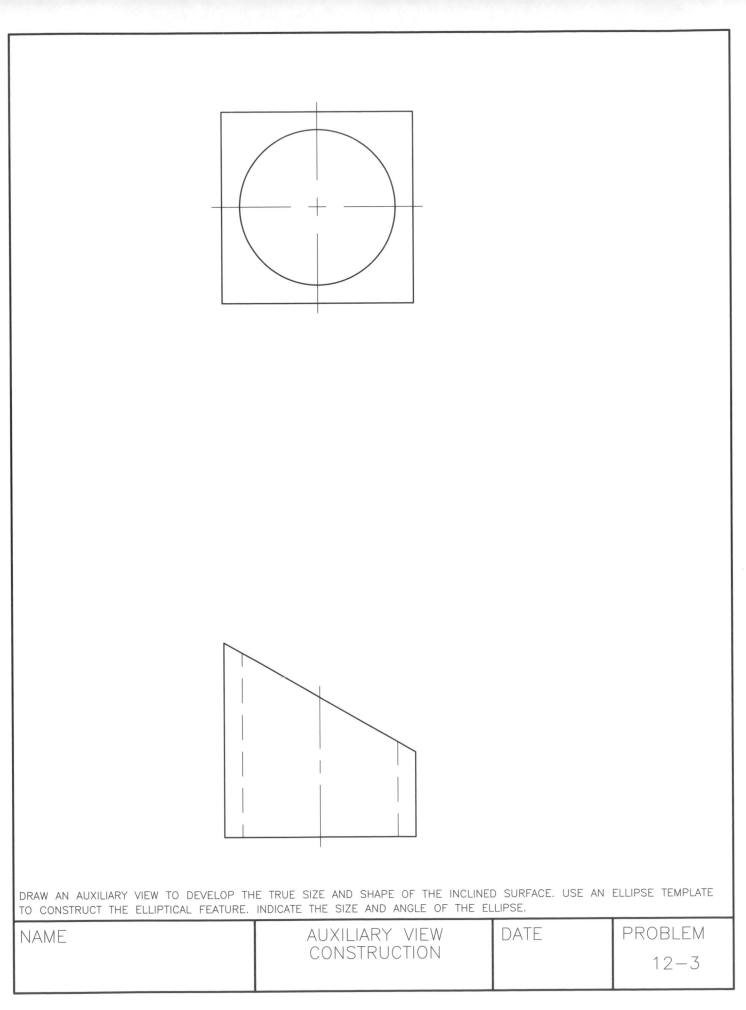

DRAW AN AUXILIARY VIEW TO DEVELOP THE TRUE SIZE AND SHAPE OF THE INCLINED SURFACE. USE AN ELLIPSE TEMPLATE TO CONSTRUCT THE ELLIPTICAL FEATURE. INDICATE THE SIZE AND ANGLE OF THE ELLIPSE.

NAME	AUXILIARY VIEW CONSTRUCTION	DATE	PROBLEM 12–3

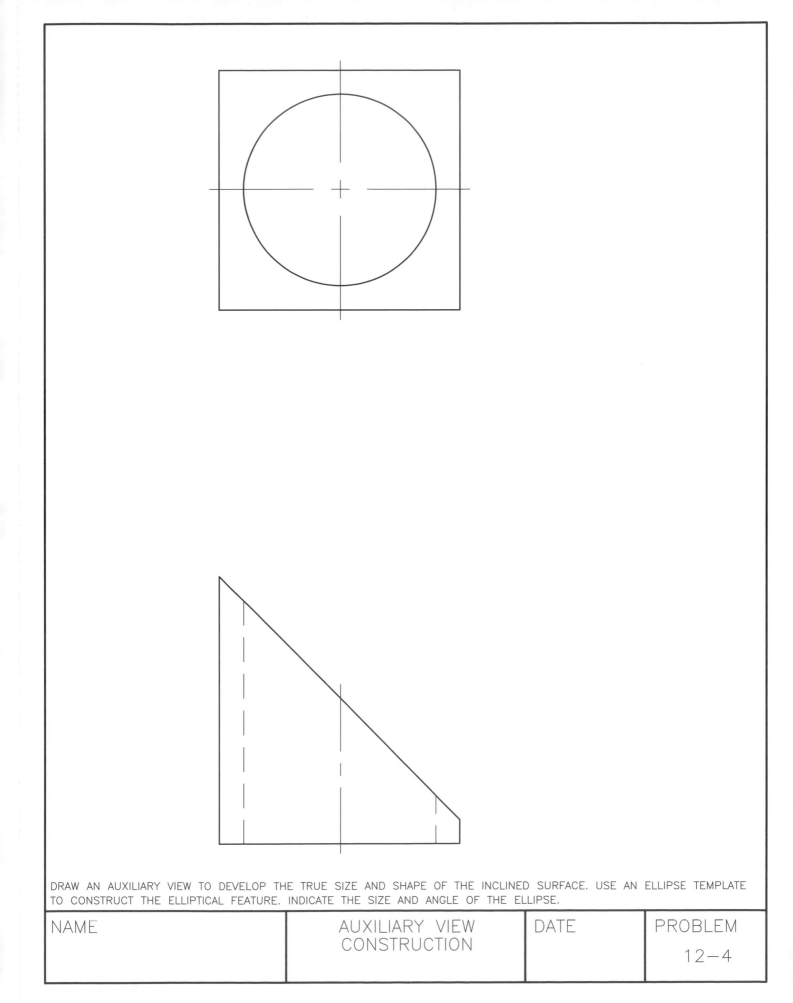

DRAW AN AUXILIARY VIEW TO DEVELOP THE TRUE SIZE AND SHAPE OF THE INCLINED SURFACE. USE AN ELLIPSE TEMPLATE TO CONSTRUCT THE ELLIPTICAL FEATURE. INDICATE THE SIZE AND ANGLE OF THE ELLIPSE.

NAME	AUXILIARY VIEW CONSTRUCTION	DATE	PROBLEM 12−4

DRAW A SECONDARY AUXILIARY VIEW OF THE OBJECT AS INDICATED BY THE LINES OF SIGHT. PROJECT A PRIMARY AUXILIARY VIEW FROM THE TOP VIEW.

NAME	SECONDARY AUXILIARY VIEW CONSTRUCTION	DATE	PROBLEM 12−5

DRAW A SECONDARY AUXILIARY VIEW OF THE OBJECT AS INDICATED BY THE LINES OF SIGHT. PROJECT A PRIMARY AUXILIARY
VIEW FROM THE TOP VIEW. LEAVE CONSTRUCTION LINES TO SHOW THE CONSTRUCTION.

NAME	SECONDARY AUXILIARY VIEW CONSTRUCTION	DATE	PROBLEM 12—6

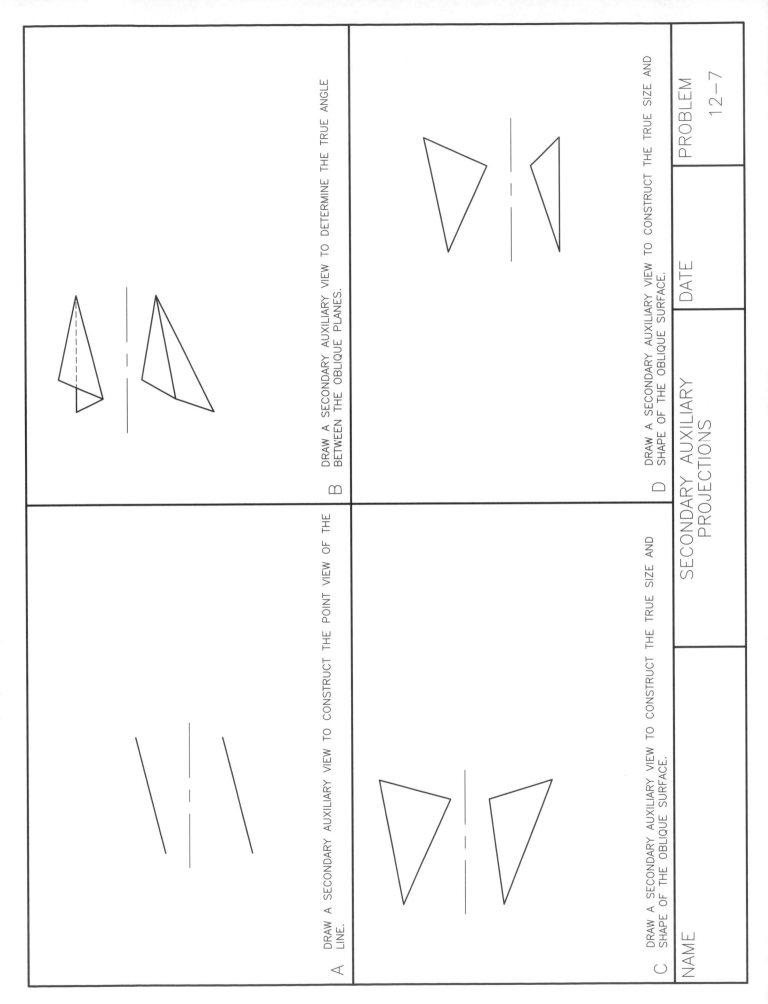

A DRAW A SECONDARY AUXILIARY VIEW TO CONSTRUCT THE POINT VIEW OF THE LINE.

B DRAW A SECONDARY AUXILIARY VIEW TO DETERMINE THE TRUE ANGLE BETWEEN THE OBLIQUE PLANES.

C DRAW A SECONDARY AUXILIARY VIEW TO CONSTRUCT THE TRUE SIZE AND SHAPE OF THE OBLIQUE SURFACE.

D DRAW A SECONDARY AUXILIARY VIEW TO CONSTRUCT THE TRUE SIZE AND SHAPE OF THE OBLIQUE SURFACE.

PROBLEM
12—7

DATE

SECONDARY AUXILIARY PROJECTIONS

NAME

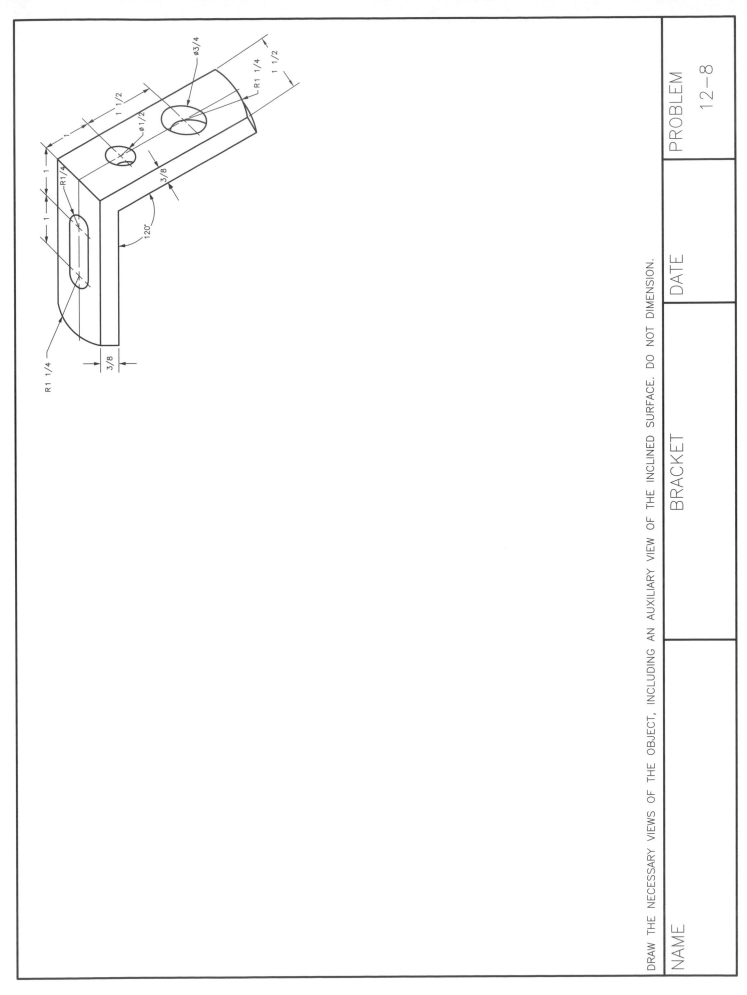

DRAW THE NECESSARY VIEWS OF THE OBJECT, INCLUDING AN AUXILIARY VIEW OF THE INCLINED SURFACE. DO NOT DIMENSION.

NAME

BRACKET

DATE

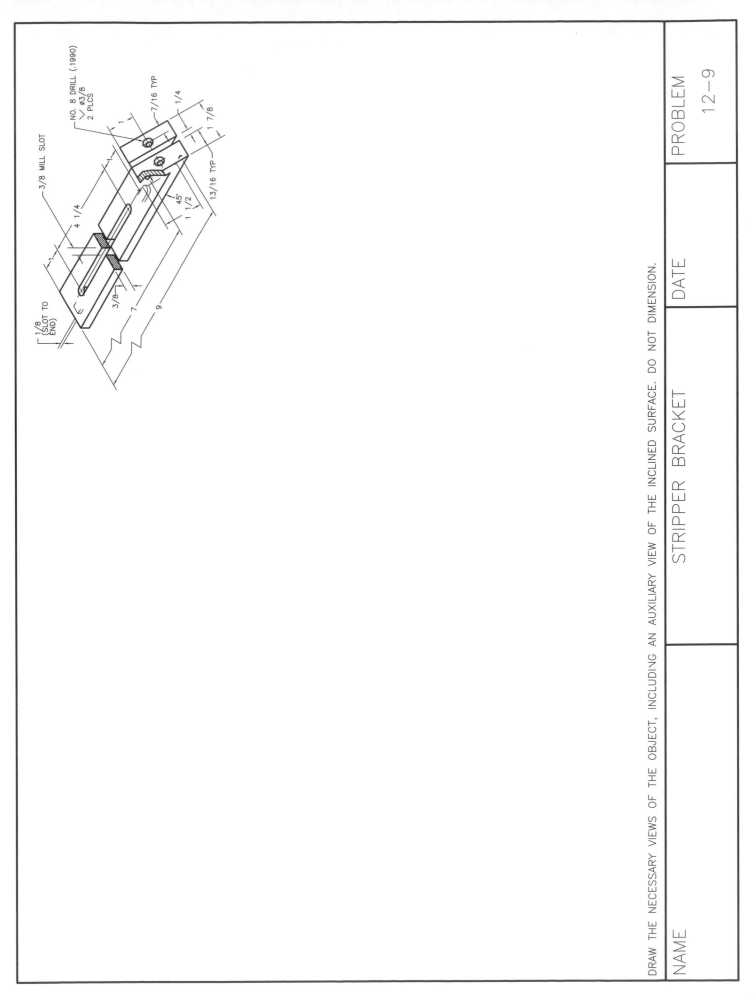

NO. 8 DRILL (.1990)
⌄ Ø3/8
2 PLCS

3/8 MILL SLOT

7/16 TYP

1/4

1 7/8

13/16 TYP

45°

1 1/2

4 1/4

1/8
(SLOT TO
END)

3/8

7

9

DRAW THE NECESSARY VIEWS OF THE OBJECT, INCLUDING AN AUXILIARY VIEW OF THE INCLINED SURFACE. DO NOT DIMENSION.

NAME

STRIPPER BRACKET

DATE

PROBLEM

12–9

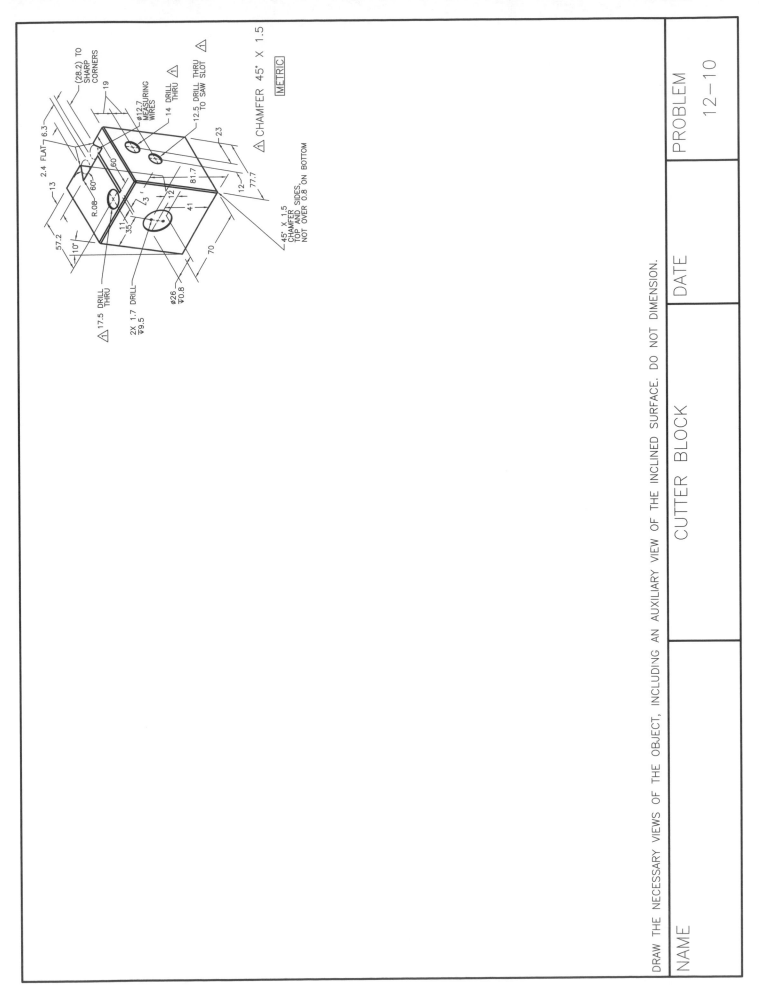

(28.2) TO SHARP CORNERS

19

2.4 FLAT ⌐ 6.3

Ø12.7 MEASURING WIRES

14 DRILL THRU △

12.5 DRILL THRU TO SAW SLOT △

△ CHAMFER 45° X 1.5

METRIC

.60

13

60

R.08

57.2

10°

11

35

3

12

41

81.7

23

77.7

12

45° X 1.5 CHAMFER TOP AND SIDES, NOT OVER 0.8 ON BOTTOM

70

△ 17.5 DRILL THRU

2X 1.7 DRILL ⊽9.5

Ø26 ⊽0.8

DRAW THE NECESSARY VIEWS OF THE OBJECT, INCLUDING AN AUXILIARY VIEW OF THE INCLINED SURFACE. DO NOT DIMENSION.

NAME

CUTTER BLOCK

DATE

PROBLEM

12−10

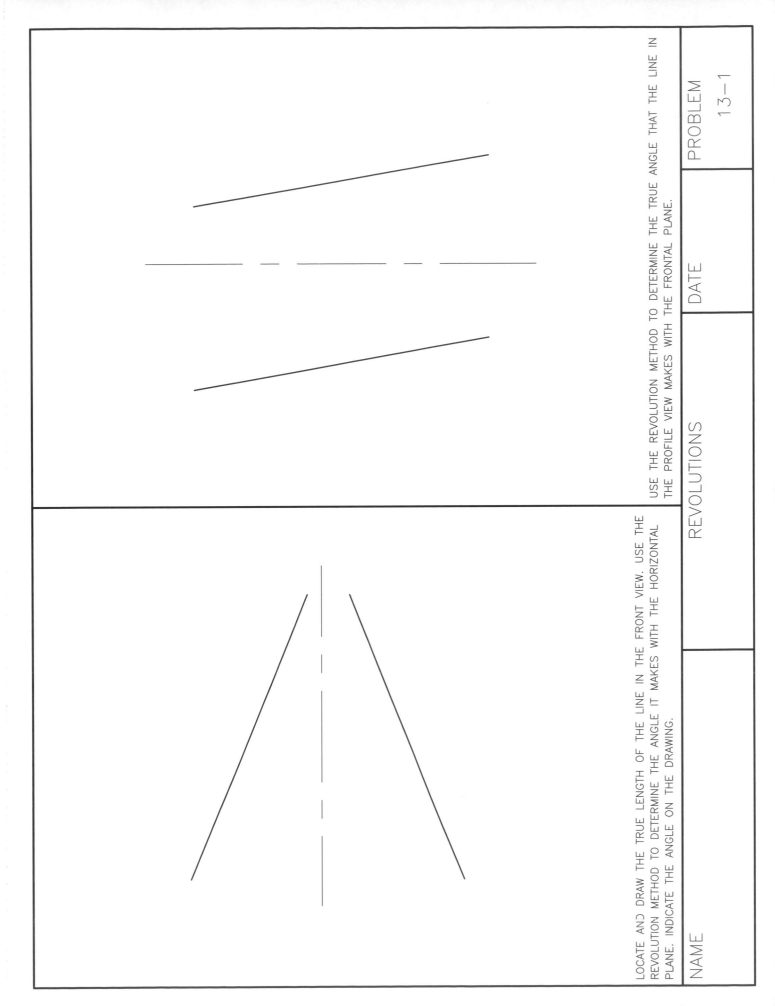

USE THE REVOLUTION METHOD TO DETERMINE THE TRUE ANGLE THAT THE LINE IN THE PROFILE VIEW MAKES WITH THE FRONTAL PLANE.

LOCATE AND DRAW THE TRUE LENGTH OF THE LINE IN THE FRONT VIEW. USE THE REVOLUTION METHOD TO DETERMINE THE ANGLE IT MAKES WITH THE HORIZONTAL PLANE. INDICATE THE ANGLE ON THE DRAWING.

NAME	REVOLUTIONS		DATE	PROBLEM
				13–1

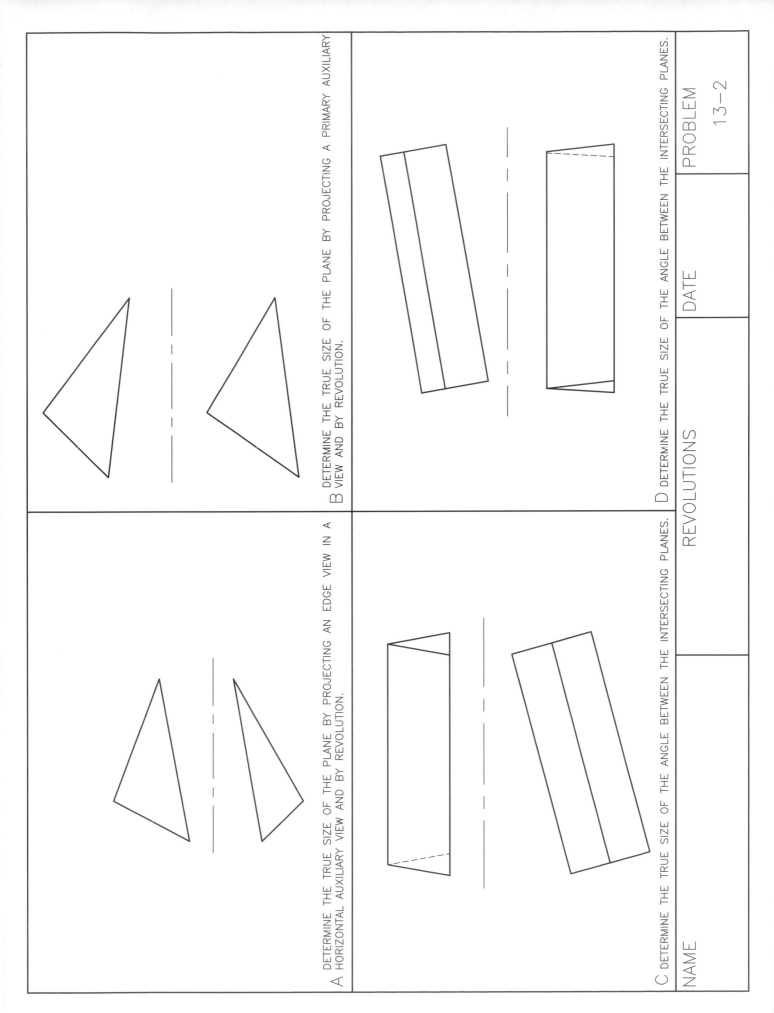

A DETERMINE THE TRUE SIZE OF THE PLANE BY PROJECTING AN EDGE VIEW IN A HORIZONTAL AUXILIARY VIEW AND BY REVOLUTION.

B DETERMINE THE TRUE SIZE OF THE PLANE BY PROJECTING A PRIMARY AUXILIARY VIEW AND BY REVOLUTION.

C DETERMINE THE TRUE SIZE OF THE ANGLE BETWEEN THE INTERSECTING PLANES.

D DETERMINE THE TRUE SIZE OF THE ANGLE BETWEEN THE INTERSECTING PLANES.

REVOLUTIONS

NAME		DATE	PROBLEM
			13-2

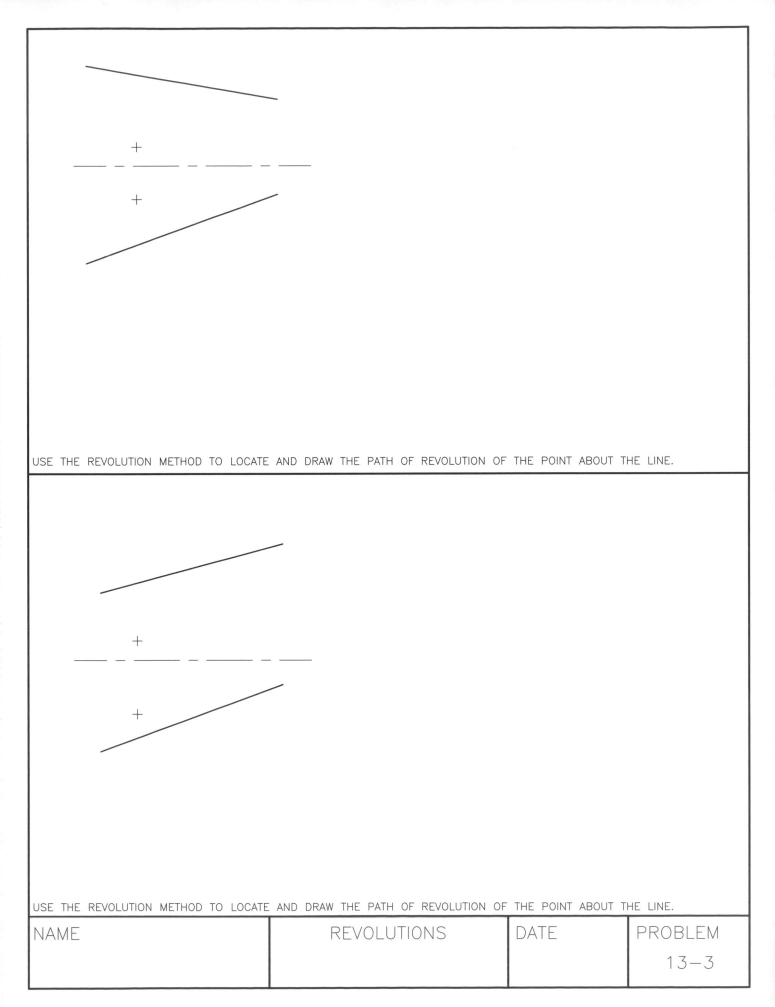

USE THE REVOLUTION METHOD TO LOCATE AND DRAW THE PATH OF REVOLUTION OF THE POINT ABOUT THE LINE.

USE THE REVOLUTION METHOD TO LOCATE AND DRAW THE PATH OF REVOLUTION OF THE POINT ABOUT THE LINE.

NAME	REVOLUTIONS	DATE	PROBLEM
			13—3

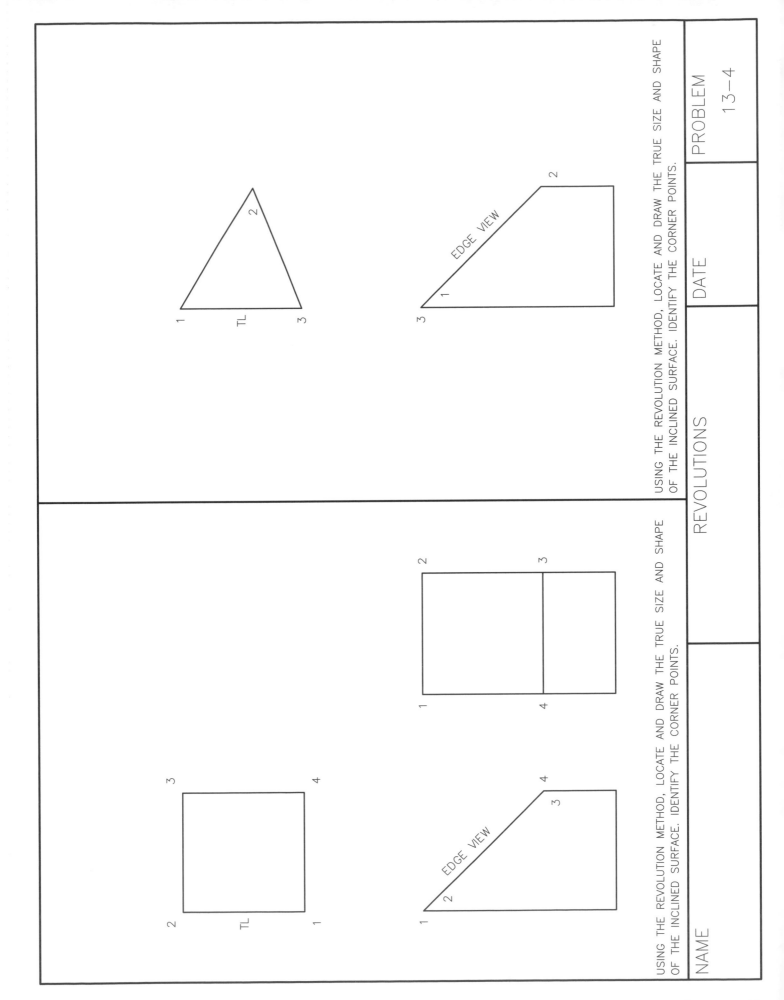

USING THE REVOLUTION METHOD, LOCATE AND DRAW THE TRUE SIZE AND SHAPE OF THE INCLINED SURFACE. IDENTIFY THE CORNER POINTS.

USING THE REVOLUTION METHOD, LOCATE AND DRAW THE TRUE SIZE AND SHAPE OF THE INCLINED SURFACE. IDENTIFY THE CORNER POINTS.

REVOLUTIONS

PROBLEM 13-4

DATE

NAME

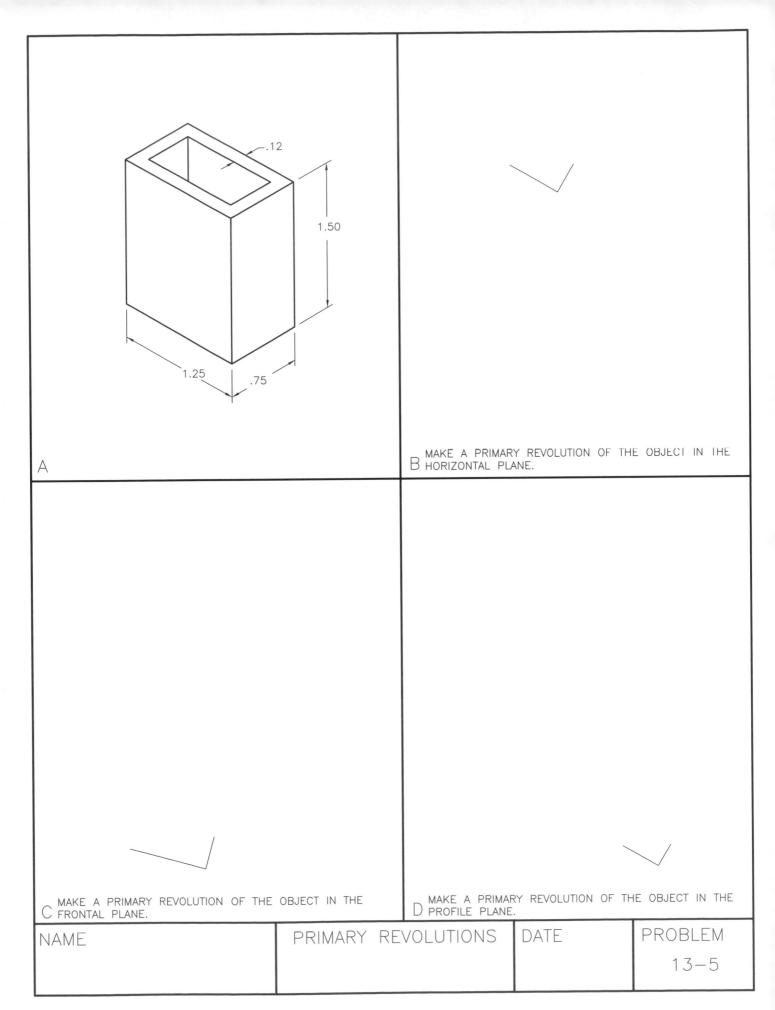

A

B MAKE A PRIMARY REVOLUTION OF THE OBJECT IN THE HORIZONTAL PLANE.

C MAKE A PRIMARY REVOLUTION OF THE OBJECT IN THE FRONTAL PLANE.

D MAKE A PRIMARY REVOLUTION OF THE OBJECT IN THE PROFILE PLANE.

NAME	PRIMARY REVOLUTIONS	DATE	PROBLEM 13-5

A DRAW THE VIEWS IN THEIR NORMAL POSITION.

MAKE A SUCCESSIVE REVOLUTION OF THE OBJECT TO PRODUCE A TRUE SIZE VIEW OF THE OBLIQUE SURFACE. DRAW THE NECESSARY VIEWS IN EACH DRAWING SPACE.

C REVOLVE THE OBJECT ON THE AXIS OF THE FRONTAL PLANE. INDICATE THE TRUE SIZE SURFACE.

B REVOLVE THE OBJECT ON THE AXIS OF THE HORIZONTAL PLANE.

SUCCESSIVE REVOLUTIONS

NAME

DATE

PROBLEM
13–6

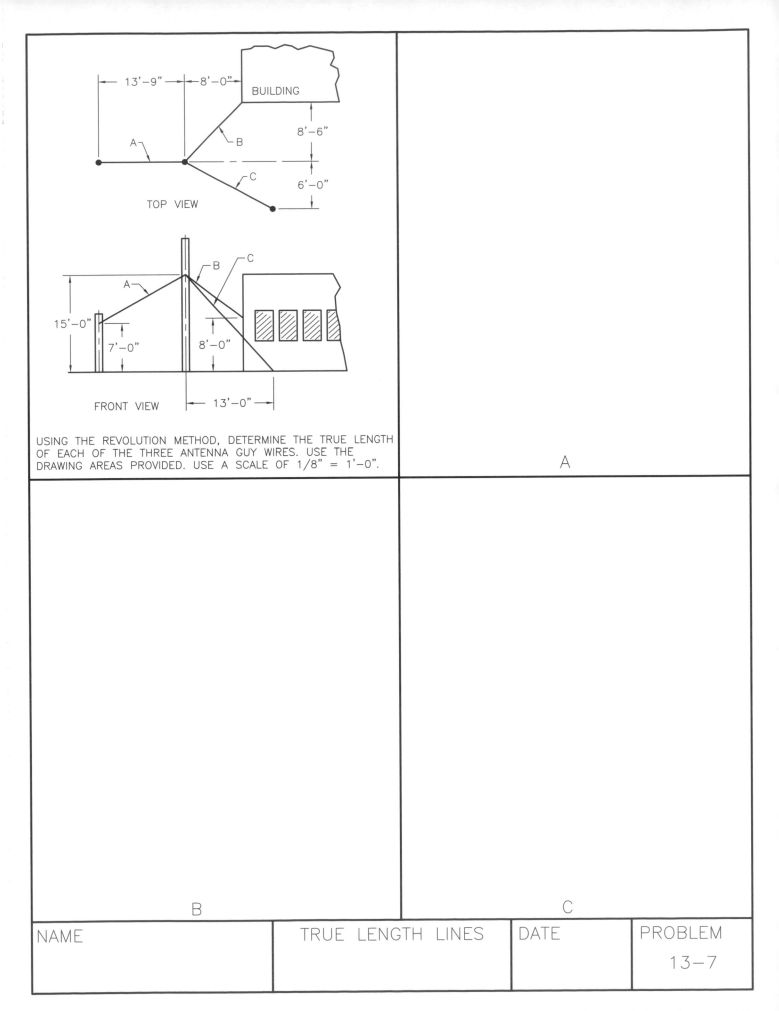

13'-9"   8'-0"
BUILDING

8'-6"

A
B

6'-0"

C

TOP VIEW

B   C
A

15'-0"

7'-0"   8'-0"

FRONT VIEW   13'-0"

USING THE REVOLUTION METHOD, DETERMINE THE TRUE LENGTH
OF EACH OF THE THREE ANTENNA GUY WIRES. USE THE
DRAWING AREAS PROVIDED. USE A SCALE OF 1/8" = 1'-0".

A

B

C

NAME	TRUE LENGTH LINES	DATE	PROBLEM
			13-7

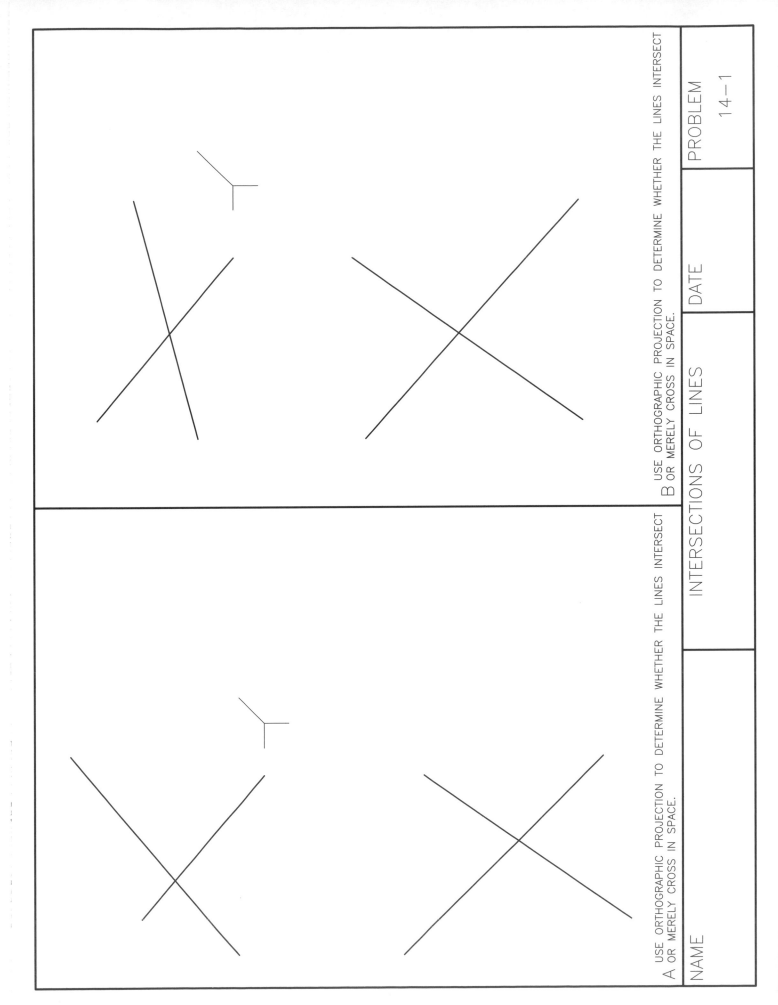

A USE ORTHOGRAPHIC PROJECTION TO DETERMINE WHETHER THE LINES INTERSECT OR MERELY CROSS IN SPACE.

B USE ORTHOGRAPHIC PROJECTION TO DETERMINE WHETHER THE LINES INTERSECT OR MERELY CROSS IN SPACE.

NAME

DATE

PROBLEM 14—1

INTERSECTIONS OF LINES

DRAW THE TOP AND FRONT VIEWS OF TWO RANDOMLY LOCATED CROSSING LINES. DETERMINE BY ORTHOGRAPHIC PROJECTION WHETHER THE LINES INTERSECT. IF THEY DO NOT, TRY TO LAY OUT TWO THAT DO IN DRAWING A AREA B.

B

INTERSECTIONS OF LINES

NAME

DATE

PROBLEM
14-2

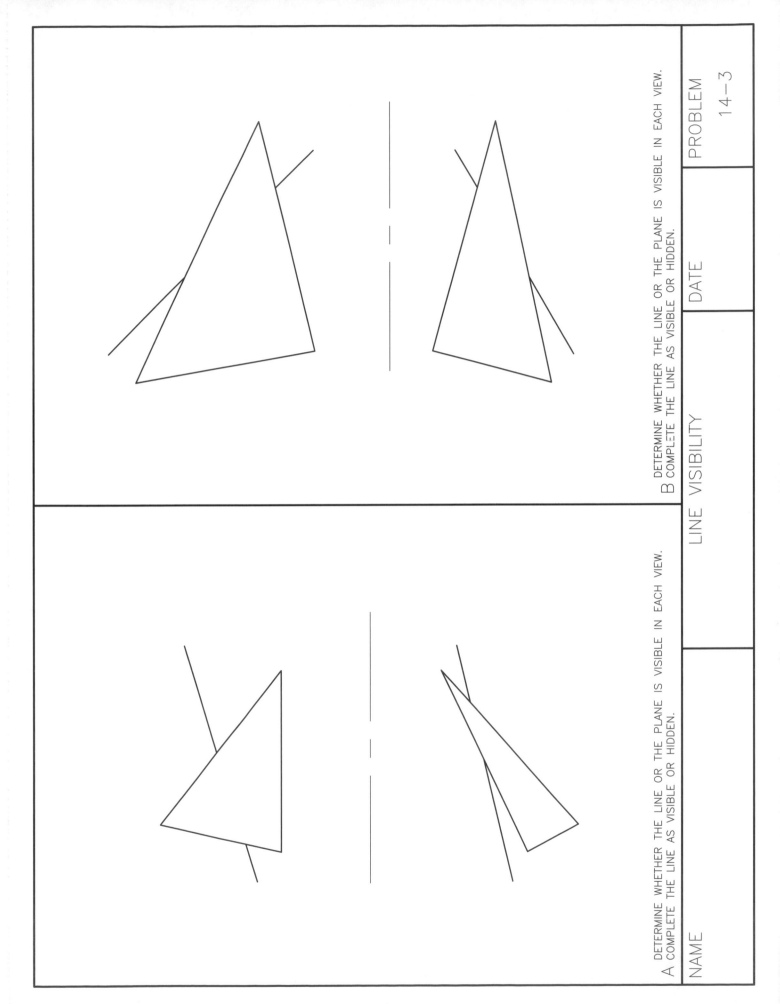

DATE

B DETERMINE WHETHER THE LINE OR THE PLANE IS VISIBLE IN EACH VIEW.
COMPLETE THE LINE AS VISIBLE OR HIDDEN.

LINE VISIBILITY

A DETERMINE WHETHER THE LINE OR THE PLANE IS VISIBLE IN EACH VIEW.
COMPLETE THE LINE AS VISIBLE OR HIDDEN.

NAME

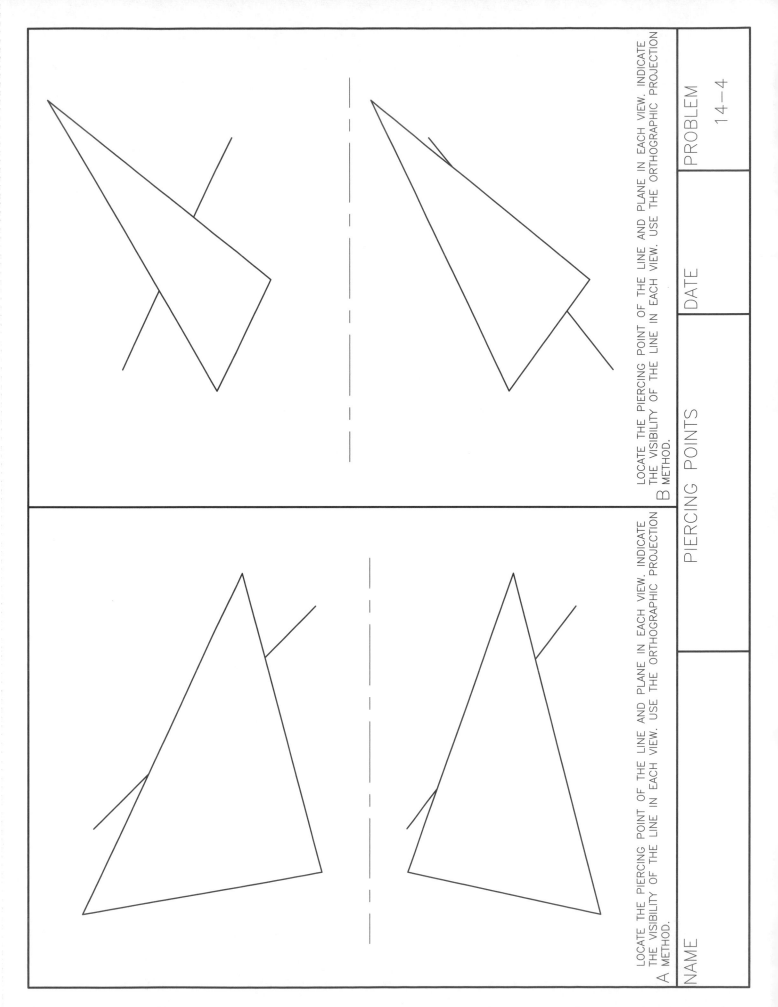

LOCATE THE PIERCING POINT OF THE LINE AND PLANE IN EACH VIEW. INDICATE THE VISIBILITY OF THE LINE IN EACH VIEW. USE THE ORTHOGRAPHIC PROJECTION A METHOD.

LOCATE THE PIERCING POINT OF THE LINE AND PLANE IN EACH VIEW. INDICATE THE VISIBILITY OF THE LINE IN EACH VIEW. USE THE ORTHOGRAPHIC PROJECTION B METHOD.

PIERCING POINTS

PROBLEM
14-4

DATE

NAME

B LOCATE THE PIERCING POINT OF THE LINE AND PLANE IN EACH VIEW. INDICATE THE VISIBILITY OF THE LINE IN EACH VIEW. USE THE AUXILIARY VIEW METHOD.

PROBLEM

14–5

DATE

PIERCING POINTS

A LOCATE THE PIERCING POINT OF THE LINE AND PLANE IN EACH VIEW. INDICATE THE VISIBILITY OF THE LINE IN EACH VIEW. USE THE AUXILIARY VIEW METHOD.

NAME

Chapter 14 Intersections **118**

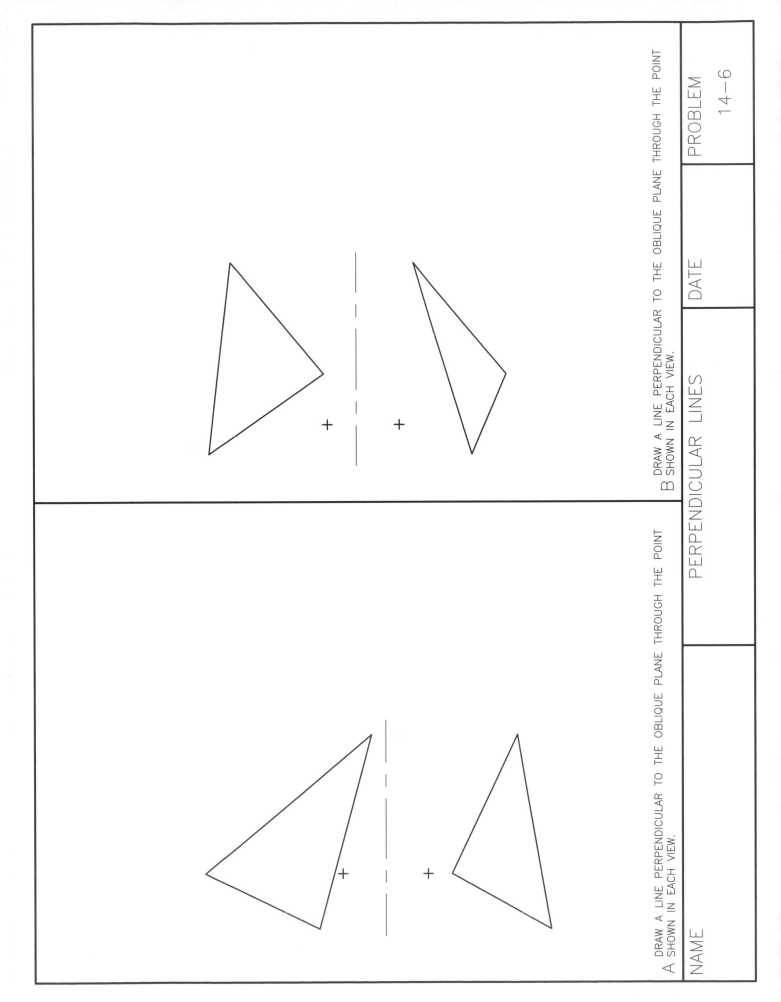

B DRAW A LINE PERPENDICULAR TO THE OBLIQUE PLANE THROUGH THE POINT SHOWN IN EACH VIEW.

PERPENDICULAR LINES

NAME

DATE

PROBLEM
14—6

LOCATE THE LINE OF INTERSECTION OF THE PLANES AND INDICATE THE VISIBILITY FOR EACH PLANE B IN THE TWO VIEWS. USE THE AUXILIARY VIEW METHOD.

INTERSECTION OF PLANES

PROBLEM
14–7

DATE

LOCATE THE LINE OF INTERSECTION OF THE PLANES AND INDICATE THE VISIBILITY FOR EACH PLANE IN THE TWO A VIEWS. USE THE ORTHOGRAPHIC PROJECTION METHOD.

NAME

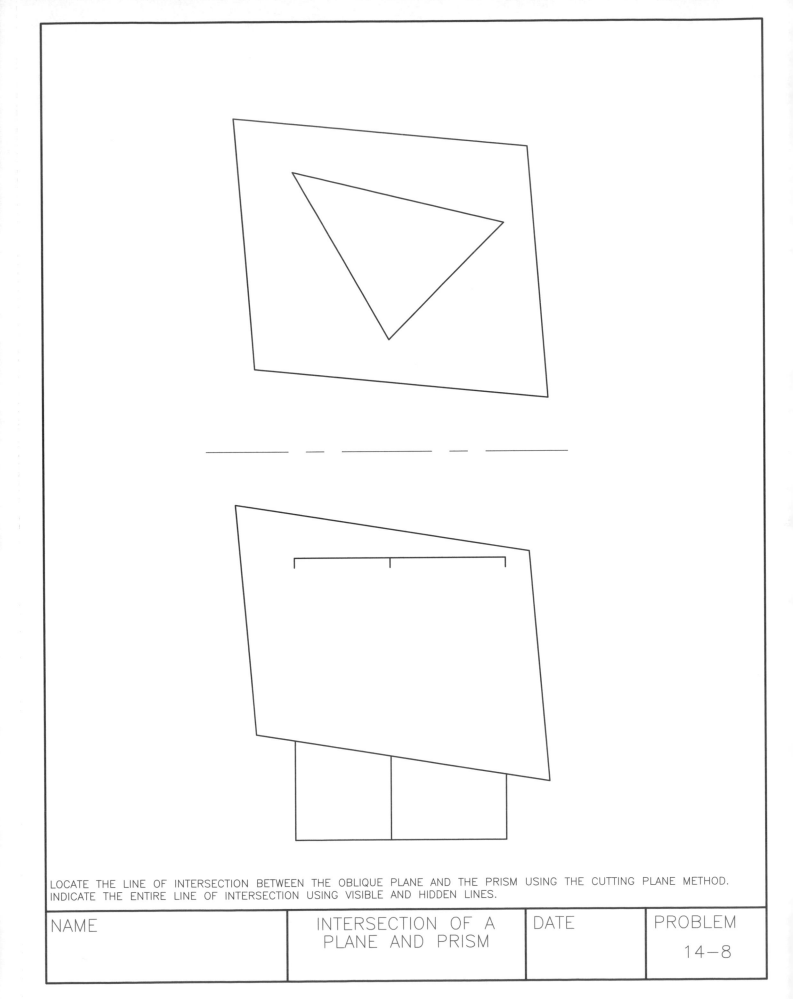

LOCATE THE LINE OF INTERSECTION BETWEEN THE OBLIQUE PLANE AND THE PRISM USING THE CUTTING PLANE METHOD.
INDICATE THE ENTIRE LINE OF INTERSECTION USING VISIBLE AND HIDDEN LINES.

NAME	INTERSECTION OF A PLANE AND PRISM	DATE	PROBLEM 14—8

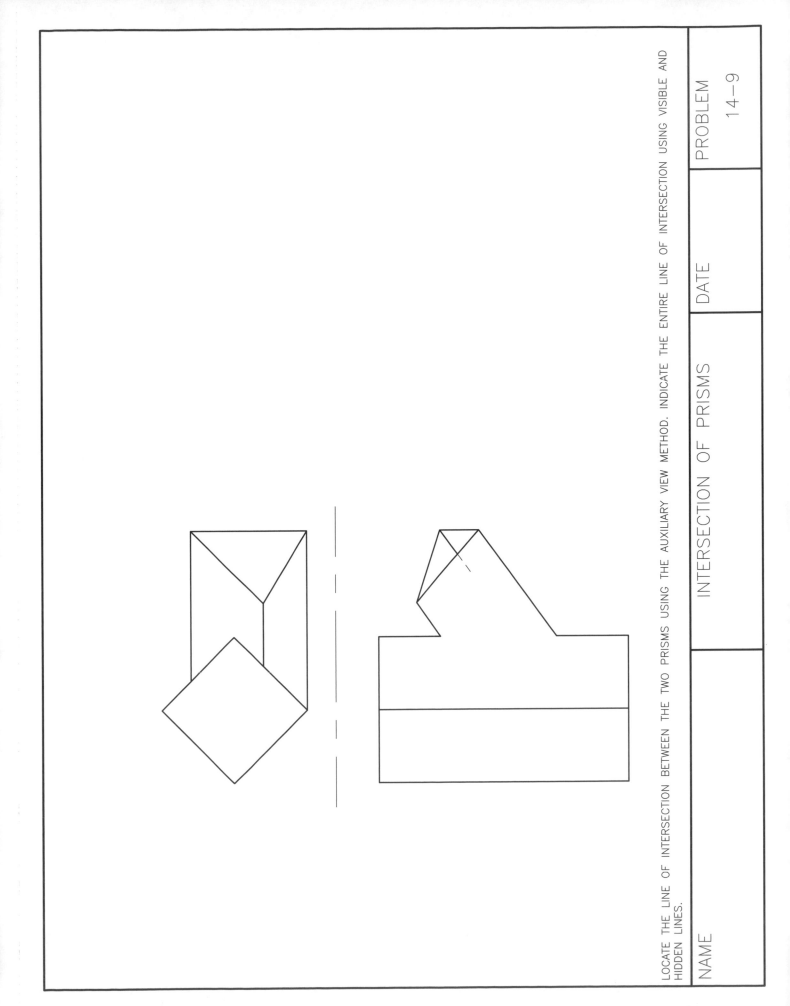

LOCATE THE LINE OF INTERSECTION BETWEEN THE TWO PRISMS USING THE AUXILIARY VIEW METHOD. INDICATE THE ENTIRE LINE OF INTERSECTION USING VISIBLE AND HIDDEN LINES.

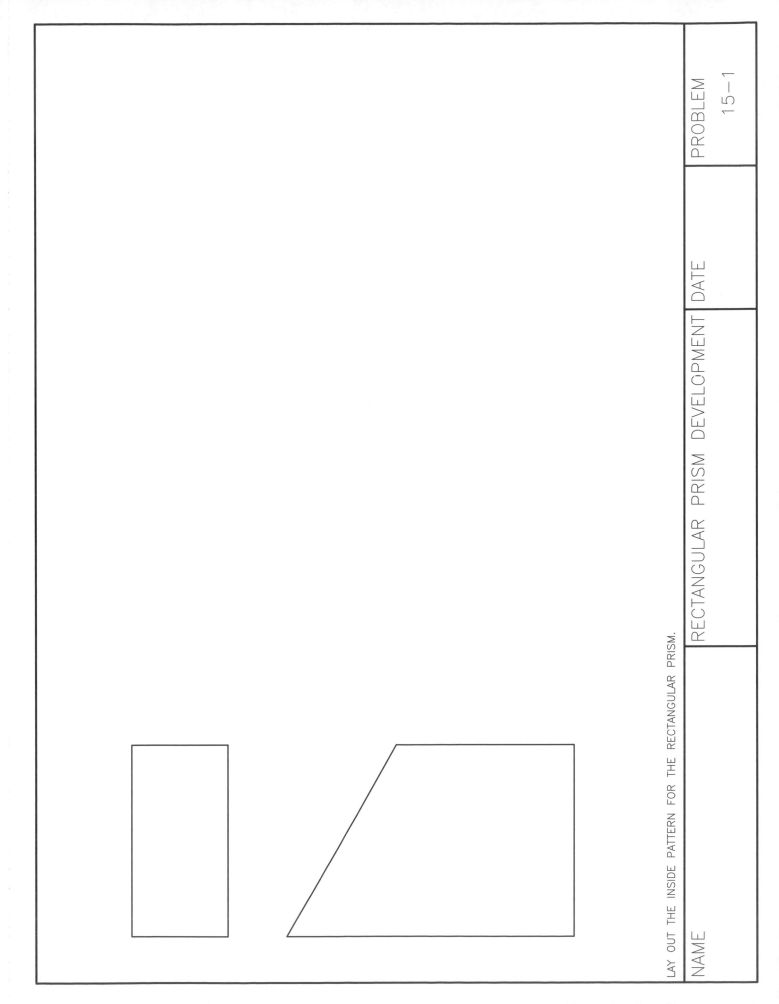

LAY OUT THE INSIDE PATTERN FOR THE RECTANGULAR PRISM.

RECTANGULAR PRISM DEVELOPMENT

PROBLEM
15–1

DATE

NAME

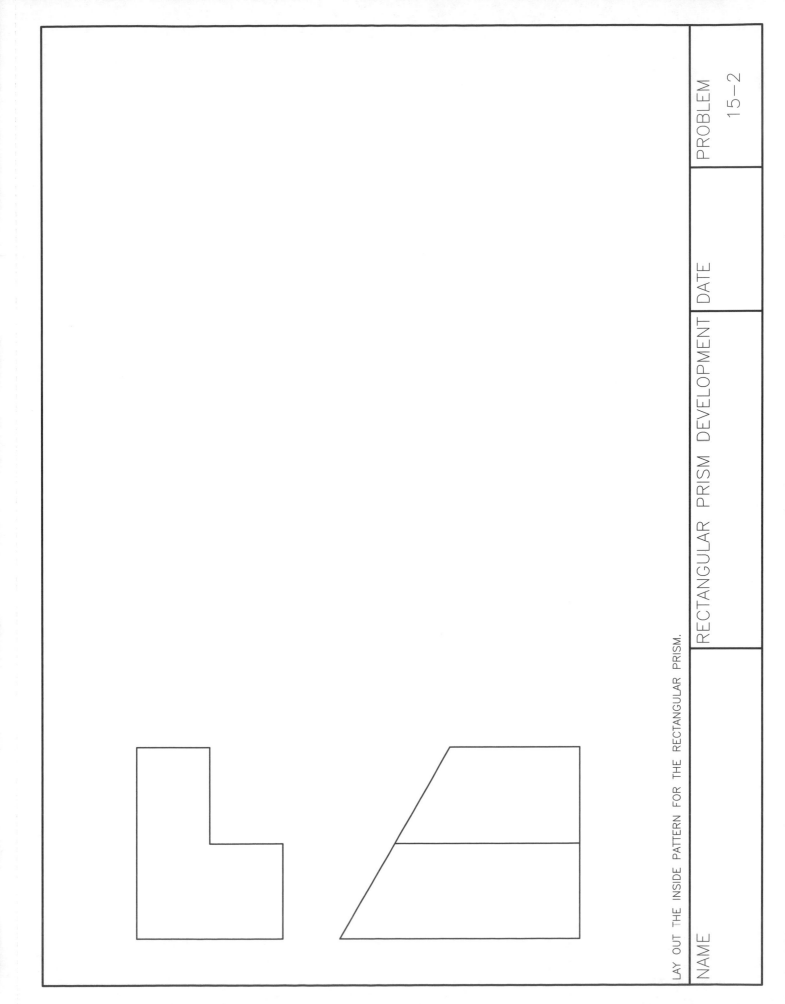

LAY OUT THE INSIDE PATTERN FOR THE RECTANGULAR PRISM.

NAME

RECTANGULAR PRISM DEVELOPMENT

DATE

PROBLEM
15-2

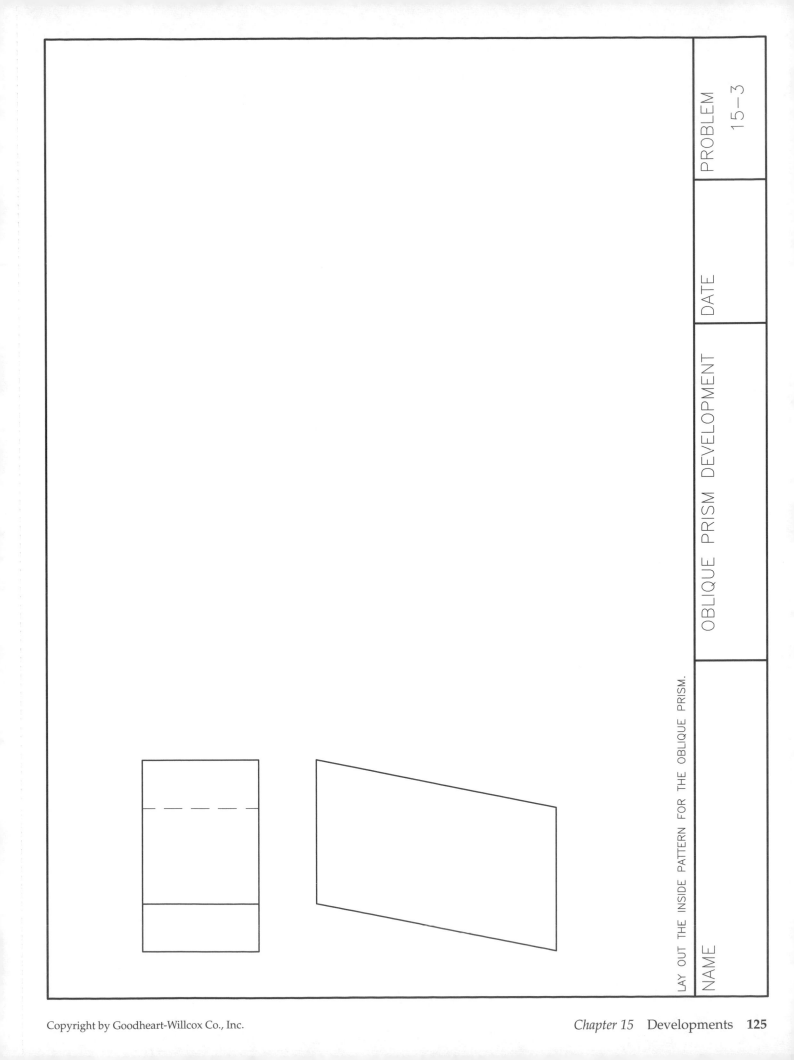

LAY OUT THE INSIDE PATTERN FOR THE OBLIQUE PRISM.

PROBLEM
15–3

DATE

OBLIQUE PRISM DEVELOPMENT

NAME

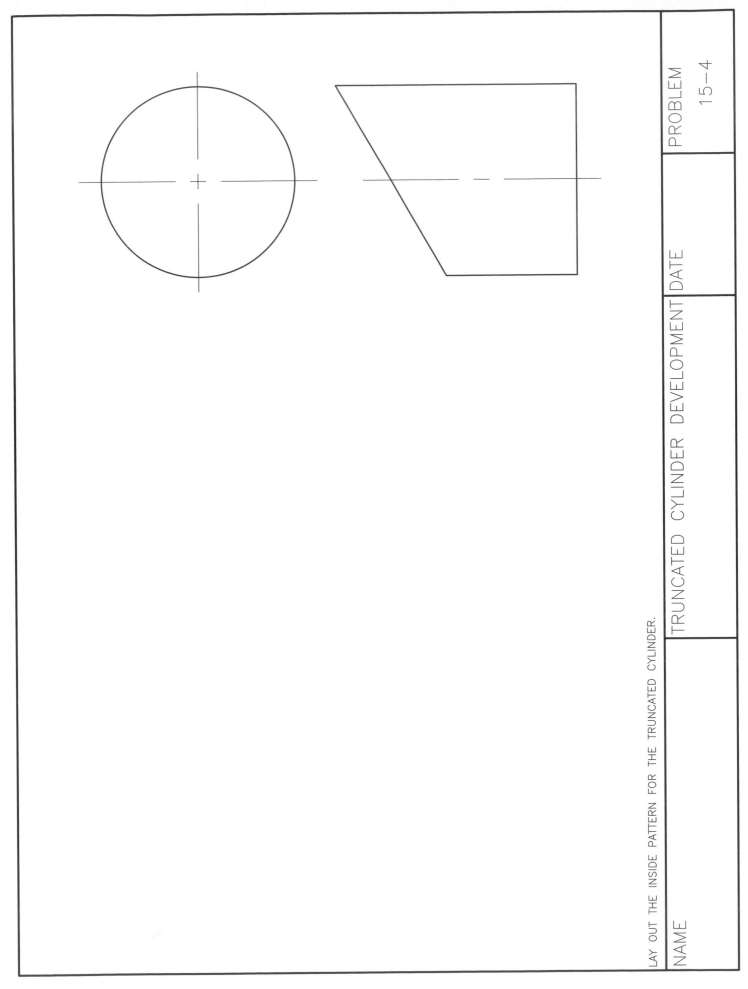

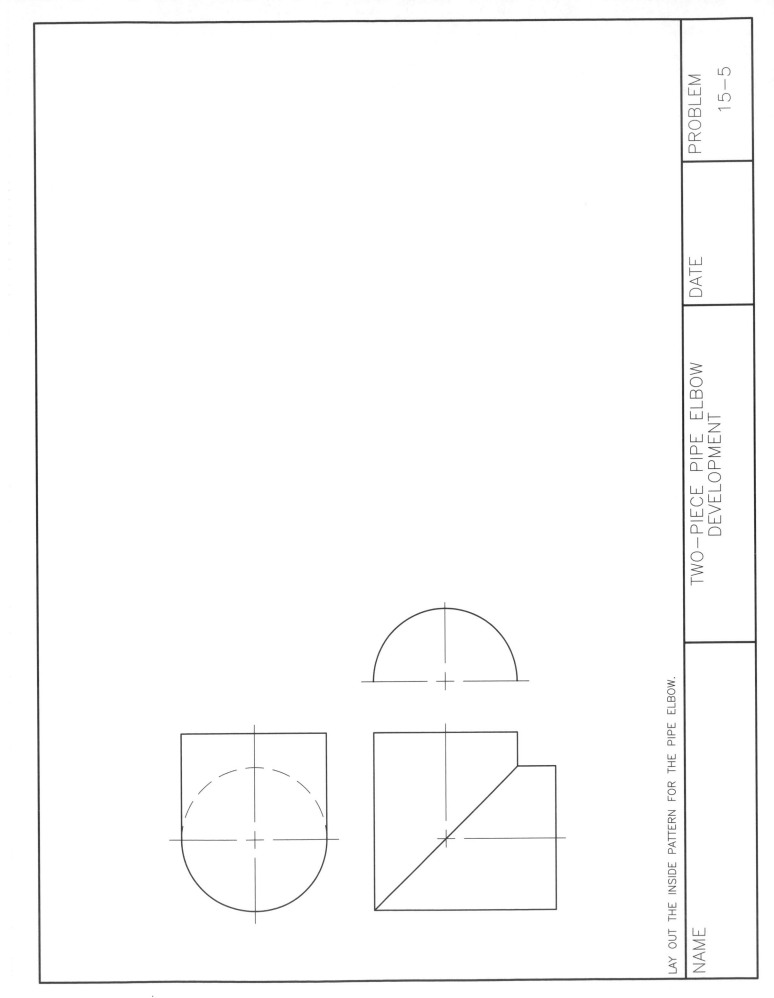

LAY OUT THE INSIDE PATTERN FOR THE PIPE ELBOW.

NAME

TWO—PIECE PIPE ELBOW
DEVELOPMENT

DATE

PROBLEM
15—5

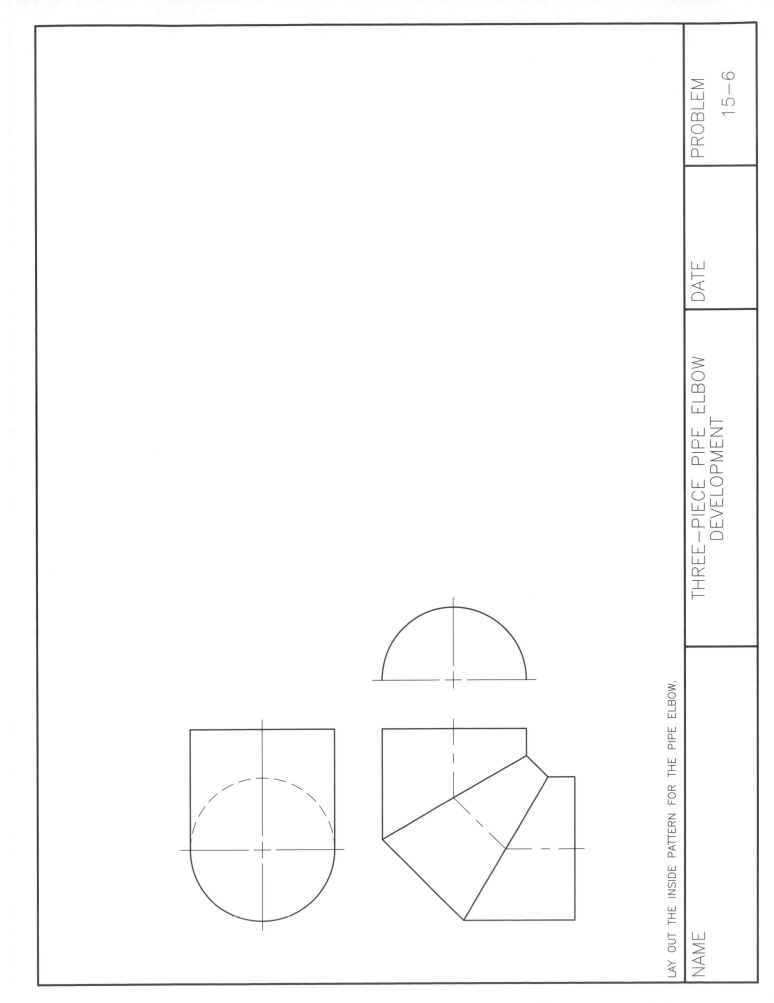

LAY OUT THE INSIDE PATTERN FOR THE PIPE ELBOW.

THREE-PIECE PIPE ELBOW DEVELOPMENT

NAME

DATE

PROBLEM
15-6

LAY OUT THE INSIDE PATTERN FOR THE OBLIQUE CYLINDER.

NAME

OBLIQUE CYLINDER DEVELOPMENT

DATE

PROBLEM
15–7

LAY OUT THE INSIDE PATTERN FOR THE TRUNCATED PYRAMID.

TRUNCATED PYRAMID DEVELOPMENT		PROBLEM
	DATE	15–8
NAME		

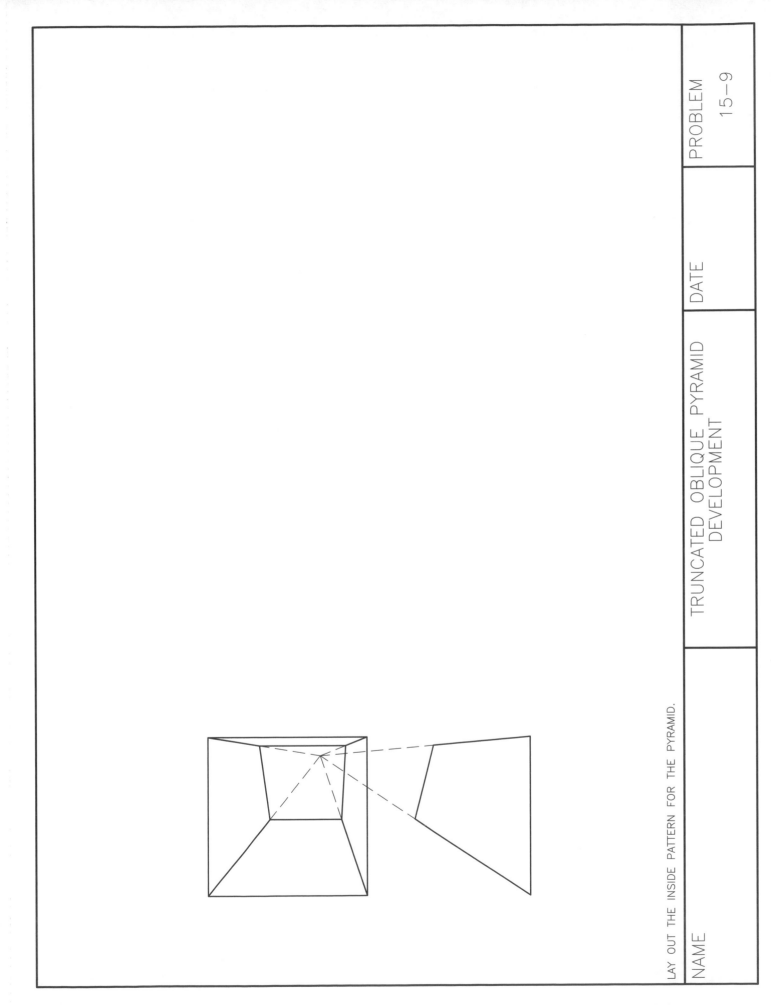

LAY OUT THE INSIDE PATTERN FOR THE PYRAMID.

NAME

DATE

PROBLEM
15–9

TRUNCATED OBLIQUE PYRAMID
DEVELOPMENT

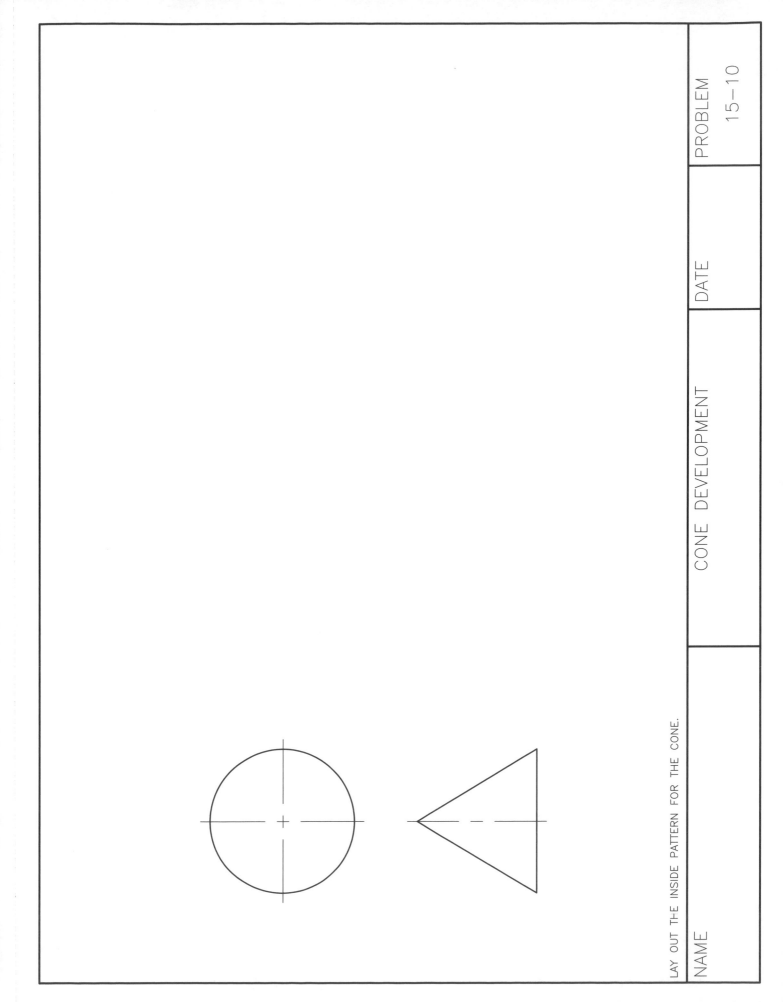

LAY OUT THE INSIDE PATTERN FOR THE CONE.

NAME

CONE DEVELOPMENT

DATE

PROBLEM
15–10

TRUNCATED CONE DEVELOPMENT

NAME

DATE

PROBLEM
15–11

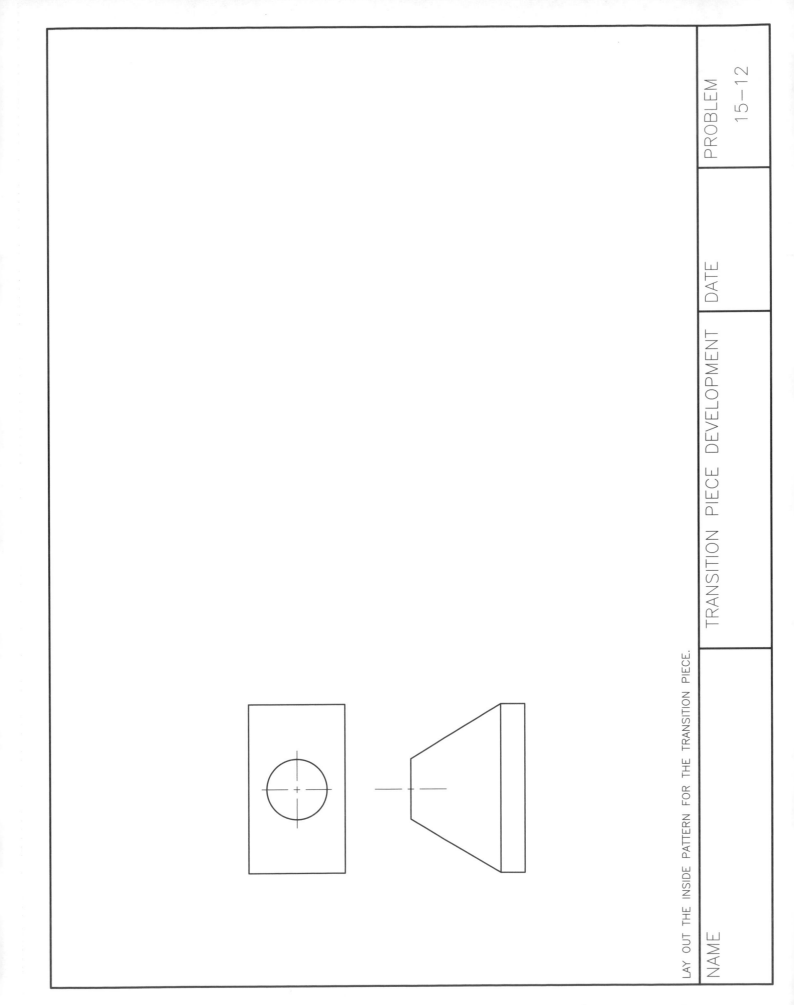

LAY OUT THE INSIDE PATTERN FOR THE TRANSITION PIECE.

NAME

TRANSITION PIECE DEVELOPMENT

DATE

PROBLEM 15–12

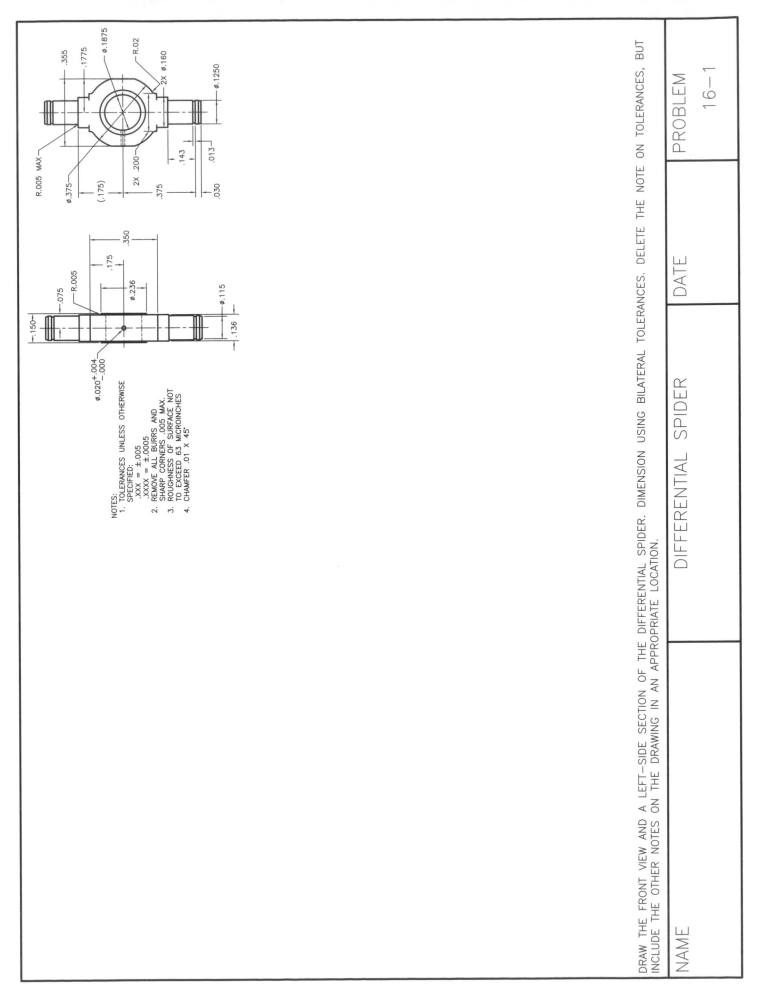

.355
.1775
Ø.1875
R.02
2X Ø.160
Ø.1250

R.005 MAX
Ø.375
(.175)
2X .200
.143
.013
.375
.030

.350
.175
R.005
Ø.236
Ø.115
.075
.150
.136
Ø.020 +.004 −.000

NOTES:
1. TOLERANCES UNLESS OTHERWISE
   SPECIFIED:
   .XXX = ±.005
   .XXXX = ±.0005
2. REMOVE ALL BURRS AND
   SHARP CORNERS .005 MAX.
3. ROUGHNESS OF SURFACE NOT
   TO EXCEED 63 MICROINCHES
4. CHAMFER .01 X 45°

DRAW THE FRONT VIEW AND A LEFT–SIDE SECTION OF THE DIFFERENTIAL SPIDER. DIMENSION USING BILATERAL TOLERANCES. DELETE THE NOTE ON TOLERANCES, BUT INCLUDE THE OTHER NOTES ON THE DRAWING IN AN APPROPRIATE LOCATION.

NAME

DIFFERENTIAL SPIDER

DATE

PROBLEM

16–1

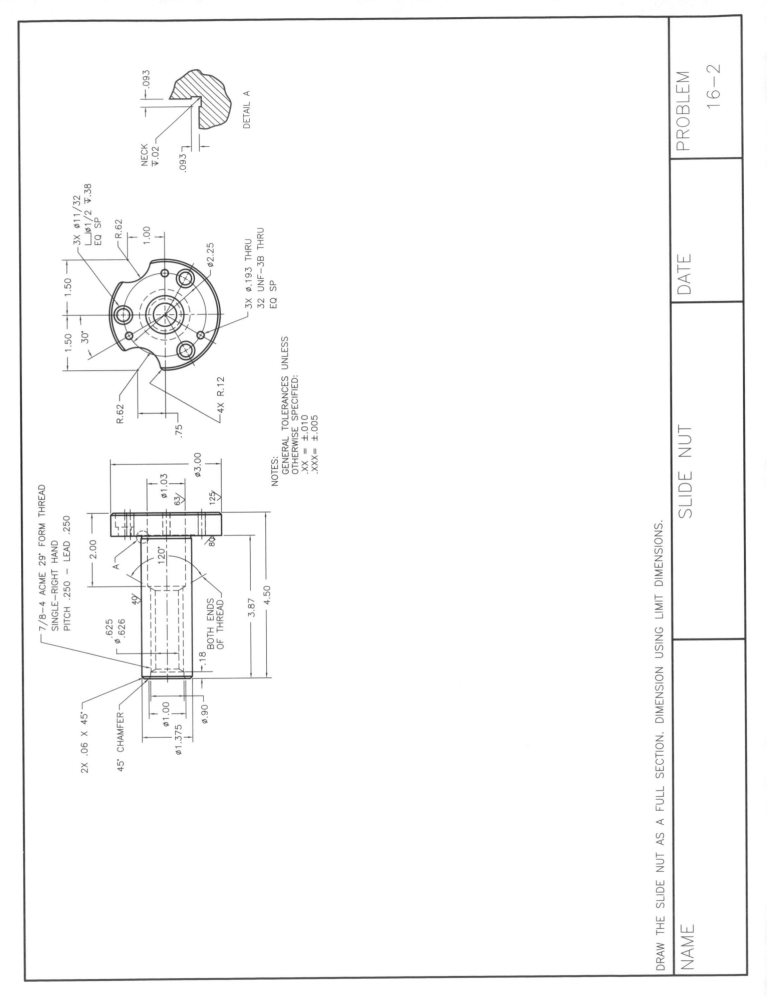

.093
NECK ∇.02
.093
DETAIL A

3X ∅11/32 ∇.38
⌴∅1/2 ∇.38
EQ SP
R.62
1.00
∅2.25
3X ∅.193 THRU
32 UNF–3B THRU
EQ SP
1.50
1.50
30°
R.62
.75
4X R.12

NOTES:
GENERAL TOLERANCES UNLESS
OTHERWISE SPECIFIED:
.XX = ±.010
.XXX= ±.005

7/8–4 ACME 29° FORM THREAD
SINGLE–RIGHT HAND
PITCH .250 – LEAD .250
∅3.00
∅1.03
63√
125√
2.00
A
120°
40°
∅.625
∅.626
3.87
4.50
.18 BOTH ENDS
OF THREAD
80√
2X .06 X 45°
45° CHAMFER
∅1.00
∅1.375
∅.90

DRAW THE SLIDE NUT AS A FULL SECTION. DIMENSION USING LIMIT DIMENSIONS.

SLIDE NUT

NAME

DATE

PROBLEM
16–2

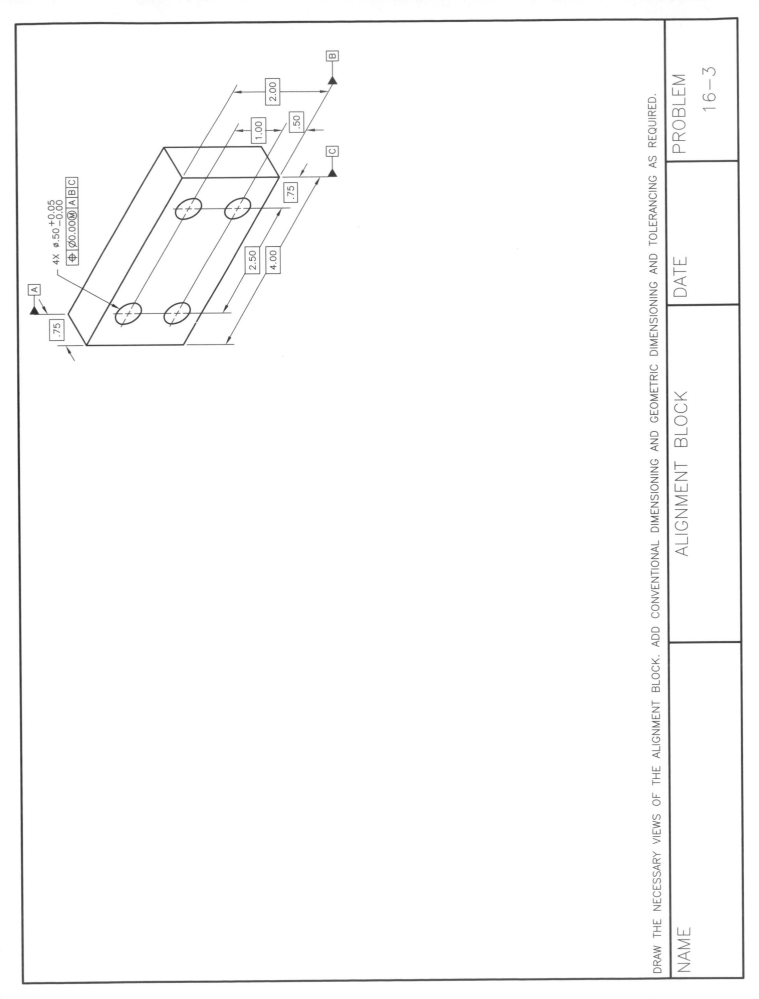

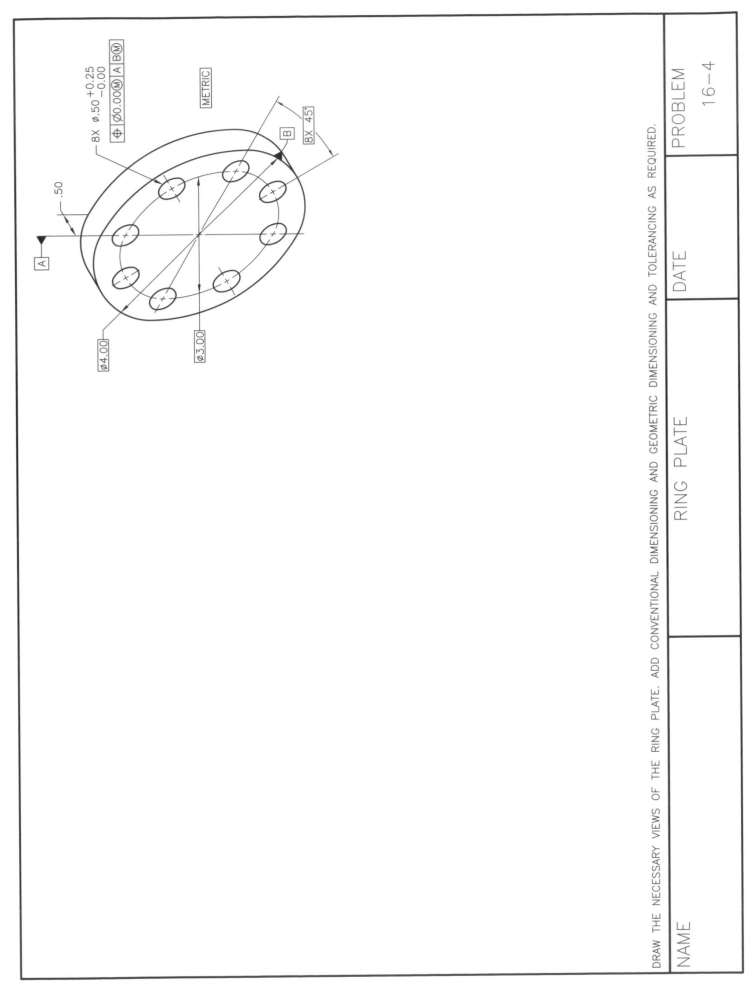

8X ⌀.50 +0.25 −0.00
⊕ ⌀0.00Ⓜ A BⓂ

METRIC

8X 45°

B

.50

A

⌀4.00

⌀3.00

NAME				RING PLATE		DATE		PROBLEM
								16–4

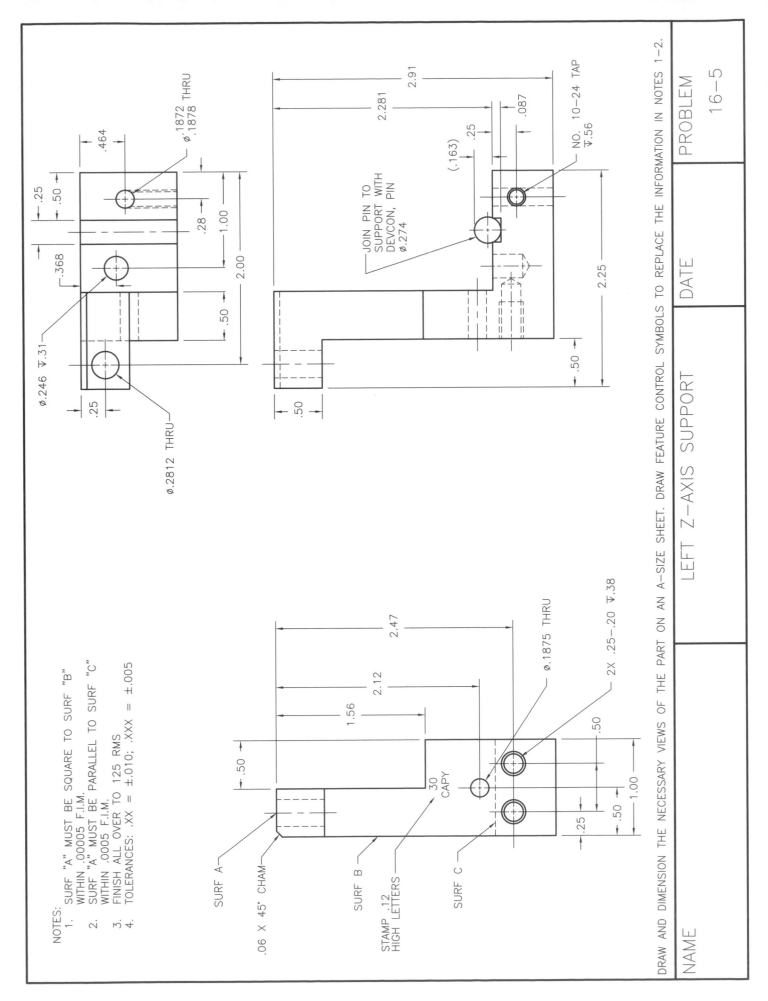

NOTES:
1. SURF "A" MUST BE SQUARE TO SURF "B"
   WITHIN .00005 F.I.M.
2. SURF "A" MUST BE PARALLEL TO SURF "C"
   WITHIN .0005 F.I.M.
3. FINISH ALL OVER TO 125 RMS
4. TOLERANCES: .XX = ±.010; .XXX = ±.005

ø.1872 THRU
ø.1878

.464
.25
.50
.28
1.00
.368
2.00
.50
ø.246 ⌵.31
.25
ø.2812 THRU

2.91
2.281
.087
.25
(.163)
JOIN PIN TO
SUPPORT WITH
DEVCON, PIN
ø.274
NO. 10–24 TAP
⌵.56
2.25
.50
.50

2.47
2.12
1.56
.50
SURF A
.06 X 45° CHAM
30
CAPY
SURF B
STAMP .12
HIGH LETTERS
SURF C
ø.1875 THRU
2X .25–20 ⌵.38
.50
1.00
.25
.50

DRAW AND DIMENSION THE NECESSARY VIEWS OF THE PART ON AN A–SIZE SHEET. DRAW FEATURE CONTROL SYMBOLS TO REPLACE THE INFORMATION IN NOTES 1–2.

NAME

LEFT Z–AXIS SUPPORT

DATE

PROBLEM
16–5

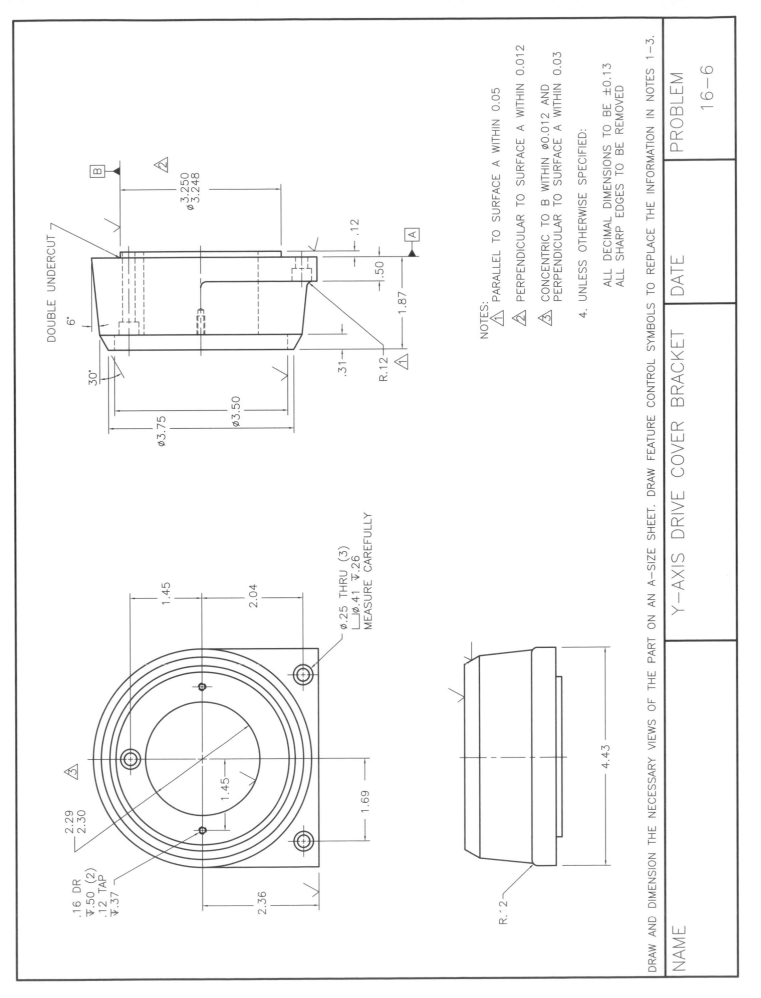

DOUBLE UNDERCUT

6°

30°

Ø3.75

Ø3.50

B

Ø3.250
Ø3.248

2

.12

.50

1.87

A

.31

R.12

1

1.45

2.04

Ø.25 THRU (3)
⌴Ø.41 ⌵.26
MEASURE CAREFULLY

1.45

1.69

2.29
2.30

3

.16 DR
⌵.50 (2)
.12 TAP
⌵.37

2.36

4.43

R.' 2

NOTES:

1 PARALLEL TO SURFACE A WITHIN 0.05

2 PERPENDICULAR TO SURFACE A WITHIN 0.012

3 CONCENTRIC TO B WITHIN Ø0.012 AND
   PERPENDICULAR TO SURFACE A WITHIN 0.03

4. UNLESS OTHERWISE SPECIFIED:

   ALL DECIMAL DIMENSIONS TO BE ±0.13
   ALL SHARP EDGES TO BE REMOVED

DRAW AND DIMENSION THE NECESSARY VIEWS OF THE PART ON AN A–SIZE SHEET. DRAW FEATURE CONTROL SYMBOLS TO REPLACE THE INFORMATION IN NOTES 1–3.

NAME	Y–AXIS DRIVE COVER BRACKET	DATE	PROBLEM
			16–6

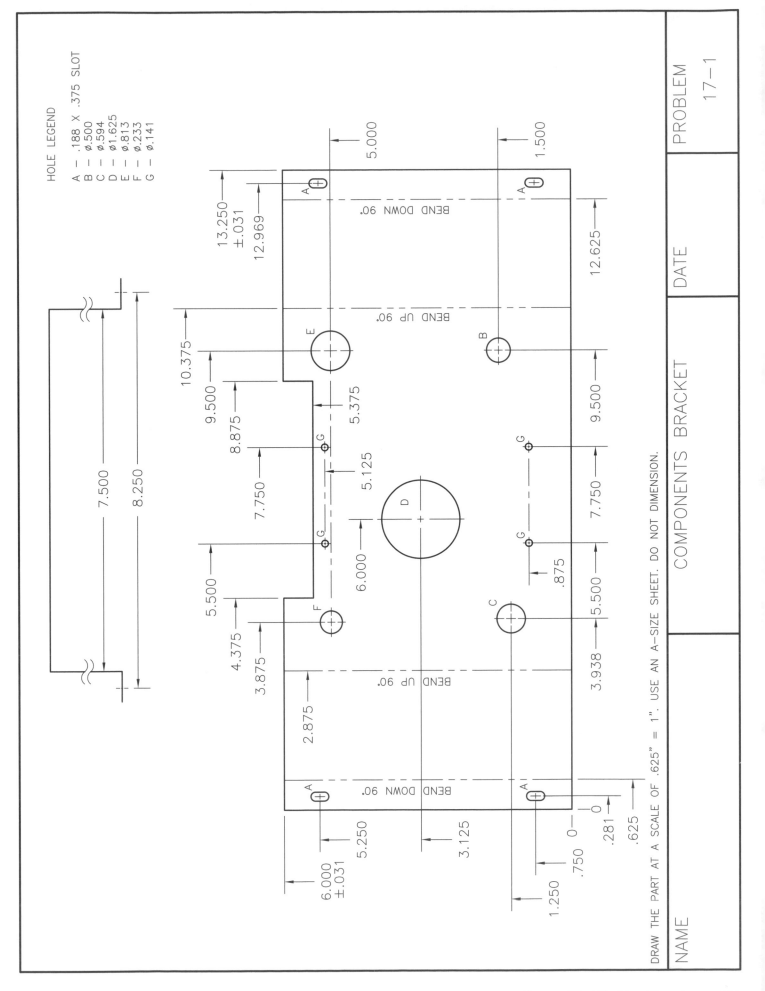

HOLE LEGEND

A — .188 X .375 SLOT
B — ⌀.500
C — ⌀.594
D — ⌀1.625
E — ⌀.813
F — ⌀.233
G — ⌀.141

DRAW THE PART AT A SCALE OF .625" = 1". USE AN A–SIZE SHEET. DO NOT DIMENSION.

NAME

DATE

PROBLEM
17–1

COMPONENTS BRACKET

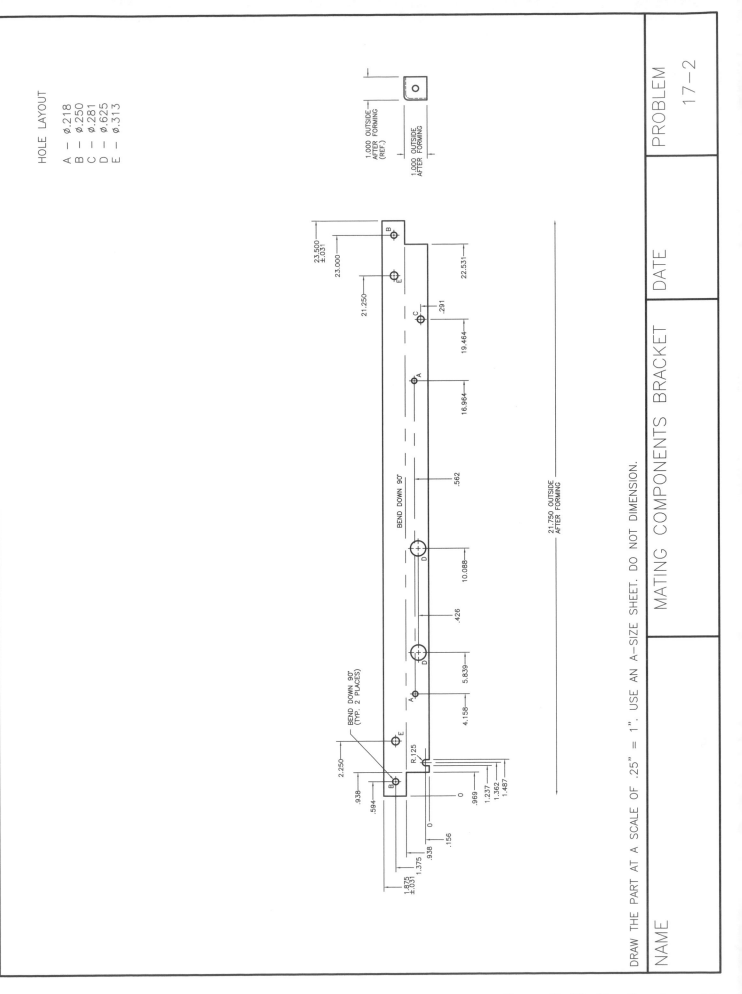

HOLE LAYOUT

A — ⌀.218
B — ⌀.250
C — ⌀.281
D — ⌀.625
E — ⌀.313

1.000 OUTSIDE AFTER FORMING (REF.)

1.000 OUTSIDE AFTER FORMING

23.500 ±.031
23.000

22.531

21.250

.291

19.464

16.964

BEND DOWN 90°

.562

21.750 OUTSIDE AFTER FORMING

10.088

.426

D

5.839

A

4.158

BEND DOWN 90° (TYP. 2 PLACES)

2.250

R.125

E

B

.938
.594

0

.969
1.237
1.362
1.487

0

.156

.938

1.875 ±.031
1.375

DRAW THE PART AT A SCALE OF .25" = 1". USE AN A–SIZE SHEET. DO NOT DIMENSION.

NAME	MATING COMPONENTS BRACKET	DATE	PROBLEM
			17–2

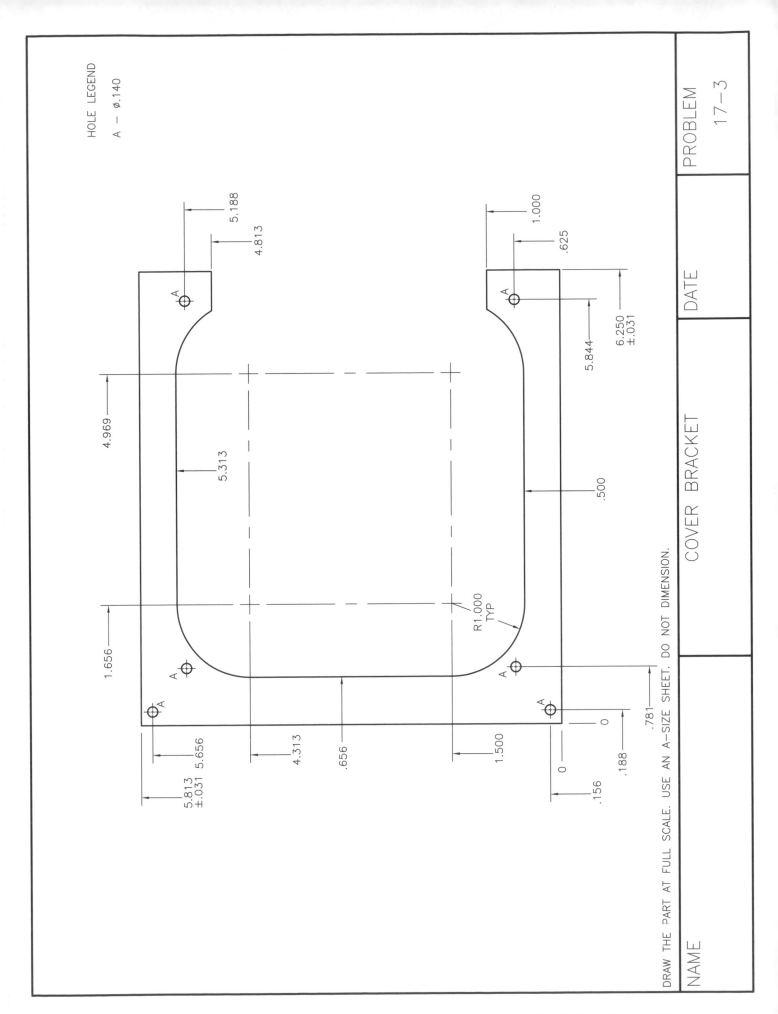

HOLE LEGEND

A – ⌀.140

5.188

4.813

1.000

.625

4.969

5.313

6.250
±.031

1.656

.500

R1.000
TYP

5.813
±.031 5.656

4.313

.656

1.500

.781

.188

.156

0

0

DRAW THE PART AT FULL SCALE. USE AN A–SIZE SHEET. DO NOT DIMENSION.

COVER BRACKET

PROBLEM
17–3

DATE

NAME

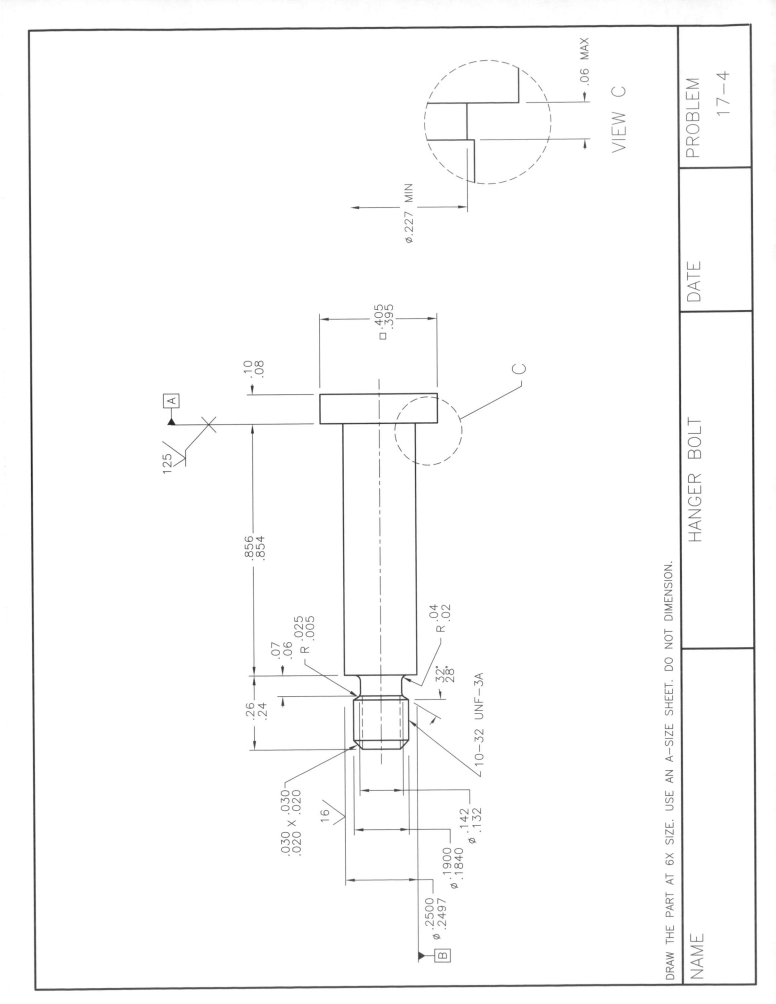

.06 MAX

VIEW C

Ø.227 MIN

Ø.405/.395

□ .405/.395

.10/.08

A

125

.856/.854

.07/.06

R .025/.005

R .04/.02

32°/28°

.26/.24

10–32 UNF–3A

.030 × .030
.020 × .020

16

Ø .142/.132

Ø .1900/.1840

Ø .2500/.2497

B

C

DRAW THE PART AT 6X SIZE. USE AN A–SIZE SHEET. DO NOT DIMENSION.

NAME

HANGER BOLT

DATE

PROBLEM
17–4

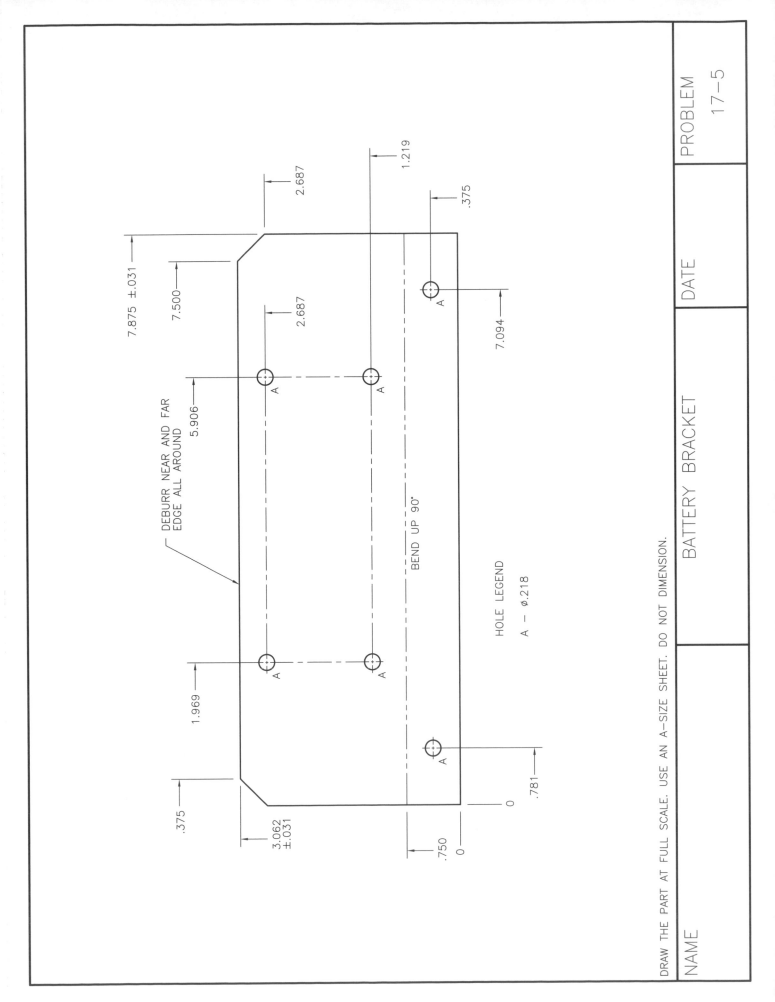

DRAW THE PART AT FULL SCALE. USE AN A-SIZE SHEET. DO NOT DIMENSION.

DEBURR NEAR AND FAR
EDGE ALL AROUND

BEND UP 90°

HOLE LEGEND

A – ⌀.218

7.875 ±.031

7.500

2.687

1.219

.375

2.687

5.906

7.094

1.969

.375

3.062
±.031

.750

.781

0

0

| NAME | DATE | BATTERY BRACKET | PROBLEM |
| | | | 17–5 |

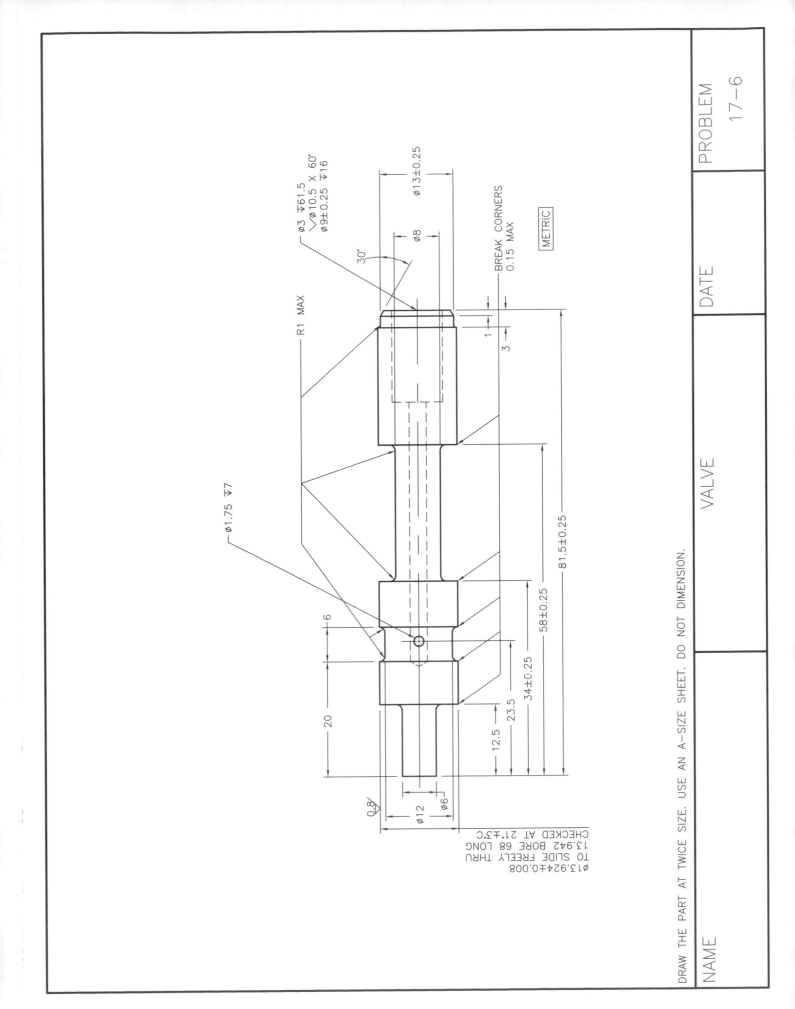

DATE

VALVE

NAME

DRAW THE PART AT TWICE SIZE. USE AN A–SIZE SHEET. DO NOT DIMENSION.

Ø3 ↧61.5
⌵Ø10.5 X 60°
Ø9± 0.25 ↧16

Ø13±0.25

Ø8

30°

R1 MAX

BREAK CORNERS
0.15 MAX

METRIC

Ø1.75 ↧7

1

3

81.5±0.25

58±0.25

6

34±0.25

23.5

20

12.5

0.8

Ø12

Ø6

CHECKED AT 21°±3°C
13.942 BORE 68 LONG
TO SLIDE FREELY THRU
Ø13.924±0.008

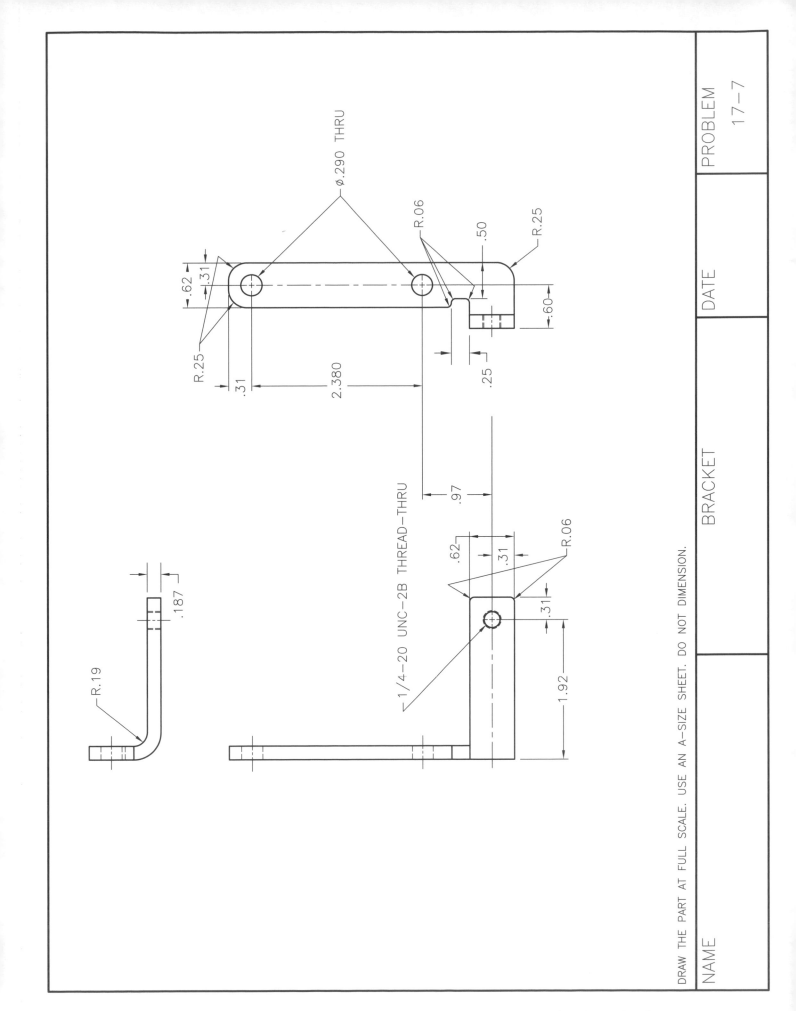

ø.290 THRU

R.06

.50

R.25

.62

.31

R.25

.31

2.380

.60

.25

1/4-20 UNC-2B THREAD-THRU

.97

R.06

.62

.31

.31

R.19

.187

1.92

DRAW THE PART AT FULL SCALE. USE AN A-SIZE SHEET. DO NOT DIMENSION.

NAME

BRACKET

DATE

PROBLEM
17-7

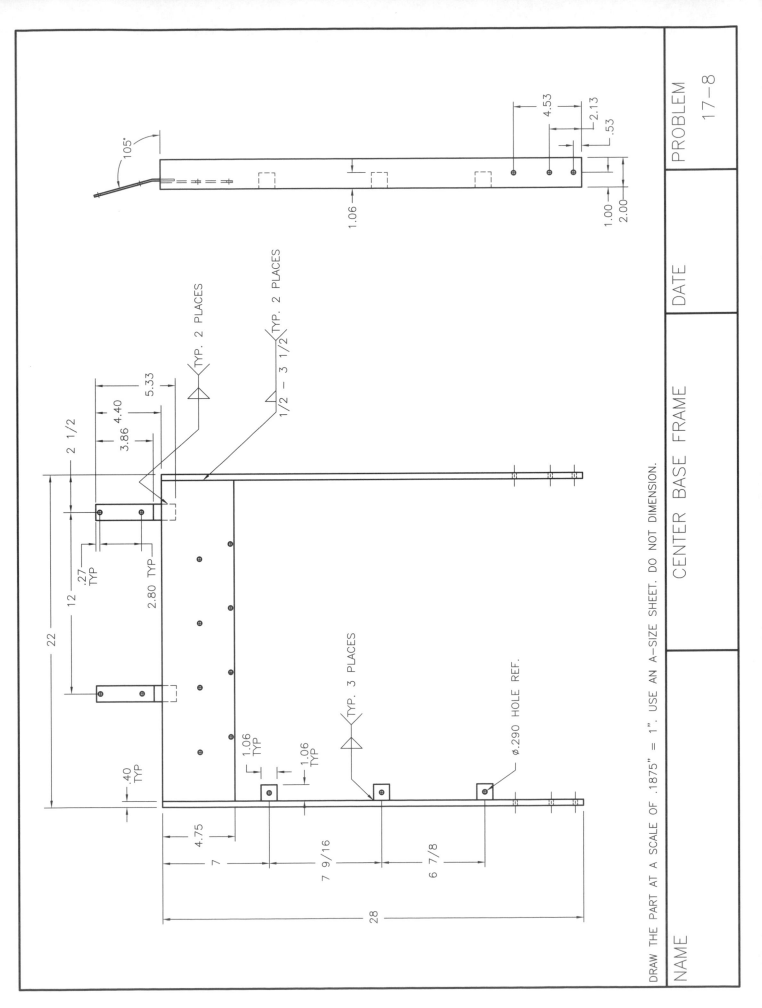

105°

4.53
2.13
.53

1.06

1.00
2.00

2 1/2

5.33
4.40
3.86

TYP. 2 PLACES

1/2 – 3 1/2
TYP. 2 PLACES

.27
TYP

2.80 TYP

12

22

TYP. 3 PLACES

Ø.290 HOLE REF.

.40
TYP

1.06
TYP

1.06
TYP

4.75

7

7 9/16

6 7/8

28

DRAW THE PART AT A SCALE OF .1875" = 1". USE AN A–SIZE SHEET. DO NOT DIMENSION.

NAME

CENTER BASE FRAME

DATE

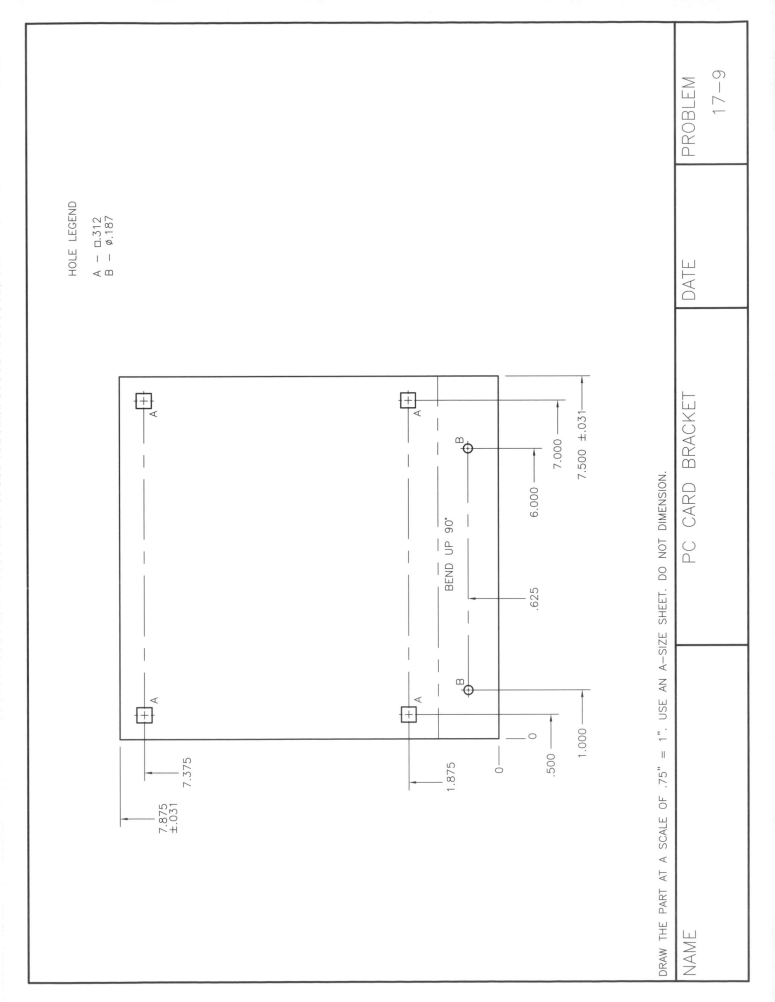

HOLE LEGEND

A – □.312
B – ⌀.187

BEND UP 90°

7.875
±.031

7.375

1.875

.500

1.000

0

0

.625

6.000

7.000

7.500 ±.031

DRAW THE PART AT A SCALE OF .75" = 1". USE AN A–SIZE SHEET. DO NOT DIMENSION.

NAME

PC CARD BRACKET

DATE

PROBLEM
17–9

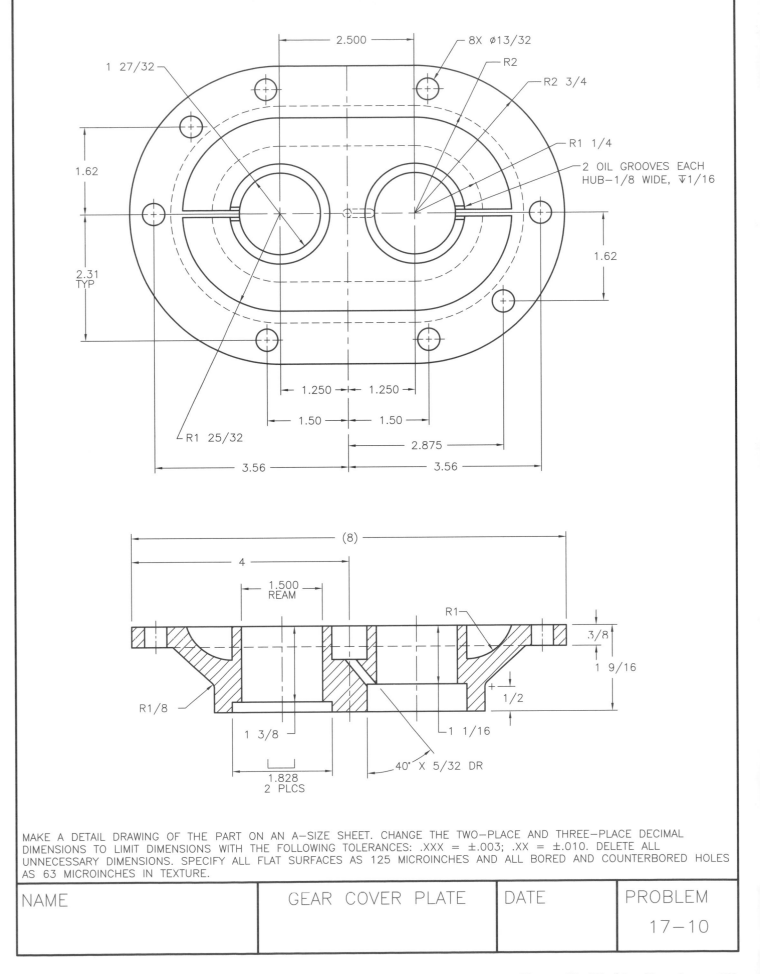

2.500

8X ⌀13/32

R2

R2 3/4

1 27/32

R1 1/4

1.62

2 OIL GROOVES EACH
HUB—1/8 WIDE, ⊻1/16

2.31
TYP

1.62

R1 25/32

1.250   1.250

1.50   1.50

2.875

3.56   3.56

(8)

4

1.500
REAM

R1

3/8

1 9/16

R1/8

1/2

1 3/8

1 1/16

40° X 5/32 DR

1.828
2 PLCS

MAKE A DETAIL DRAWING OF THE PART ON AN A—SIZE SHEET. CHANGE THE TWO—PLACE AND THREE—PLACE DECIMAL
DIMENSIONS TO LIMIT DIMENSIONS WITH THE FOLLOWING TOLERANCES: .XXX = ±.003; .XX = ±.010. DELETE ALL
UNNECESSARY DIMENSIONS. SPECIFY ALL FLAT SURFACES AS 125 MICROINCHES AND ALL BORED AND COUNTERBORED HOLES
AS 63 MICROINCHES IN TEXTURE.

| NAME | GEAR COVER PLATE | DATE | PROBLEM |
| | | | 17—10 |

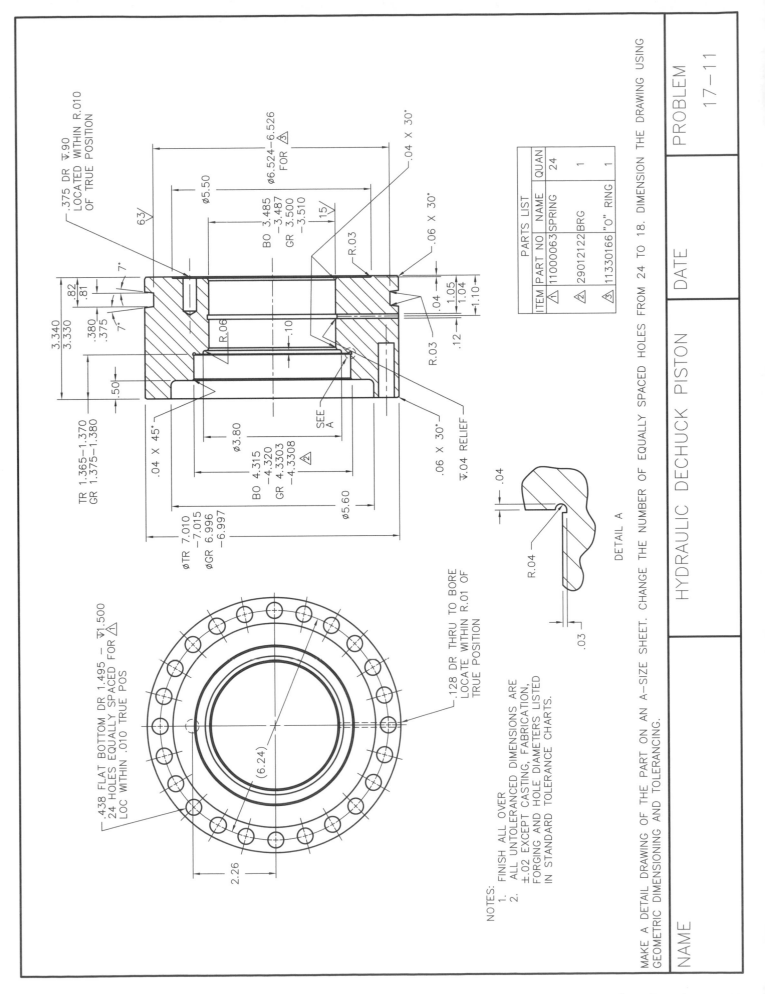

NOTES:
1. FINISH ALL OVER
2. ALL UNTOLERANCED DIMENSIONS ARE ±.02 EXCEPT CASTING, FABRICATION, FORGING AND HOLE DIAMETERS LISTED IN STANDARD TOLERANCE CHARTS.

DETAIL A

PARTS LIST			
ITEM	PART NO	NAME	QUAN
⚠	11000063	SPRING	24
⚠	29012122	BRG	1
⚠	11330166	"O" RING	1

MAKE A DETAIL DRAWING OF THE PART ON AN A–SIZE SHEET. CHANGE THE NUMBER OF EQUALLY SPACED HOLES FROM 24 TO 18. DIMENSION THE DRAWING USING GEOMETRIC DIMENSIONING AND TOLERANCING.

NAME

HYDRAULIC DECHUCK PISTON

DATE

PROBLEM
17–11

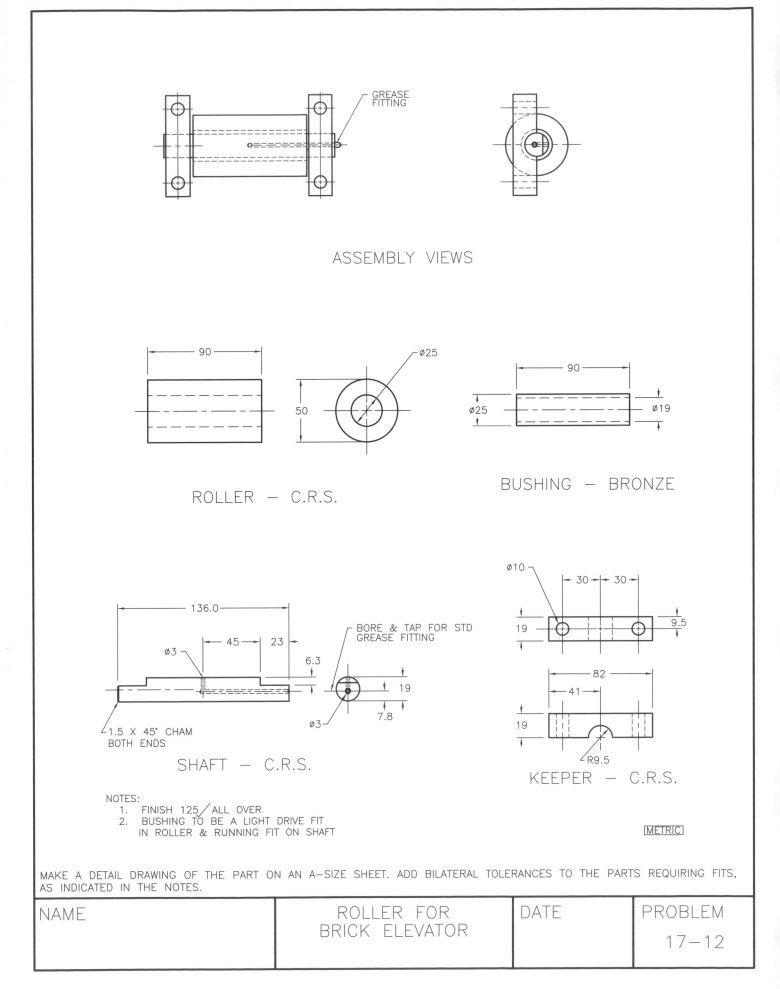

GREASE
FITTING

ASSEMBLY VIEWS

90

Ø25

50

ROLLER – C.R.S.

90

Ø25   Ø19

BUSHING – BRONZE

136.0

45   23

Ø3

6.3

BORE & TAP FOR STD
GREASE FITTING

19

7.8

Ø3

1.5 X 45° CHAM
BOTH ENDS

SHAFT – C.R.S.

Ø10

30   30

19   9.5

82

41

19

R9.5

KEEPER – C.R.S.

NOTES:
1.   FINISH 125/ ALL OVER
2.   BUSHING TO BE A LIGHT DRIVE FIT
     IN ROLLER & RUNNING FIT ON SHAFT

METRIC

MAKE A DETAIL DRAWING OF THE PART ON AN A–SIZE SHEET. ADD BILATERAL TOLERANCES TO THE PARTS REQUIRING FITS,
AS INDICATED IN THE NOTES.

NAME	ROLLER FOR BRICK ELEVATOR	DATE	PROBLEM 17–12

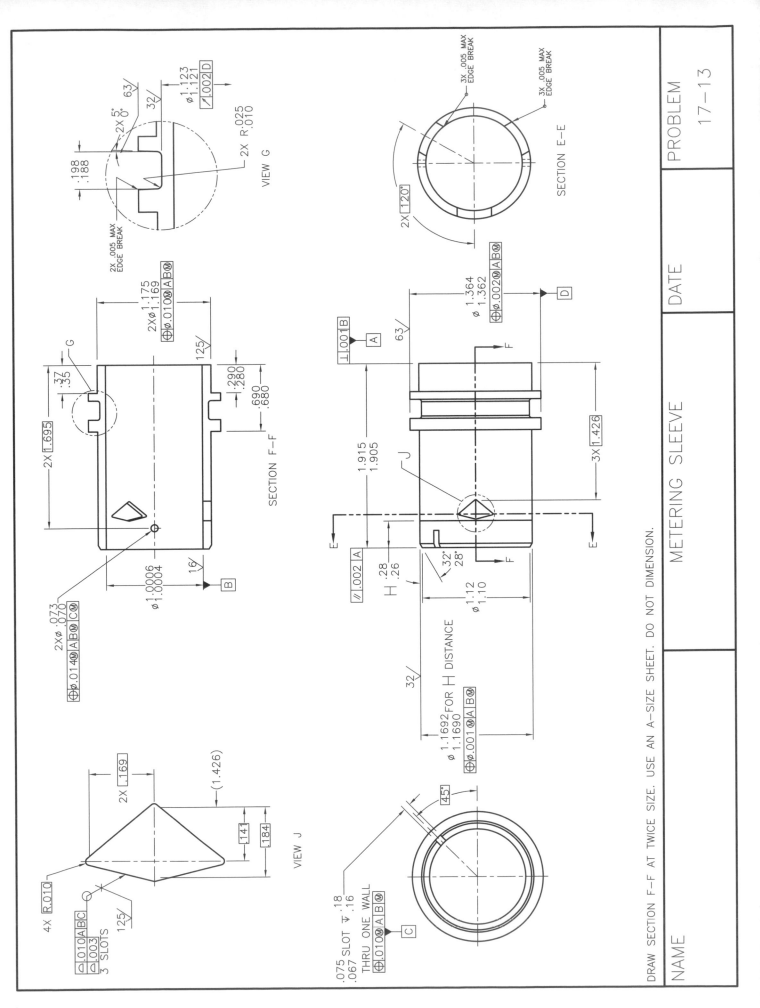

DATE

METERING SLEEVE

NAME

DRAW SECTION F-F AT TWICE SIZE. USE AN A-SIZE SHEET. DO NOT DIMENSION.

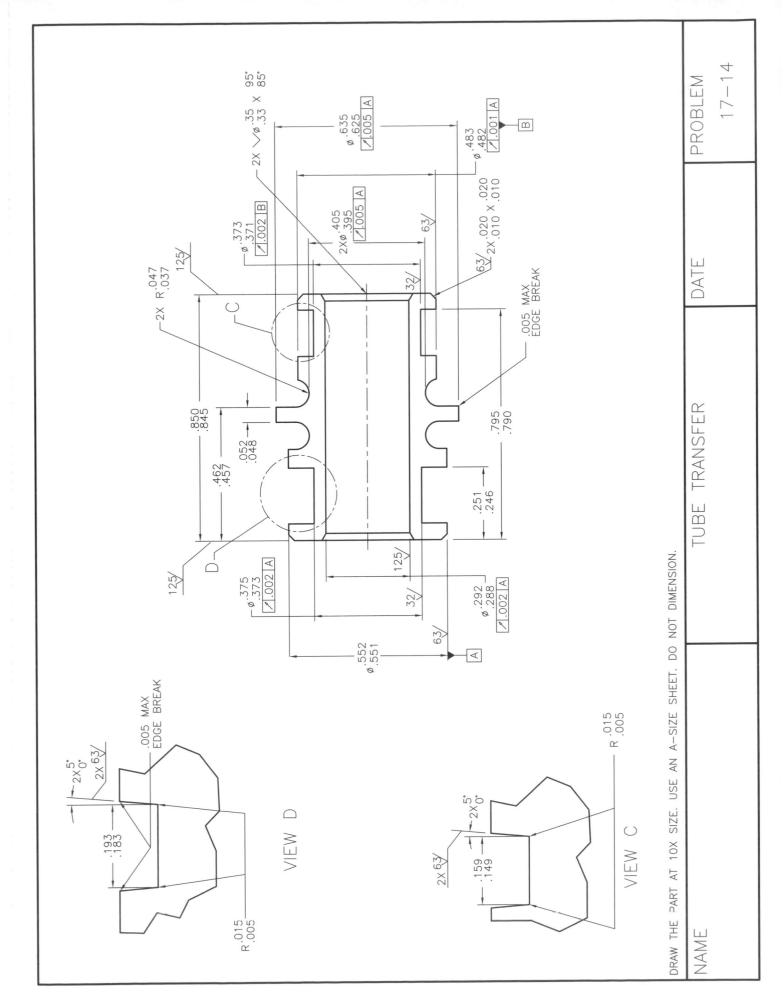

VIEW D

VIEW C

DRAW THE PART AT 10X SIZE. USE AN A-SIZE SHEET. DO NOT DIMENSION.

TUBE TRANSFER

NAME

DATE

PROBLEM
17–14

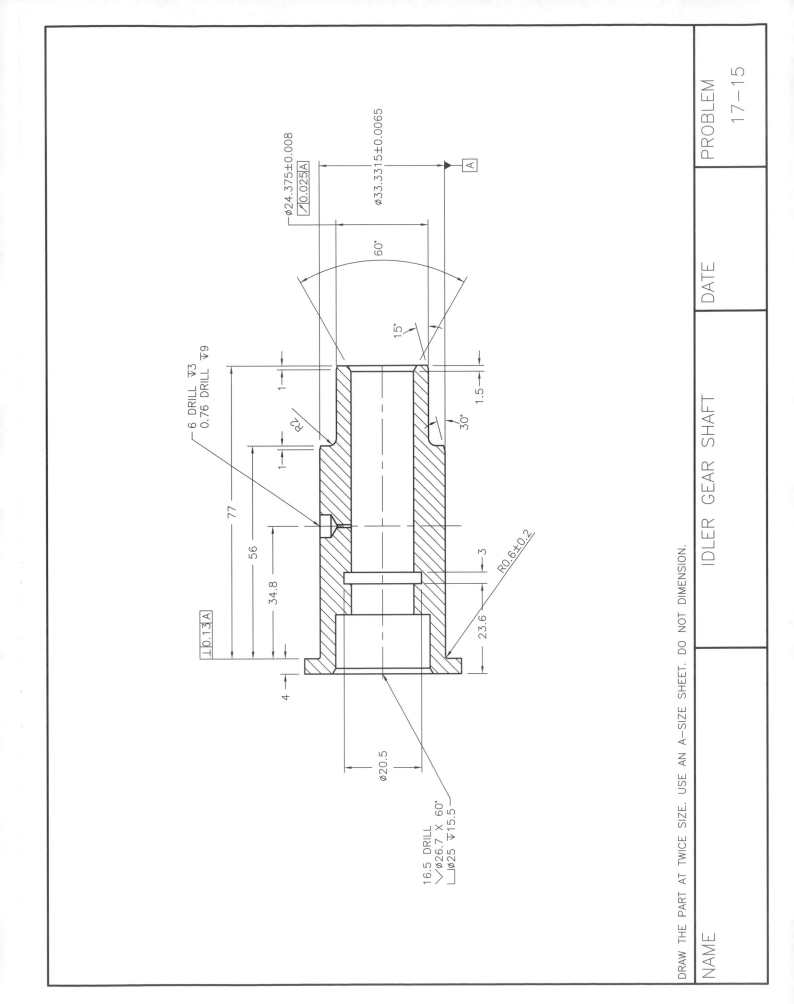

ø24.375±0.008
⌀0.025Ⓐ
ø33.3315±0.0065
Ⓐ
60°
15°
1.5
30°
1
R2
1
6 DRILL ⩗3
0.76 DRILL ⩗9
77
56
34.8
⊥0.13 A
4
3
R0.6±0.2
23.6
ø20.5
16.5 DRILL
⩗ø26.7 X 60°
⊔ø25 ⩗15.5

NAME

DRAW THE PART AT TWICE SIZE. USE AN A–SIZE SHEET. DO NOT DIMENSION.

IDLER GEAR SHAFT

DATE

PROBLEM
17–15

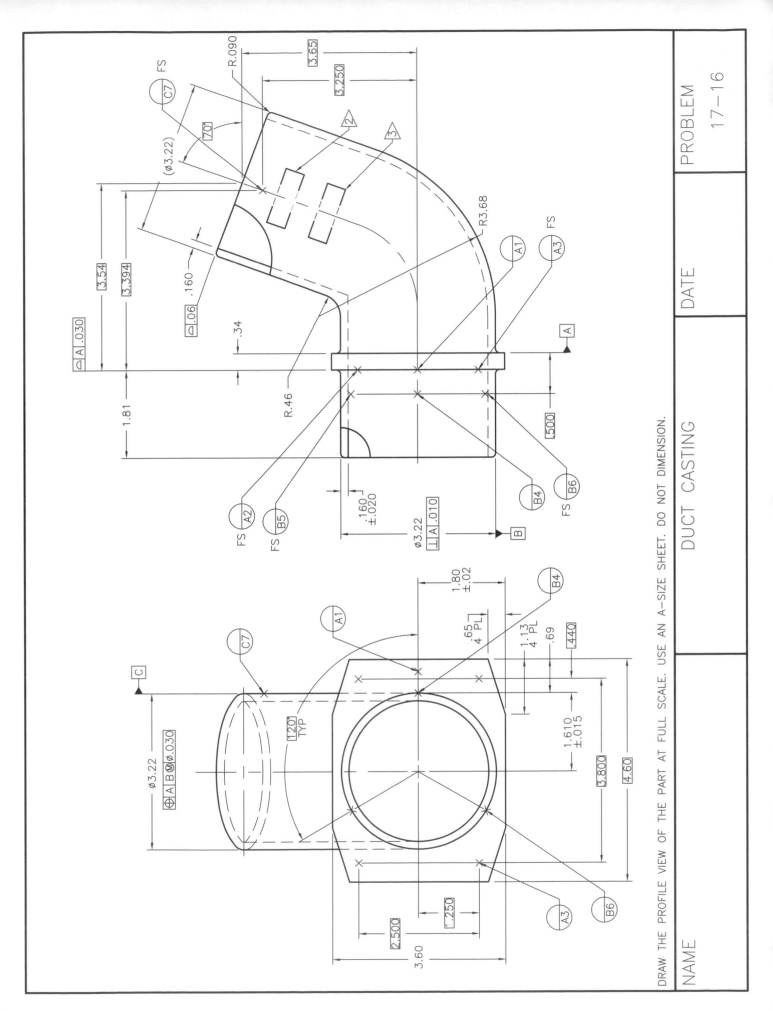

DRAW THE PROFILE VIEW OF THE PART AT FULL SCALE. USE AN A-SIZE SHEET. DO NOT DIMENSION.

NAME

DATE

DUCT CASTING

PROBLEM
17–16

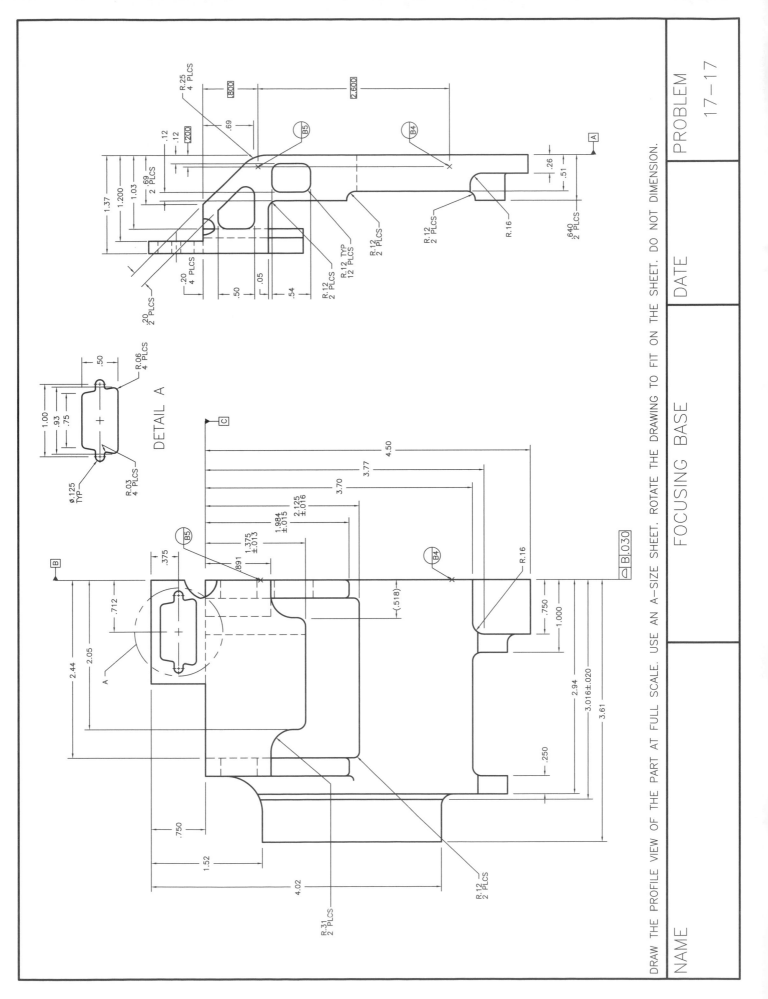

DETAIL A

DRAW THE PROFILE VIEW OF THE PART AT FULL SCALE. USE AN A-SIZE SHEET. ROTATE THE DRAWING TO FIT ON THE SHEET. DO NOT DIMENSION.

| NAME | FOCUSING BASE | DATE | PROBLEM 17-17 |

DRAW A HEXAGONAL HEAD BOLT AND NUT AND A REGULAR HEAD BOLT AND NUT. FOR BOTH FASTENERS, DRAW A SIMPLIFIED REPRESENTATION AND SPECIFY A NOMINAL SIZE OF 1/2", A BODY LENGTH OF 3", AND A THREAD LENGTH OF 2". DIMENSION THE THREADS WITH A NOTE.

| NAME | BOLTS AND NUTS | DATE | PROBLEM |
| | | | 18—1 |

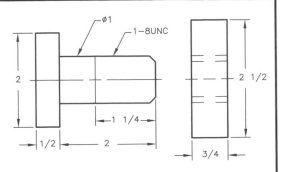

DRAW DETAILED, SCHEMATIC, AND SIMPLIFIED REPRESENTATIONS OF THE THREADED BLOCK. INCLUDE A SECTION VIEW WITH EACH REPRESENTATION. DO NOT DIMENSION.

NAME	THREADED BLOCK	DATE	PROBLEM
			18-2

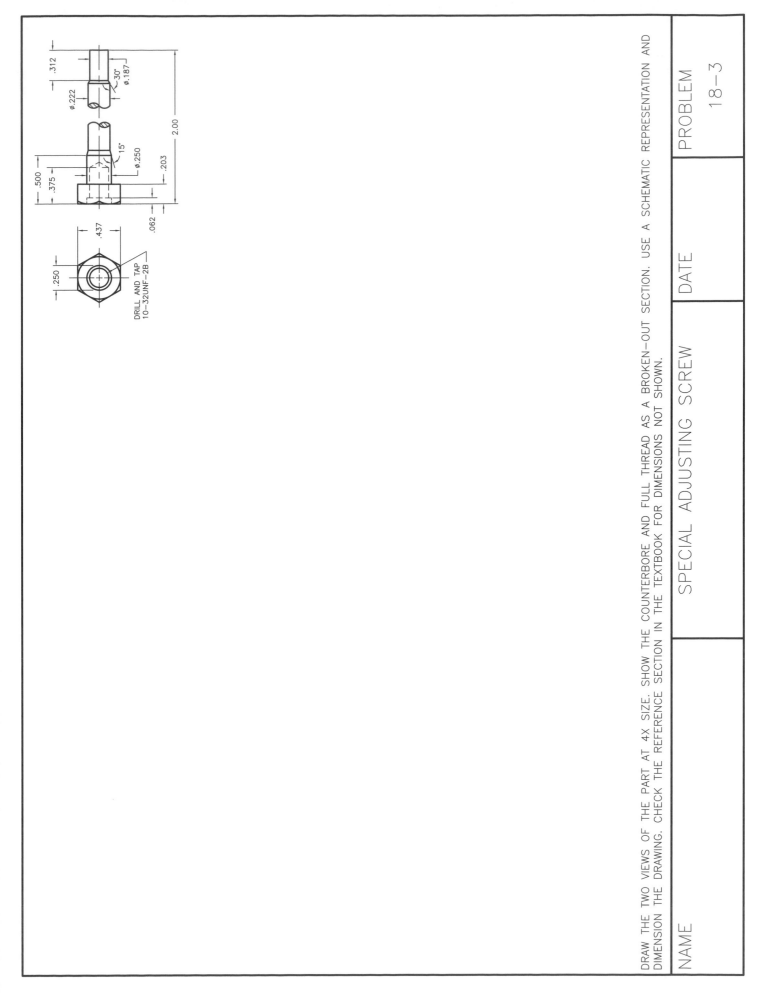

.312
30°
Ø.187
Ø.222
2.00
15°
Ø.250
.500
.375
.203
.062
.437
.250
DRILL AND TAP
10–32UNF–2B

DRAW THE TWO VIEWS OF THE PART AT 4X SIZE. SHOW THE COUNTERBORE AND FULL THREAD AS A BROKEN–OUT SECTION. USE A SCHEMATIC REPRESENTATION AND DIMENSION THE DRAWING. CHECK THE REFERENCE SECTION IN THE TEXTBOOK FOR DIMENSIONS NOT SHOWN.

NAME		SPECIAL ADJUSTING SCREW	DATE	PROBLEM 18–3

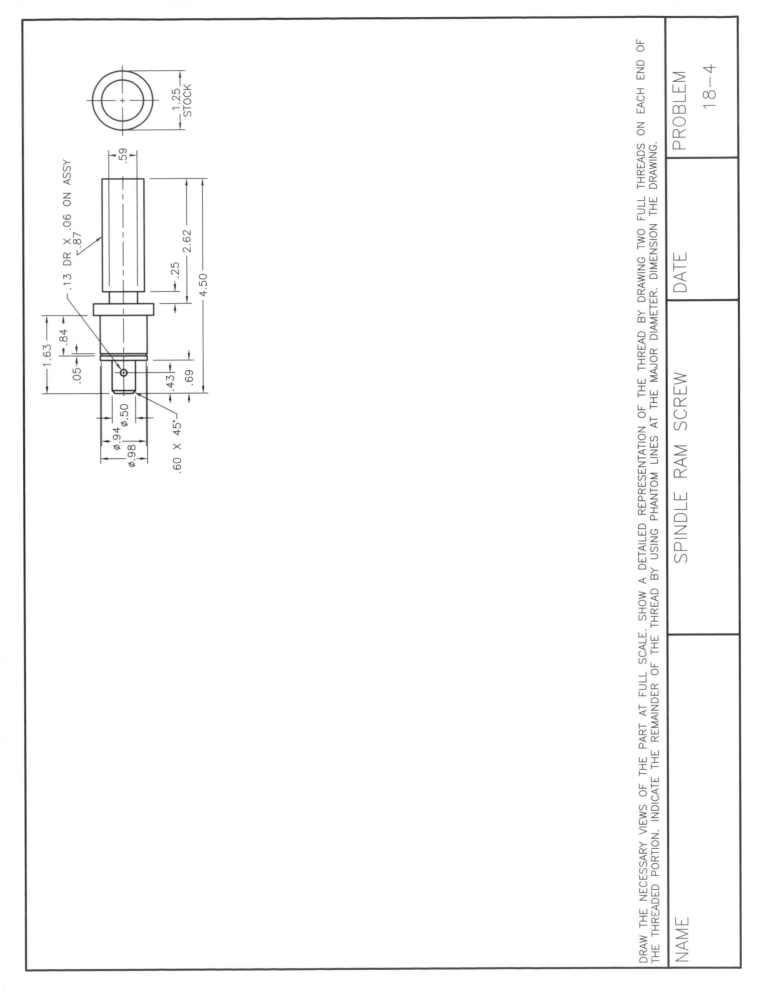

1.25
STOCK

.59

.13 DR X .06 ON ASSY

.87

.25

2.62

4.50

1.63

.84

.05

.43

.69

⌀.94

⌀.50

⌀.98

.60 X 45°

DRAW THE NECESSARY VIEWS OF THE PART AT FULL SCALE. SHOW A DETAILED REPRESENTATION OF THE THREAD BY DRAWING TWO FULL THREADS ON EACH END OF THE THREADED PORTION. INDICATE THE REMAINDER OF THE THREAD BY USING PHANTOM LINES AT THE MAJOR DIAMETER. DIMENSION THE DRAWING.

NAME

SPINDLE RAM SCREW

DATE

PROBLEM

18–4

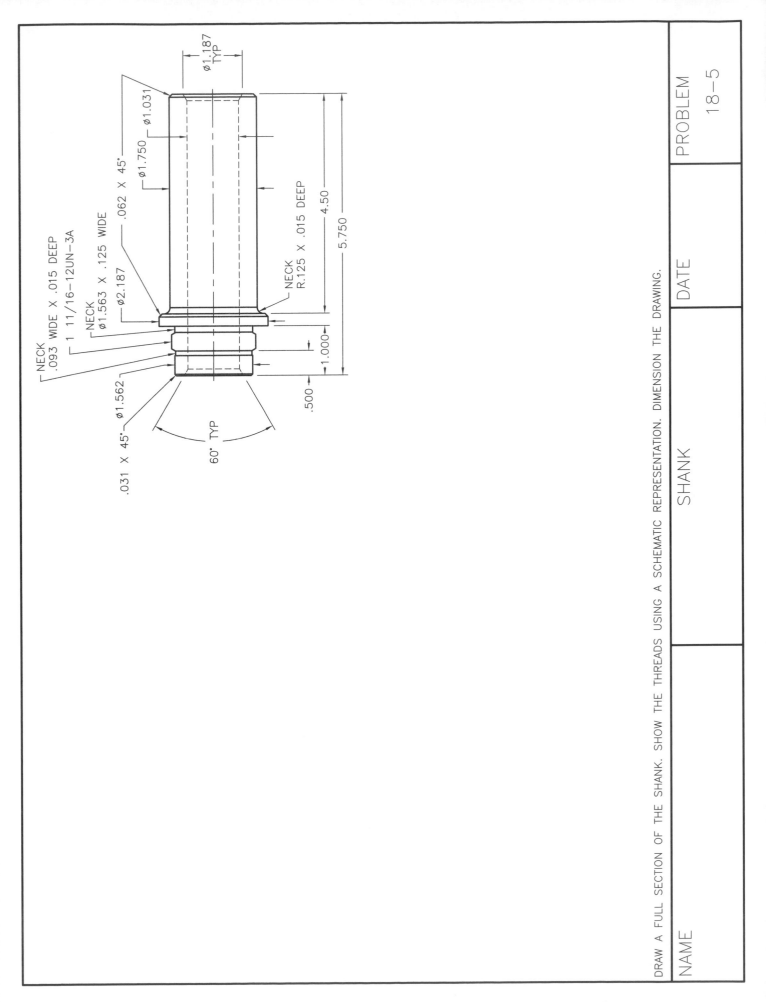

Ø1.187
TYP

Ø1.031

Ø1.750

.062 X 45°

NECK
.093 WIDE X .015 DEEP

1 11/16-12UN-3A

NECK
Ø1.563 X .125 WIDE

Ø2.187

4.50

5.750

NECK
R.125 X .015 DEEP

1.000

.500

Ø1.562

.031 X 45°

60° TYP

DRAW A FULL SECTION OF THE SHANK. SHOW THE THREADS USING A SCHEMATIC REPRESENTATION. DIMENSION THE DRAWING.

NAME

SHANK

DATE

PROBLEM
18-5

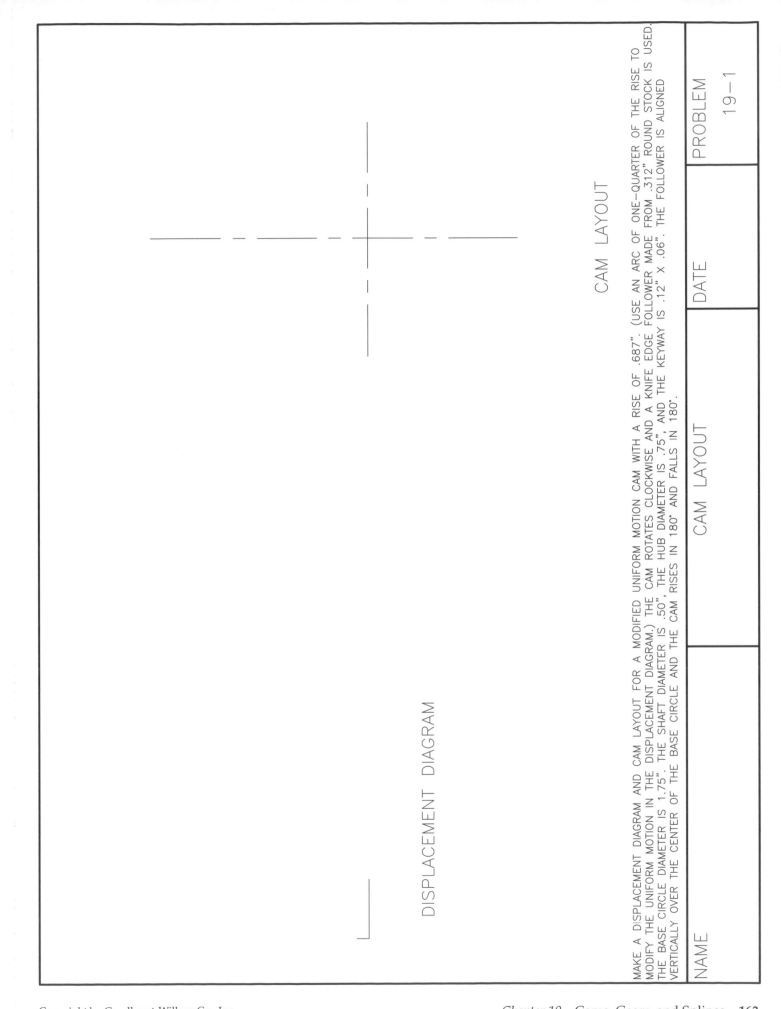

DISPLACEMENT DIAGRAM

CAM LAYOUT

MAKE A DISPLACEMENT DIAGRAM AND CAM LAYOUT FOR A MODIFIED UNIFORM MOTION CAM WITH A RISE OF .687". (USE AN ARC OF ONE-QUARTER OF THE RISE TO MODIFY THE UNIFORM MOTION IN THE DISPLACEMENT DIAGRAM.) THE CAM ROTATES CLOCKWISE AND A KNIFE EDGE FOLLOWER MADE FROM .312" ROUND STOCK IS USED. THE BASE CIRCLE DIAMETER IS 1.75". THE SHAFT DIAMETER IS .50", THE HUB DIAMETER IS .75", AND THE KEYWAY IS .12" X .06". THE FOLLOWER IS ALIGNED VERTICALLY OVER THE CENTER OF THE BASE CIRCLE AND THE CAM RISES IN 180° AND FALLS IN 180°.

NAME	CAM LAYOUT	DATE	PROBLEM
			19–1

DESIGN A CAM THAT WILL OPEN AND CLOSE A VALVE ON AN AUTOMATIC HOT-WAX SPRAY AT A CAR WASH IN ONE REVOLUTION. TO OPEN THE VALVE, THE CAM FOLLOWER MUST MOVE .562". THE VALVE IS TO OPEN IN 20° OF CAM ROTATION, REMAIN OPEN FOR 320°, CLOSE IN 10°, AND REMAIN CLOSED FOR 10°. THE CAM OPERATES AT MODERATE SPEED. YOU ARE TO SELECT THE APPROPRIATE CAM MOTION, BASE CIRCLE SIZE, AND TYPE OF CAM FOLLOWER. MAKE A FULL-SIZE WORKING DRAWING OF THE DISPLACEMENT DIAGRAM AND THE CAM.

NAME		CAM DESIGN PROBLEM	DATE	PROBLEM
				19-2

MAKE A WORKING DRAWING OF A SPUR GEAR IN SIMPLIFIED CONVENTIONAL FORM. DRAW CIRCULAR AND SECTION VIEWS. USE A SHAFT DIAMETER OF .75", A HUB DIAMETER OF 1.5", A HUB WIDTH OF 1.00", A FACE WIDTH OF .50", AND A KEYWAY WITH DIMENSIONS OF 1/8" X 1/16". THE GEAR HAS 40 TEETH, A DIAMETRAL PITCH OF 8, AND A PRESSURE ANGLE OF 20°. COMPUTE VALUES FOR THE PITCH DIAMETER, CIRCULAR THICKNESS, AND WHOLE DEPTH. INCLUDE THE GEAR DATA IN A TABLE ON THE DRAWING.

NAME		DATE	PROBLEM
	SPUR GEAR		19-3

MAKE A DETAIL DRAWING OF A BEVEL GEAR IN SIMPLIFIED CONVENTIONAL FORM. DRAW CIRCULAR AND SECTION VIEWS. USE A SHAFT DIAMETER OF 1.00", A HUB DIAMETER OF 2.125", A HUB WIDTH OF 1.25", AND A KEYWAY WITH DIMENSIONS OF 1/8" X 1/16". THE GEAR HAS 36 TEETH, A DIAMETRAL PITCH OF 12, A PRESSURE ANGLE OF 20°, A FACE WIDTH OF .53", AND A MOUNTING DISTANCE OF 1.875". COMPUTE VALUES FOR THE PITCH DIAMETER, CIRCULAR PITCH, WHOLE DEPTH, ADDENDUM, AND DEDENDUM. INCLUDE THE GEAR DATA IN A TABLE ON THE DRAWING.

| NAME | BEVEL GEAR | DATE | PROBLEM |
| | | | 19–4 |

DESIGN A GEAR ASSEMBLY INVOLVING TWO GEARS, OR A WORM GEAR AND A WORM, TO ACHIEVE A DEFINITE RATIO. OBTAIN BASIC SPECIFICATIONS FOR GEARS FROM A MACHINIST'S HANDBOOK OR FROM A GEAR CATALOG. MAKE AN ASSEMBLY DRAWING OF THE GEARS. ADD THE NECESSARY DIMENSIONS AND SPECIFICATIONS TO THE DRAWING.

GEAR ASSEMBLY

NAME		DATE	PROBLEM
			19-5

PREPARE DRAWINGS AS INDICATED IN THE FOLLOWING PROBLEMS FOR THE HOUSE ILLUSTRATED IN THE FLOOR PLAN BELOW. USE A SEPARATE SHEET FOR EACH DRAWING. THE DRAWINGS ARE BEST SUITED FOR B- OR C-SIZE SHEETS.

FLOOR PLAN—SHEET 1
PREPARE A WORKING DRAWING OF THE FLOOR PLAN OF THE HOUSE. USE AN APPROPRIATE DRAWING SCALE. INCLUDE ALL NECESSARY DIMENSIONS AND NOTES.

FOUNDATION PLAN—SHEET 2
PREPARE A FOUNDATION PLAN FOR THE HOUSE. USE AN APPROPRIATE DRAWING SCALE. THERE IS NO BASEMENT AND THE FOUNDATION CONSISTS OF A 36" STEM WALL ON A FOOTING. ON THE SAME SHEET, PREPARE A CONSTRUCTION DETAIL DRAWING SHOWING ANY BEAMS AND PIERS NECESSARY IN THE FOUNDATION TO SUPPORT THE FLOOR AND INTERIOR WALLS. ADD THE NECESSARY DIMENSIONS AND NOTES.

ELECTRICAL PLAN—SHEET 3
TRACE THE FLOOR PLAN AND PREPARE AN ELECTRICAL PLAN FOR THE HOUSE. USE AN APPROPRIATE DRAWING SCALE. CHECK YOUR LOCAL ELECTRICAL CODE FOR THE REQUIREMENTS ON SPACING FOR THE WALL OUTLETS. SHOW LINES TO SWITCHES ON ALL OUTLETS CONTROLLED BY SWITCHES. ADD THE NECESSARY DIMENSIONS AND NOTES.

ELEVATION PLAN—SHEET 4
PREPARE A DRAWING OF THE FRONT ELEVATION OF THE HOUSE. USE AN APPROPRIATE DRAWING SCALE. ADD THE NECESSARY DIMENSIONS AND NOTES.

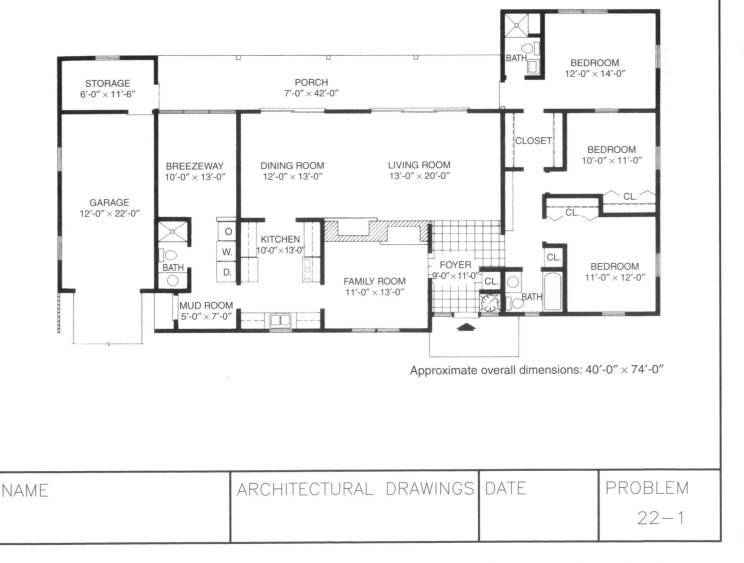

Approximate overall dimensions: 40'-0" × 74'-0"

NAME	ARCHITECTURAL DRAWINGS	DATE	PROBLEM
			22-1

DRAW AND LABEL THE FOLLOWING COMPONENT SYMBOLS. USE THE SPACE PROVIDED TO THE RIGHT. DRAW EACH COMPONENT TO THE SAME RELATIVE SIZE AND INCLUDE THE COMPONENT DESIGNATION AND PART INFORMATION.

A. BATTERY, 9 VOLTS, BT_1

B. SWITCH, SINGLE—POLE, SINGLE—THROW, S_1

C. AMMETER, M_1

D. RESISTOR, 4700 OHMS, R_1

E. LAMP, INCANDESCENT, DIAL LAMP, DS_1

NAME	ELECTRICAL SYMBOLS	DATE	PROBLEM
			24—1

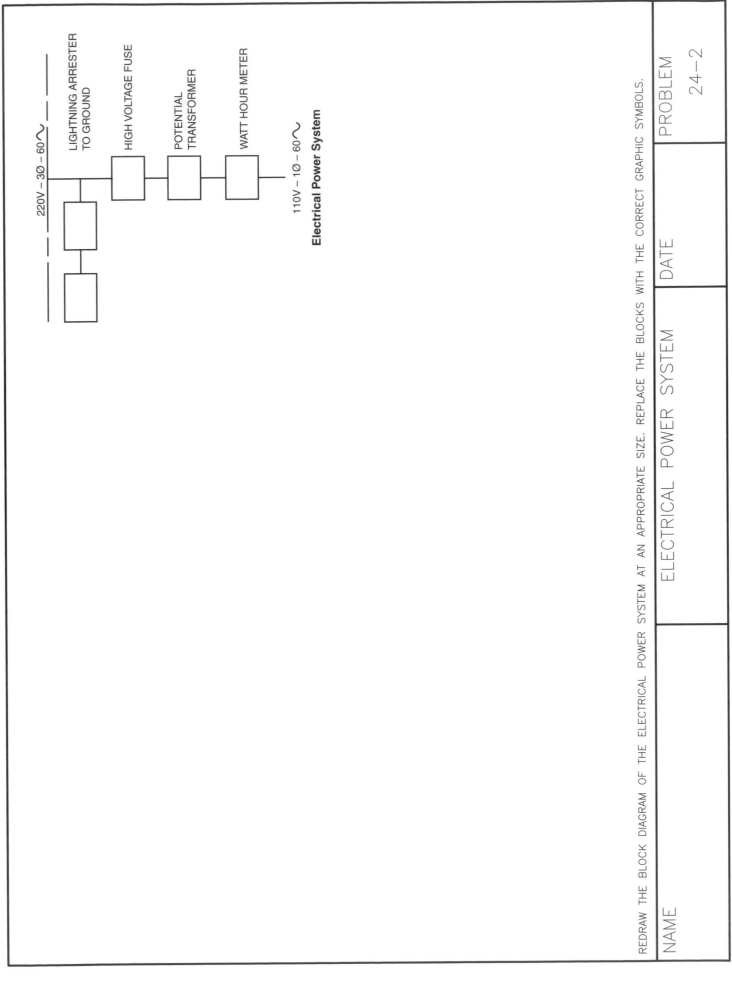

220V – 3∅ – 60 ~

LIGHTNING ARRESTER
TO GROUND

HIGH VOLTAGE FUSE

POTENTIAL
TRANSFORMER

WATT HOUR METER

110V – 1∅ – 60 ~

Electrical Power System

REDRAW THE BLOCK DIAGRAM OF THE ELECTRICAL POWER SYSTEM AT AN APPROPRIATE SIZE. REPLACE THE BLOCKS WITH THE CORRECT GRAPHIC SYMBOLS.

NAME	ELECTRICAL POWER SYSTEM	DATE	PROBLEM 24–2

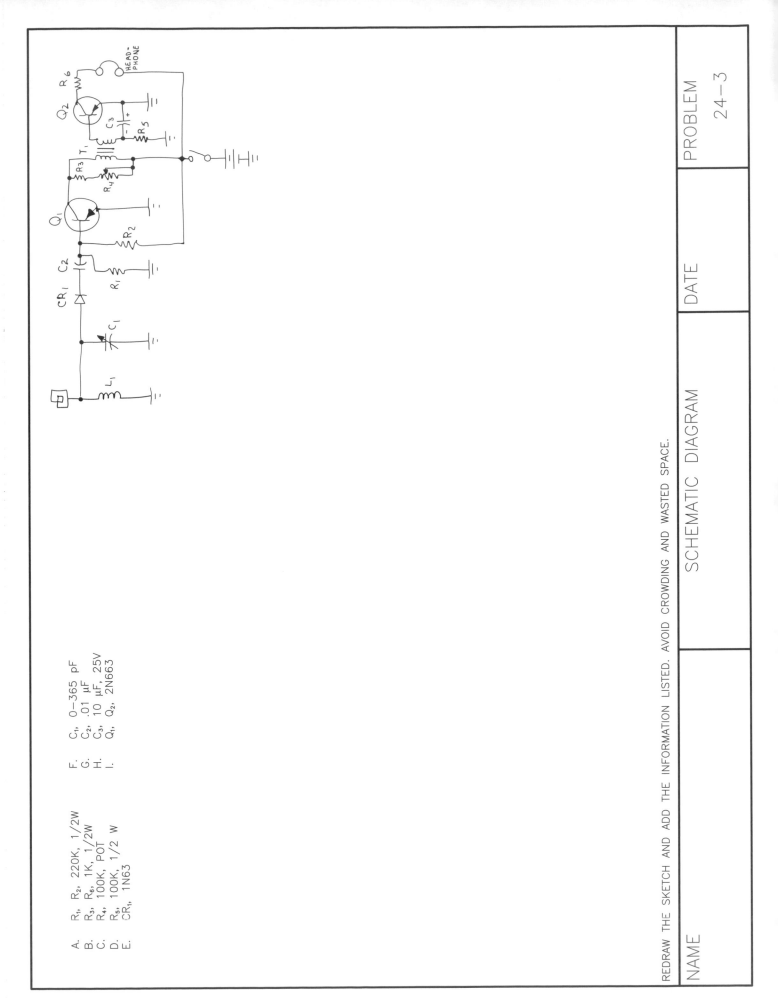

A. R₁, R₂, 220K, 1/2W
B. R₃, R₆, 1K, 1/2W
C. R₄, 100K, POT
D. R₅, 100K, 1/2 W
E. CR₁, 1N63

F. C₁, 0–365 pF
G. C₂, .01 μF
H. C₃, 10 μF, 25V
I. Q₁, Q₂, 2N663

REDRAW THE SKETCH AND ADD THE INFORMATION LISTED. AVOID CROWDING AND WASTED SPACE.

NAME

DATE

PROBLEM
24–3

SCHEMATIC DIAGRAM

SELECT AN APPROPRIATE SCALE AND CONTOUR INTERVAL AND PLOT THE CONTOURS, AS WELL AS THE NATURAL AND CONSTRUCTED FEATURES, FOR THE GRID SURVEY SHOWN BELOW. USE THE GIVEN ELEVATION DATA AND INTERPOLATION TO LOCATE PLOTTING POINTS. IN THE SPACE BELOW THE CONTOUR MAP, DRAW A PROFILE MAP SHOWING THE SHAPE OF THE TERRAIN AT LINE 3 THROUGH THE MAP SECTION. EXAGGERATE THE SCALE TO EMPHASIZE CHANGES IN ELEVATION.

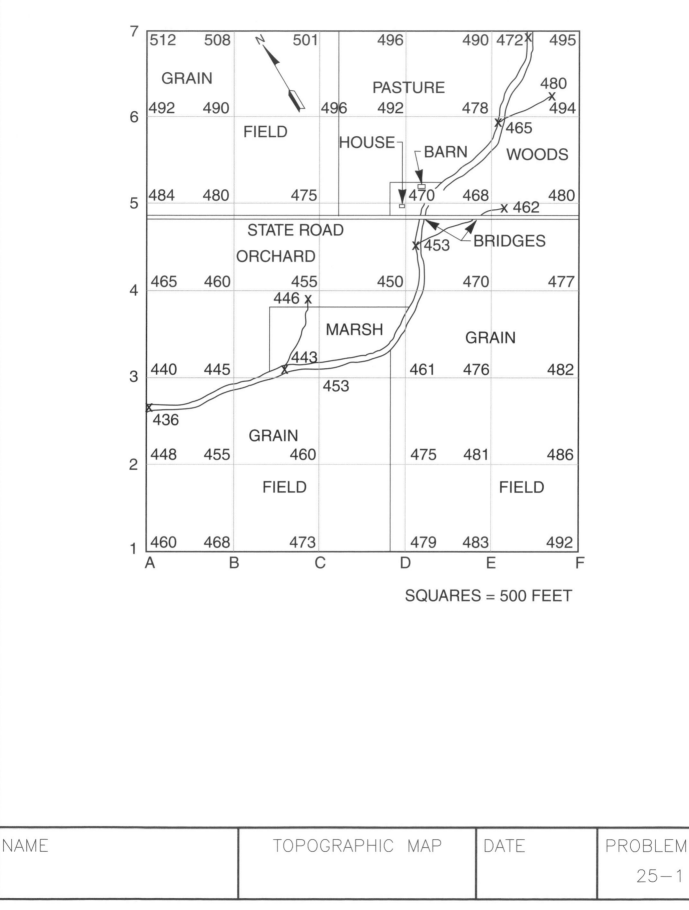

SQUARES = 500 FEET

NAME	TOPOGRAPHIC MAP	DATE	PROBLEM
			25–1

LAY OUT THE MAP TRAVERSE SHOWN USING THE GIVEN LINE AND STATION DATA. INDICATE THE NORTH DIRECTION ON THE MAP, AND THEN ORIENT THE FIRST STATION AND BACKSIGHT LINE WITH IT. USE THE FOLLOWING STATION POINTS. LAY OUT A CLOSED TRAVERSE AFTER LOCATING STATION 3 AND INDICATE THE DIRECTION AND DISTANCE.

A. STATION 2: RIGHT DEFLECTION ANGLE = 75°; DISTANCE FROM STATION 1 = 129'
B. STATION 3: RIGHT DEFLECTION ANGLE = 138°30'; DISTANCE FROM STATION 2 = 162.5'

STATION 1

S 17° W
114'

| NAME | MAP TRAVERSE | DATE | PROBLEM |
| | | | 25—2 |

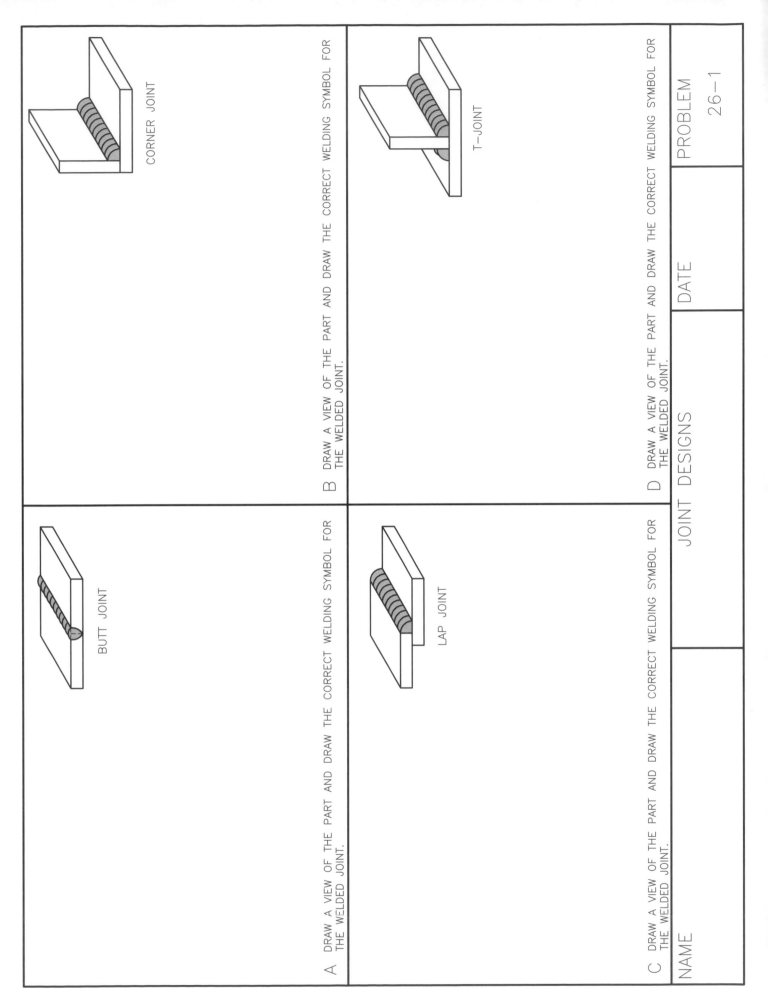

CORNER JOINT

T-JOINT

BUTT JOINT

LAP JOINT

A   DRAW A VIEW OF THE PART AND DRAW THE CORRECT WELDING SYMBOL FOR THE WELDED JOINT.

B   DRAW A VIEW OF THE PART AND DRAW THE CORRECT WELDING SYMBOL FOR THE WELDED JOINT.

C   DRAW A VIEW OF THE PART AND DRAW THE CORRECT WELDING SYMBOL FOR THE WELDED JOINT.

D   DRAW A VIEW OF THE PART AND DRAW THE CORRECT WELDING SYMBOL FOR THE WELDED JOINT.

NAME

JOINT DESIGNS

DATE

PROBLEM

26-1

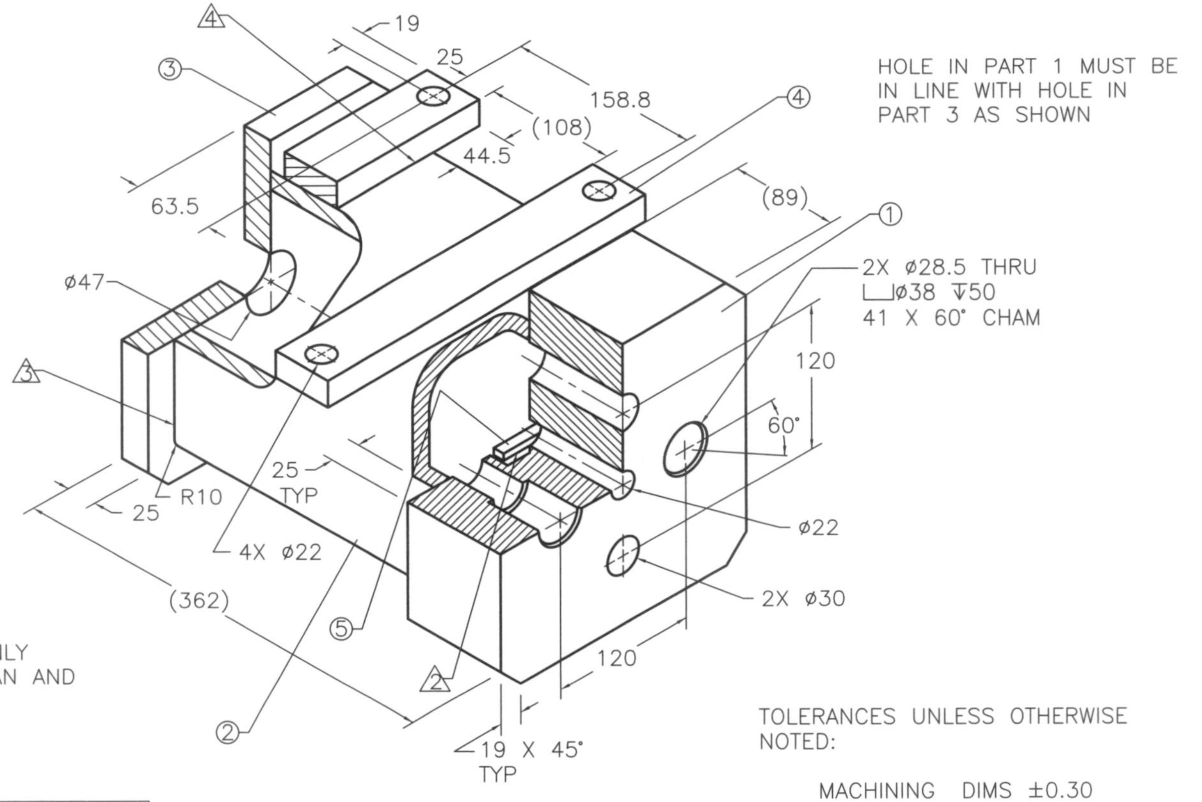
19
25
158.8
(108)
44.5
63.5
(89)
ø47
R10
25
25
TYP
4X ø22
(362)
2X ø28.5 THRU
⌴ø38 ↧50
41 X 60° CHAM
120
60°
ø22
2X ø30
120
19 X 45°
TYP
1
2
3
4
5

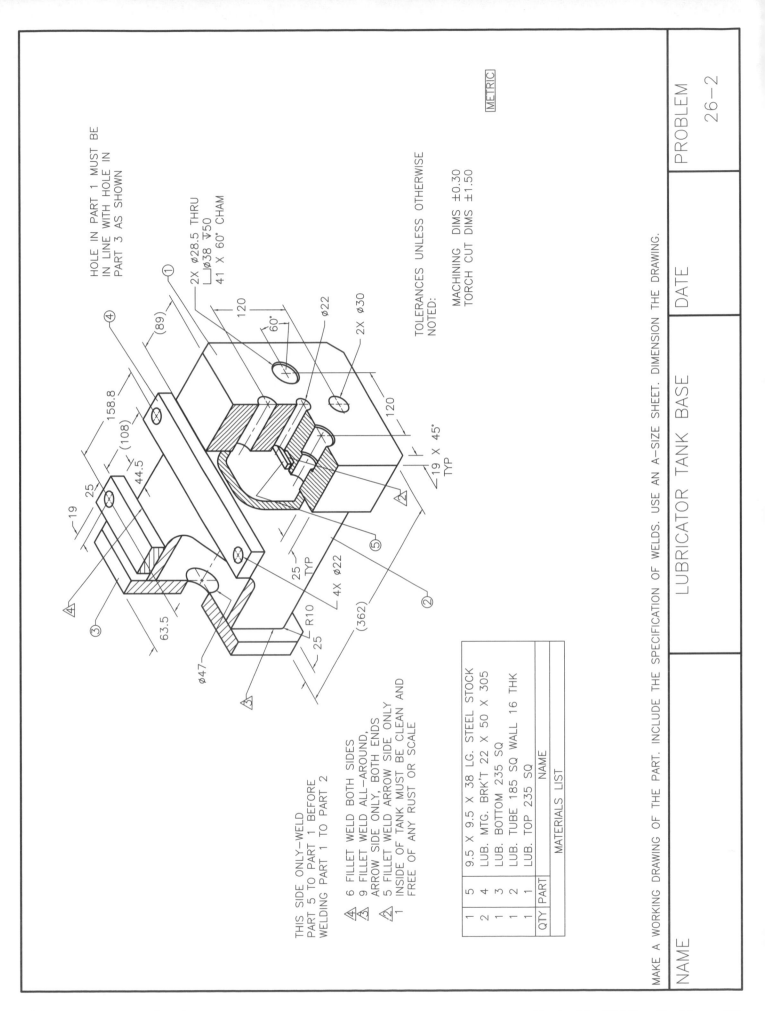

HOLE IN PART 1 MUST BE IN LINE WITH HOLE IN PART 3 AS SHOWN

THIS SIDE ONLY—WELD PART 5 TO PART 1 BEFORE WELDING PART 1 TO PART 2

4 6 FILLET WELD BOTH SIDES
3 9 FILLET WELD ALL—AROUND, ARROW SIDE ONLY, BOTH ENDS
2 5 FILLET WELD ARROW SIDE ONLY
1 INSIDE OF TANK MUST BE CLEAN AND FREE OF ANY RUST OR SCALE

TOLERANCES UNLESS OTHERWISE NOTED:

MACHINING DIMS ±0.30
TORCH CUT DIMS ±1.50

METRIC

1	5	9.5 X 9.5 X 38 LG. STEEL STOCK
2	4	LUB. MTG. BRK'T 22 X 50 X 305
1	3	LUB. BOTTOM 235 SQ
1	2	LUB. TUBE 185 SQ WALL 16 THK
1	1	LUB. TOP 235 SQ
QTY	PART	NAME
MATERIALS LIST		

MAKE A WORKING DRAWING OF THE PART. INCLUDE THE SPECIFICATION OF WELDS. USE AN A-SIZE SHEET. DIMENSION THE DRAWING.

NAME	LUBRICATOR TANK BASE	DATE	PROBLEM 26—2

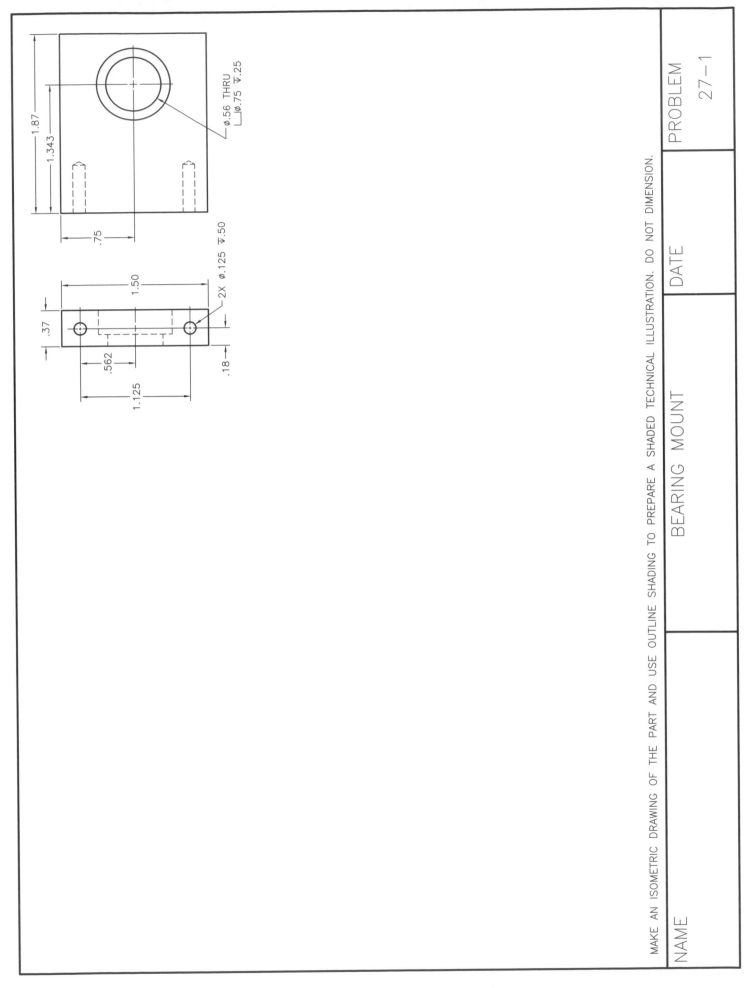

ø.56 THRU
⌴ø.75 ▽.25

1.87
1.343
.75

1.50
.37
.562
1.125
.18
2X ø.125 ▽.50

MAKE AN ISOMETRIC DRAWING OF THE PART AND USE OUTLINE SHADING TO PREPARE A SHADED TECHNICAL ILLUSTRATION. DO NOT DIMENSION.

NAME

BEARING MOUNT

DATE

PROBLEM
27-1

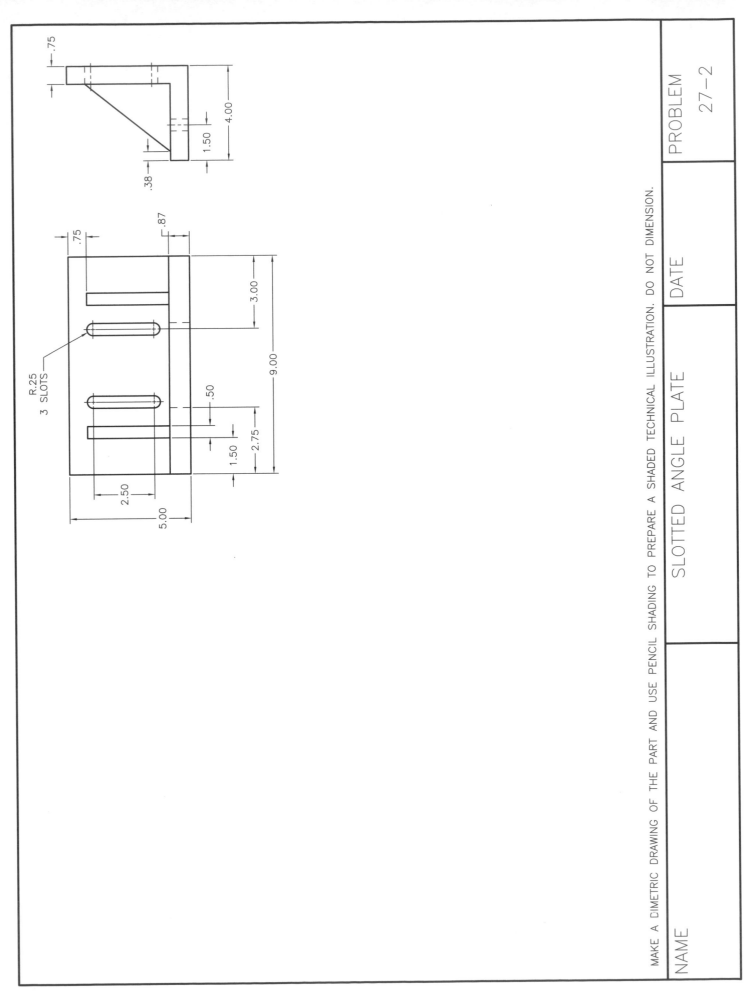

.75

4.00

1.50

.38

.87

.75

3.00

9.00

.50

1.50

2.75

R.25
3 SLOTS

2.50

5.00

PROBLEM
27-2

DATE

SLOTTED ANGLE PLATE

NAME

PREPARE A LINE GRAPH COMPARING THE NUMBER OF PEOPLE EMPLOYED IN SERVICE–PRODUCING INDUSTRIES TO THOSE IN GOODS–PRODUCING INDUSTRIES. USE THE FOLLOWING DATA. SUBSTITUTE ACTUAL DATES FOR YEARS.

	PAST		PRESENT	FUTURE	
	10 YRS	5 YRS		5 YRS	10 YRS
SERVICE (MILLIONS OF WORKERS)	24.8	27.2	34.0	47.6	59.7
GOODS (MILLIONS OF WORKERS)	27.3	26.0	24.8	28.5	30.0

NAME		DATE	PROBLEM
	LINE GRAPH		28–1

PROBLEM

DATE

NAME